Large-Scale
Software Architecture

Large-Scale Software Architecture

A Practical Guide using UML

Jeff Garland
CrystalClear Software Inc.

Richard Anthony
Object Computing Inc.

JOHN WILEY & SONS, LTD

Email (for orders and customer service enquiries): cs-books@wiley.co.uk
Visit our Home Page on www.wileyeurope.com or www.wiley.com

Other Wiley Editorial Offices

John Wiley & Sons Inc., 111 River Street, Hoboken, NJ 07030, USA

Jossey-Bass, 989 Market Street, San Francisco, CA 94103-1741, USA

Wiley-VCH Verlag GmbH, Boschstr. 12, D-69469 Weinheim, Germany

John Wiley & Sons Australia Ltd, 33 Park Road, Milton, Queensland 4064, Australia

John Wiley & Sons (Asia) Pte Ltd, 2 Clementi Loop #02-01, Jin Xing Distripark, Singapore 129809

John Wiley & Sons Canada Ltd, 22 Worcester Road, Etobicoke, Ontario, Canada M9W 1L1

Library of Congress Cataloging-in-Publication Data

(to follow)

British Library Cataloguing in Publication Data

A catalogue record for this book is available from the British Library

ISBN 0 470 84849 9
Typeset in 10½/13pt Sabon by Keytec Typesetting, Bridport, Dorset

Contents

3 Software Architecture and the Development Process   **39**

Preface

The purpose of this book is to describe practical representations and techniques for the development of large-scale software architectures. The goal is to enable other software architects, developers, and managers to become more effective as a direct result of our experiences on several large-scale software development projects. We describe the techniques and architectural representations we have utilized successfully.

This book is intended to be a **practical guide**. Our goal is to be brief. We cover only the essential information to guide software architects in defining the software architecture, providing pointers to further reading in lieu of detailed descriptions of this literature. Ideally, we can help software development teams avoid the common practice of capturing the architecture after the software has been developed instead of utilizing the architecture as a tool to guide the software development.

The Unified Modeling Language (UML) is used throughout this book. We reduce the myriad of UML constructs to a precious few that we have found to be most useful. Leveraging the recent IEEE 1471 standard for software intensive systems, we describe several architectural viewpoints that are helpful in the development and documentation of software architectures. After reading this book, you will understand these viewpoints and techniques that will improve the modeling of your system's software architecture.

The focus of this book will be the software architecture of **large-scale systems**. Typically, this means **enterprise** systems and large **distributed** systems. However, most of the viewpoints and techniques discussed here will apply to **smaller projects** and embedded systems. A typical large-scale software project will include:

- Large quantities of source code (typically millions of lines)

- Large numbers of developers (potentially hundreds, often geographically distributed)

- High complexity of interaction between components

- Extensive use of off-the-shelf components

- Multiple programming languages

- Multiple persistence mechanisms (files, relational databases, object databases)

- Multiple hardware platforms

- Distribution of components over several hardware platforms

- High concurrency

Dealing with the complexity of large-scale systems can be a challenge for even the most experienced software designers and developers. Large software systems contain millions of elements, which interact to achieve the system functionality. The interaction of these elements is far from obvious, especially given the artifacts created for a typical software project. These artifacts are especially critical as new team members are added and at different phases of the project. These phases include development, integration, testing and maintenance of the system. Even more challenging, however, these elements must be understood and modified as the required functionality of the system evolves. To do this correctly requires an understanding of how the elements interact as well as the underlying principles of the design.

Unfortunately, humans are ill equipped to manage complexity. Human short-term memory can typically hold between five and nine items simultaneously. Communication among team members is critical to cooperation and yet often uses imprecise language that frequently creates miscommunication. Providing a shared language of discussion can greatly enhance communication. Recently software has begun to develop some of the complexity management methods similar to those utilized in other engineering domains. These include the UML, object-modeling techniques, Design Patterns, and use of pre-fabricated software components and frameworks.

Architecture-based development is often recommended as a technique for dealing with the complexity of large-scale projects. However, there is still little agreement about how to develop and describe software architecture effectively. The agreement usually ends with the use of UML for design, although this is not universal either. The UML provides a huge set of constructs for describing the software architecture, and includes many extensibility features. However, this flexibility creates a large number of possibilities for software architecture representation. In addition, most of the books and articles on software architecture and UML do not address large-scale development. The literature typically doesn't provide guidelines on how to get started in the definition of the software architecture, and doesn't provide specific representations which convey appropriate information to the stakeholders in a software architecture. This book is an attempt to meet these needs, which are critical to the software architect and the software development team.

Some areas where this book will provide practical guidance include:

- Modeling of architectural constructs, including components, subsystems, dependencies, transactions, and interfaces

- Modeling of environmental elements, including processes, nodes, and physical databases

- Insight into useful techniques for development of software architectures

- Various software architecture development processes

- Roles and responsibilities of the software architect and the architecture team

- Traps and pitfalls of architecture development

- Utilization of reusable and off-the-shelf software frameworks and components

- Addressing non-functional requirements such as performance and maintainability

This book does not purport to describe the best or only way to represent software architecture. Some systems may require additional representations from the ones shown in this book, and others may require only a subset of those shown here. However, most software development projects could benefit from at least some of the techniques and architecture representations described here.

In this book, we stick closely to the UML without major extensions. In some cases, this results in some limitations in formality or model semantics. Regardless of these limitations, these viewpoints have helped us solve complex problems in large systems. Note that over the course of several projects, the views described within were upgraded to utilize the UML. In many cases, we were using ad-hoc notations before the UML had reached its current state. In addition, future changes to the UML and the associated profiles may allow for improvements of the architecture views described in the book. Any that we are aware of are highlighted. Finally, although the focus is on modeling architecture with the UML, we discuss other representations where appropriate.

While a major portion of the book focuses on the application of the UML to software architecture, we also discuss the **role of the software architect** and how architecture development fits within the software development process. We have applied the architectural viewpoints described within on several projects across different organizations and within different development processes. Large projects tend to utilize relatively formal processes for which the described viewpoints fit nicely. However, we have also used these viewpoints and techniques on projects using highly iterative and **agile processes**. We believe that architecture-based development does not need to imply heavy-weight processes.

The **intended audience** for this book includes those practitioners who are currently in the role of software architect, those who are currently software developers or designers and who will soon be in this role, and developers working on large-scale software development who want to better understand successful techniques for software architecture. We have assumed the reader has a working knowledge of the UML and at least a few years experience as a software developer or designer. Experience in the role of software architect or on a software architecture team would allow the reader to gain even more from reading this book.

This **book is organized** to provide general information and overview in the first chapters and discussion of specific architectural viewpoints in the later chapters. Chapter 1 provides our view of what 'software architecture' means. Chapters 2–3 discuss roles and process related to architecture. Chapter 4 gives an overview of a banking system example we use to illustrate the various viewpoints in the later chapters. Chapter 5 summarizes the UML diagrams and the viewpoints described in later chapters. Chapters 6–10 discuss and describe the various viewpoints of software architecture. Chapter 11 describes architecture development techniques and principles.

At the end of each chapter is a **recommended reading** list of key books and papers. These references contain additional information on the topics covered in that chapter. Many of the books, papers, and Web page references in the recommended readings provide detail in areas where we only touch lightly. This list is intended to contain the information we have found most useful. The books and papers are summarized in the Bibliography. URLs can be found at the book's web site.

Chapter 1 introduces the **definition of software architecture** and other terms. In addition, the UML-based architecture viewpoints are introduced and compared with other contemporary architecture methods.

Chapter 2 describes the **role of the software architect**. This includes topics such as the skills and background required to be an effective software architect, the ways an organization can support the architect, and the organization and structure of the software architecture team.

Chapter 3 discusses how software architecture relates to the overall **software development process** and describes processes for the development of software architecture. Topics include the creation of an effective review process, development of software infrastructure, technology roadmap management, process traps and pitfalls, and a brief discussion on tools.

Chapter 4 gives an overview of the **banking system example** that will be used to illustrate the architectural viewpoints described in the remainder of the book.

Chapter 5 provides a quick overview of the **UML diagrams and concepts** used in later chapters to build architectural viewpoints.

Chapter 6 provides an overview of representations and techniques for defining system context and performing **domain analysis**. Included is a discussion of conceptual diagrams, context views, and views used for domain analysis.

Chapter 7 explains architecture representations to facilitate **component development**. This includes the Component View, Component Interaction View, and Component State Views. Component messaging and interfaces are also discussed.

Chapter 8 discusses **subsystem and layer representations**. These views include the Layered Subsystem View and the Subsystem Interface Dependency View. These views serve as some of the fundamental diagrams utilized for software architecture.

Chapter 9 describes **transaction and logical data modeling**. This includes a discussion of mapping designs to relational databases.

Chapter 10 discusses representations for the modeling of **physical system** constructs, including nodes, databases, and process. These include Physical Data Views, Process Views, and Deployment Views.

Chapter 11 describes various **tips and techniques** essential to the development of software architectures. This includes architectural patterns, system partitioning, legacy and COTS utilization, and design techniques.

Chapter 12 puts it all together and has some **final remarks**. This includes some thoughts on becoming a software architect.

The Appendix provides **summaries** of all the **architectural viewpoints**.

This book provides a useful addition to the growing set of literature on software architecture in that it is a concise collection of key information, it is focused on large-scale software architecture, and it provides a set of key informative architectural viewpoints utilizing UML. We hope you will enjoy this book and find it to contain much of the key information required by the software architect. We welcome comments and discussion on this book at our website, *http://www.largescalesoftwarearchitecture.info/*.

Jeff Garland

Richard Anthony

Acknowledgments

We would like to thank the many individuals that helped make this book possible.

Our reviewers gave up their own valuable time to provide us very useful input that helped us to improve the overall quality of the book. These reviewers included Brad Appleton, Thomas Bichler, David DeLano, Robert Hanmer, Ralph Johnson (and his Software Architecture Class Participants), Patrick McDaid, Robert Nord, Micki Tugenberg, and Eoin Woods.

Thanks also to Linda Rising for inspiring us and helping us get this project started. In addition, we would like to thank our editor, Gaynor Redvers-Mutton. Without her enthusiasm and support, this book would not have been possible.

Finally, we would like to thank our families for their patience and support.

1

Introduction

1.1   What is Software Architecture?

The many web pages and books on software architecture have provided dozens, if not hundreds, of definitions of software architecture and related terms. Given this plethora of definitions, we must settle on a set of key definitions for the purposes of communicating software architecture concepts. What follows are some key definitions required for a discussion of software architecture. Additional definitions can be found in the recommended readings located at the end of this chapter.

The Institute of Electrical and Electronic Engineers (IEEE) recently issued a recommended practice regarding Software Architecture: IEEE 1471. The definitions we provide in this book are closely aligned with IEEE 1471. These include definitions of system, stakeholder, architect, architecture, architectural views, and architectural viewpoints. IEEE 1471 defines the following key terms:

- **System** is a set of components that accomplishes a specific function or set of functions.

- '**Architecture** is the fundamental organization of a system embodied in its components, their relationships to each other, and to the environment, and the principles guiding its design and evolution'.

- **Architectural Description** is a set of products that document the architecture.

- **Architectural View** is a representation of a particular system or part of a system from a particular perspective.

- **Architectural Viewpoint** is a template that describes how to create and use an architectural view. A viewpoint includes a name, stakeholders, concerns addressed by the viewpoint, and the modeling and analytic conventions.

The IEEE definitions are intentionally general, to cover many types of software architecture, and are not specific enough to provide detailed guidance to architects and developers of large-scale systems. As such, a large portion of the book is devoted to the description of specific **architectural viewpoints,** defined in the UML, which can be applied to many different large-scale development projects. In addition, most of these viewpoints can also be applied to smaller development efforts. In this book, these viewpoints are illustrated as **architectural views** for an example system introduced in Chapter 4.

The **System Architecture** is the set of entities, the properties of those entities, and relationships among them that define structure of the system. The **Software Architecture** is the set of software components, subsystems, relationships, interactions, the properties of each of these elements, and the set of guiding principles that together constitute the fundamental properties and constraints of a software system or set of systems.

Software Architecting refers to the analysis, design, documentation, review, approval, and other related activities concerned with the definition and management of the software architecture. **Architectural Views** provide representations of the architecture that can be used to guide construction, manage, explore, train personnel, test, and perform other engineering tasks related to creation and maintenance of the software system. Some uses for views include:

- Capturing the design decisions both early on, and as enhancements are made

- Capturing information about the runtime environment for the software

- Providing constraints on the lower-level design and implementation

- Providing input to the structure of the development organization

- Designing the system to meet the software reliability, availability, maintainability, and performance requirements

- Facilitating communication among the project teams

- Communicating the software capabilities and constraints to various developers, testers, and others

For each of these views there is a group of associated **Stakeholders**. The stakeholders may include project and program managers, development team managers and technical leads, system engineers, the test organization, and individual developers. This group of stakeholders may be building the early versions of the software, or may be making maintenance modifications to software that has existed for some time. The architectural views are used to communicate with the stakeholders and, as such, must be carefully crafted to communicate the appropriate information at the appropriate level of detail to the set of associated stakeholders for that view.

While the definition of software architecture terminology provided above is useful, the definitions are still somewhat fuzzy since some of the terms used in the definitions are not themselves clearly defined. The following sections of this chapter will help refine and clarify these definitions.

Architecting software is primarily about software design – design in the large. Thus, the focus of architecture is on the arrangement of the larger aspects of software systems such as subsystems and components rather than classes and objects. To model software systems in the large requires examining both the static or build-time view and the dynamic or runtime behaviors of the software.

Another way of thinking about software architecture is to think about some of the typical questions that can be answered by views of the architecture:

- What are the subsystems or components of the software?

- What are the responsibilities of the components?

- What are the interfaces provided/consumed by these subsystems or components?

- What subsystems or components are impacted by a change to the software?

- How much retesting is required if we change this component?

- What components are involved in installing this change?

- How are parts of the system to be physically distributed?

- How will a change impact the performance of the system?

- What development teams are impacted by a change to this interface?

- How much effort is involved in the development of this functionality?

Since the software architecture being defined is often part of an even larger system, it is often useful to concentrate on the subset of the system for which a particular architecture is being defined. Examples of this type of system subset include a set of components being developed by a particular development team or a set of components that will be developed rather than purchased. This subset of the system can be referred to as the **system under design**. This means that even though only part of a larger system is being designed, any external entities can be considered external to the system under design. This approach allows architectural definition to focus on the parts of the system that are critical and delay concerns about parts of the system which are not yet defined.

1.1.1   What software architecture is not

The software architecture does not include the hardware, network, or physical plant architecture. As such, the software architecture description is not intended to convey the complete description of the system, only the software within that system and any context needed to create the software. As an example, information such as hardware model number, hardware configuration information, routers, or LAN cards is not the focus in software architecture views. Other views, tables, or documents may be used to specify this type of information. However, this type of information should be included or referenced if it influences the software design.

In general, the software architecture description should not duplicate information found in other sources, such as requirements documents or marketing information. Duplication causes extra rework when these other documents change.

The software architecture description must be kept at the appropriate level of detail. The team that defines the architecture must keep each view at the right level of detail and avoid showing more than one level of detail in a particular view, unless the reasons for doing so are clear and agreed upon in advance.

Low-level implementation details should not be included in the software architecture description. For example, a context or subsystem view should not include details about the implementation mechanism for a particular interface. In addition, descriptions of specific implementation mechanisms such as compiler optimizations, shared versus static libraries, COTS class or method names, or file format should not be included in the software architecture views.

1.1.2 Attributes of software architecture

Many different attributes or qualities are of interest in software architecture. These qualities are important because they impact the design and development of many different parts of the software. Some of these qualities include:

- Cultural adaptability – support for multiple languages and cultural differences

- Security – prevent unauthorized access

- Data integrity – does not corrupt or provide bad data

- Maintainability characteristics

    o   Portability – can software be ported to other platforms

    o   Changeability – ability to add new functions and change existing functions

      ■   Fragility – changes to fragile software tend to break existing functions

      ■   Rigidity – software is difficult to change even in simple ways

      ■   Duplication – software with duplication strewn throughout is more difficult to maintain because it is larger and because change is not localized

    o   Understandability – can the software be understood so that changes can be made

    o   Debugging support – support for multiple levels of online debugging

- Testability – software can be tested effectively (impacts changeability)

- Usability – a measure of the effectiveness of the human interface

- Operational system aspects:
  - ○ Availability – percentage of the time system is functioning
  - ○ Manageability – ability to inspect and manage executing components
  - ○ Upgradeability – can system be upgraded while running, how difficult are upgrade procedures
  - ○ Reliability – ability to perform required functions over specified period of time
  - ○ Recoverability – time required to recover from a failure
- Performance
  - ○ Response – is the response fast enough for normal and extreme usage scenarios
  - ○ Scalability – system capacity/throughput can be increased or decreased as necessary
  - ○ Capacity/Throughput – handle heavy loads and still maintain response
- Safety – system does not create hazards in the real world

All of these attributes of the architecture are typical concerns for the architecture team. Members of the architecture team need to constantly evaluate the software architecture to determine if it meets the desired goals with respect to these characteristics. At first blush, this evaluation seems straightforward, but it is not. Increasing one attribute often results in a non-linear decrease in a different attribute. For example, an increase in modifiability might reduce performance. An increase in changeability might negatively impact testability. In addition, the requirements with respect to these properties are not easy to specify. Many of these attributes can only be assessed qualitatively given current tools and practice. Architects must constantly prioritize and manage the trade-offs between these attributes for a given project.

Some of these properties also imply that architects are concerned with implementation mechanisms. For example, mechanisms involving data persistence, transactions, and component error handling often need consistent approaches in order to meet the architectural goals. This often means coping with how to integrate legacy components alongside new components.

To a large extent, the practice of software architecture is the attempt to balance a series of fuzzy trade-offs for the system stakeholders over what are often immensely complex systems. Looking at the whole system at once is simply not possible. Architects need tools to break down problems and reason about the parts, the interaction of the parts, and how the entire system fits together.

1.1.3 Definitions of other key architecture-related terms

The following are a few other definitions that are required for understanding the discussions in the remainder of the book. We recommend the reader rely on the recommended readings for a complete set of architecture-related definitions. Terms that are associated with a particular aspect of software architecture, for example terms associated with the analysis and design process, are defined in the appropriate sections later in this book.

The following terms will provide a clearer understanding of concepts key to large-scale software architecture:

Architectural Patterns – define a general set of element types and their interactions. Examples of Architectural Patterns include *Pipes and Filters*, *Model–View–Controller*, and *Reflection*.

Architectural Style – As the term coined by Garlan and Shaw, it is an idiomatic pattern of system organization. For example, a client–server system is an architectural style. Many of the original architectural styles have been reformulated as patterns.

Build Systems – Development teams typically employ a set of tools that facilitate the translation of a large source code base into a set of libraries and executables in an orderly manner. This usually involves interacting with configuration management tools as well as tools such as the 'Make' utility that utilizes software dependencies to perform incremental builds.

Commercial Off-the-Shelf (COTS) Products – These include software components that are purchased from software vendors or obtained from open source. Some authors use the term 'common' in place of the term commercial to prevent confusion with using the term 'commercial' for open source software.

Component – A construct that groups implementation constructs and provides/consumes a set of interfaces. A component is a modular and easily replaceable implementation construct. The UML definition includes executable processes, applets, EJB, and code libraries as part of the component definition. Some authors further categorize components to include conceptual or logical components. However, we define views only in terms of the runtime aspects of components.

Domain – A domain is an area of concern. For example, the 'problem domain' defines the 'what' aspect of the system under design. The 'solution domain' is the 'how' aspect. A large complex problem is often broken into sub-domains that address only one aspect of the larger problem.

Model – A representation used to understand or document one or more aspects of a problem or solution. With the UML, the model is often kept in a tool that will support the creation of multiple views. In this case, the tool can provide the ability to keep a series of partial views of a complex model consistent.

Top-Level Software Architecture Description – The set of views of the system that encompass the highest-level perspective of the software. This perspective tends to focus on subsystems and components as documented in the top-level software design document.

Subsystem – A collection of classes and components that are grouped to form a development package. These subsystems need to be defined in such a way as to facilitate having them assigned to different, possibly geographically diverse, development teams.

1.1.4 Other types of architectures

Architecture is used in conjunction with many adjunct terms such as technical architecture, business architecture, enterprise architecture, reference architecture, product line architecture, and information architecture. To some extent, all these 'architectures' have confused and obscured the definition of software architecture. The following list will briefly describe some of these in order to clarify how they relate to software architecture:

Enterprise Architecture is generally defined in terms of its constituent architectures. These include the business architecture, application architecture, technology architecture, software infrastructure architecture, and information architecture. The enterprise architecture provides the vision and consistent principles that cross all the constituent architecture types and addresses objectives such as security, flexibility, make versus buy decisions, and reuse.

The **Business Architecture** defines the key business strategies, organization, goals, and related business processes. The software architecture should be complementary with the business architecture. We must remember that the final goal of most software is to make the business successful, not simply to produce an elegant software design.

At the enterprise level, the **Application Architecture** may be more of a set of guidelines on how the various software architectures should be constructed consistently across the enterprise. For a specific product, the application architecture is the software architecture for that product.

The **Technology/Infrastructure Architecture** refers to the network connectivity, hardware upon which the software runs, network routers, operating systems, and other technologies that facilitate the communication among the distributed software components and support the execution environment of the software.

The **Data Architecture**, sometimes referred to as the Information Architecture, refers to how the data is structured, stored, and handled either in the enterprise or for a particular project. The definition of the data architecture involves the specification of the number and type of databases, the logical and physical database design, the allocation of data to servers, the strategy for data replication and archival, as well as the strategy and design of a data warehouse.

The U.S. Army's Joint Technical Architecture – Army (JTA-Army) provides the following definition:

> A *Technical Architecture* is the minimal set of rules governing the arrangement, interaction, and interdependence of the parts or elements that together may be used to form an information system. Its purpose is to ensure that a conformant system satisfies a specified set of requirements. It is the build code for the Systems Architecture being constructed to satisfy Operational Architecture requirements.

A **Product-line Architecture** is used to define a set of products that are developed by a company or organization within the company. The similarities within that set of products allow for sharing of design and implementation information among the various teams developing the products. In this way, the products can be more consistent in the way they are designed, developed, tested, supported, and in their appearance to the end user. In addition, these products can be developed in a more cost-effective manner, due to the design and implementation reuse potential.

The term **Reference Architecture** refers to the definition of an architecture for a particular application domain. An example domain might be satellite ground control systems or telecommunications switch network management. The reference architecture describes the high-level set of elements involved in applications from a particular domain along with their interactions. These elements must intentionally be left at a high level to apply to a large number of systems for that particular domain. Reference architectures are often used to focus on subsystem definition rather than application process level definition. Reference architecture definitions also provide an excellent framework for development of a specific system in that application domain and can save the software architects a significant amount of time rediscovering these elements. In addition, the naming conventions used in the reference architecture provide a common language for architects and application developers to communicate. The functional and interface definitions provided in the reference architecture also provide an opportunity for third-party COTS products to be developed that can be used by software architects for significant portions of the final system.

The techniques and many of the architectural views described in this book can also be used for developing product-line, data, and reference architectures.

1.2 Why Architect?

It has become standard practice in the software industry to engage in a process of software analysis and design along with coding. This design facilitates understanding the structure of the developed software. Architecting simply recognizes the need to focus on the bigger picture of the software design and to provide guidance to the development team designers. At the software architecture level, we're more interested in the subsystems, components, and interfaces than in the classes and methods.

According to Hofmeister, software architecture:

> *provides a design plan – a blueprint of the system, and that it is an abstraction to help manage the complexity of the system. ... The purpose of the software architecture is not only to describe the important*

aspects for others, but to expose them so that the architect can reason about the design.

As described earlier in this chapter, the software architecture is a place to capture early design decisions, provide constraints on the lower-level design and implementation, and provide the organizational structure for the development team. Getting the architecture defined well up front saves a great deal of pain and trouble throughout the development process. The goal is that a well-defined architecture will produce a system that will be easier to design, develop, and maintain.

A good architectural representation (sometimes any meaningful architectural representation) is often missing completely from projects that have been under development for some time. Often the role of the software architect is to capture the existing architecture, then make recommendations for improvements for future releases. We have been in this position, and it can be quite frustrating. Major design changes may be required to repair the damage from the lack of a software architecture, but convincing management to make these changes may be an impossible task. Our hope is that the emphasis on good software architecture practices will allow the software architect to get the architecture right up front. In this way, the architect will not be the victim of a bad architecture and can avoid playing catch-up to try to fix a bad architecture.

Here is a list of some of the uses for the software architecture description:

Training is essential for new team members. Anyone who has been assigned to an existing software project can appreciate the need for a well-documented software architecture to quickly bring developers up to speed. In addition, this information can be used to train customers, managers, testers, and operations personnel for the software system. New architects will likely need to be trained since most teams do not stay the same over the full life of a system.

Making modifications to the system must be done carefully so existing functionality is not broken. A common maintenance need is to describe the impact or scope of a change and hence the regression testing required to ensure correctness of the change. This process should start with a careful analysis of the existing software architecture, which includes the static and dynamic aspects of the system.

Testers need to understand the system and its interfaces, at both the subsystem level and the component level, to perform white box testing. In addition, key process interactions are captured in the architecture views. Finally, each interface should have associated performance information that can be verified by the test organization.

Ensuring architectural attributes such as testability, reliability, availability, maintainability, and performance is another important use of the architectural description. To reason about these attributes of software, there is a need to explore and document these attributes of the software structure.

Verification of requirements – Architectural modeling will often expose missing, invalid, or inconsistent requirements.

Project management – When the architecture moves beyond the preliminary state, project managers can use the information to structure the development organizations and identify work to be performed by specific development teams. Project managers can use the architecture to identify interface elements to be negotiated among the development teams. This can be useful when contract or project negotiations need to take place to reduce functionality or move functionality to a later build.

Operating a system – Large systems such as telephone switches that support 24×7 operations often require human operators to run and interact with the system. Some of these may be users, but others will perform system administration functions. The operations staff often needs an understanding of the software structure to perform their job.

1.3   Architectural Viewpoint Summary

The following summarizes the architectural viewpoints described in later chapters. These viewpoints are built by applying the various UML diagram types to specific architecture development tasks. Each viewpoint has specific modeling goals and stakeholders. Additionally, we have used the IEEE 1471 framework to describe the rationale for each of the viewpoints. These descriptions should assist those attempting to apply these viewpoints. Appendix A provides a detailed summary of these viewpoints.

The viewpoints in Table 1.1 provide a set of highly abstracted software descriptions. The Context View provides a summary of the system boundary and the external entities that interact with the system. The analysis views provide an abstract set of entities focused on modeling the problem rather than the solution.

Table 1.1   Conceptual and analysis viewpoint summary

Viewpoint	UML diagram type	Description	Chapter
Analysis Focused	Class	Describe system entities in response to a scenario. Often referred to as a view of participating classes or VOPC.	6
Analysis Interaction	Interaction	Interaction diagram between objects for analysis.	6
Analysis Overall	Class	Combination of all classes from all focused analysis viewpoints.	6
Context	Use Case	Show the external system actors and the system under design.	6

Table 1.2 describes a set of viewpoints targeted at describing the software design. The Component, Component Interaction, and Component State Views provide a mapping of the logical runtime structures, their functionality, and their intercommunications. The Subsystem Interface Dependency View provides a

Table 1.2   Logical design viewpoints

Viewpoint	UML diagram type	Description	Chapter
Component	Component	Illustrate component communications.	7
Component Interaction	Interaction	Interactions among components.	7
Component State	State/Activity	State transition/activity diagram for a component or for a set of components.	7
Layered Subsystem	Package	Illustrate layering and subsystems design.	8
Logical Data	Class	Show critical data views used for integration.	9
Subsystem Interface Dependency	Class	Illustrate subsystem dependencies and interfaces.	8

visualization of subsystem dependencies and interfaces. The Layered Subsystem View provides a highly abstracted view of all the subsystems. Finally, the Logical Data View provides a description of data models shared between components.

The final set of viewpoints (Table 1.3) is focused on the environment and physical aspects of the software, such as database deployment, that can impact architectural qualities of the system. The Deployment View shows the mapping of hardware and software for distributed systems. The Physical Database View illustrates the physical deployment structures of databases. The Process View shows the execution threads of the system and often the mapping to components. The Process State View shows the dynamic states for a process.

Table 1.3   Environment/Physical viewpoint summary

Viewpoint	UML diagram type	Description	Chapter
Deployment	Deployment	Mapping of software to hardware for distributed systems.	10
Physical Data	Deployment	Physical view of a particular database.	10
Process	Deployment	Show the processes of a particular system instance.	10
Process State	State	Show the dynamic states of a process.	10

Why These Viewpoints – Isn't This Too Many? Where are the others?

So why this particular set of viewpoints? These viewpoints are based on our architectural development experiences on several large-scale projects. These projects are from different domains, including telecommunications, financial systems, and others. We have spent a large amount of time over the years trying to apply various techniques to the real-world work of developing and communicating software architectures. In our experience, the viewpoints discussed here have broad application across many types of systems.

Many of the ideas incorporated in the viewpoints precede the UML. We have reworked our previously ad-hoc notations to utilize the UML. Several of the viewpoints in this book highlight the utilization of parts of the UML not frequently discussed in the current literature, with the majority of articles focused on the modeling of classes and objects. With only a couple of exceptions, all of the viewpoints focus on constructs larger than the class and object, such as components and subsystems.

In these days of Agile Methods, it might be inferred from the number of viewpoints described here that a heavyweight process needs to be employed. This is not the case. The viewpoints should be used only where they provide useful benefit to the project. In addition, there is no requirement that a particular viewpoint be maintained. A viewpoint can be sketched on a whiteboard, information absorbed by the participants, understanding gained, and then the whiteboard erased. This is discussed further in Chapter 5.

Obviously missing from these viewpoints is a staple of software architects: the UML use case diagram. This does not imply that we oppose the application of use cases for requirements definition. Rather, we leave out use case diagrams, for several reasons. First, in our experience they do not contribute greatly to the understanding of the software architecture. Second, non-experts are frequently confused by the meaning of the use case diagrams. Often the relationship lines are interpreted as data flow. A simple list of use cases avoids these issues and serves as an excellent tool for requirements management. Finally, we focus less on use cases here since there is already a large body of literature on use cases.

Another frequently cited 'architectural view' missing here is the implementation or code view. These views use the UML notations to provide a pictorial view of the source files and dependencies. In our experience, these views are inferior to using tables or performing analysis of the source code. Automated tools and build systems are an essential part of creating large systems. These systems often provide the ability to analyze and understand the details of the implementation far better than UML diagrams.

Often, overall views of large software systems become overwhelming. An overall view usually requires architecture-size paper to print, which necessarily limits distribution and use. As a result, we sometimes describe a single viewpoint that covers both a 'focused' and 'overall' variation of a view. In these cases, a series of focused views is often developed as the basis for an overall view. However, if the stakeholders and intent of the focused and overall perspectives are different a new viewpoint is created. The idea of focusing a view is critical to enabling development of large systems. In Chapter 5, in the discussion of managing model complexity, we describe the focusing principles that underlie the derivation of many of these viewpoints. Specific projects might create other viewpoints using these principles.

Frequently several views will be used together. For example, in the design of components and interfaces it is common to create a Component View, a Component Interaction View, and a Component State View. A series of interaction views is then used to elaborate the details of the Component View and validate the component structure. The state view describes the overall dynamics of a collection of components without showing the details of the sequencing of operations.

1.4   Other Software Architecture Approaches

Much of the current literature uses different meanings for the term architectural view. In the following sections, therefore, the term view does not always match IEEE 1471. The following sections will briefly map our approach to several of the other current software architecture approaches.

1.4.1   The 4+1 Views

One architecture approach, the 4+1 Views described by Philippe Kruchten, has become a widespread approach for architecture representation. This scheme defines several key views of a system.

- **Logical View** – This is the logical representation of the key packages and subsystems within the software system under design. It omits any implementation or physical details.

- **Process View** – This view will define how the various operating system threads, tasks, or processes communicate with one another.

- **Deployment View** – This defines the way the actual processes are instantiated and deployed on the physical hardware.

- **Implementation View** – This view describes how the actual software is implemented and usually includes concepts such as the actual source code, the directory structure of the code, and the library structure of the system.

- **Use-Case View** – This view contains the body of use cases that must be defined to understand the behavior of the system.

Obviously, since the 4+1 views preceded IEEE 1471, they do not meet the definition of views as specified in the standard. The 4+1 views are more closely aligned with an IEEE 1471 viewpoint. The 4+1 views describe a collection of representations that provide guidance for software architects. These views tend to be more suggestive than proscriptive. As a result, they have been applied differently in various papers and books.

However, in large part, the viewpoints we discuss are within the spirit of the 4+1 views. Most of the architecture viewpoints described in this book would fit within the definitions of the Logical, Deployment, and Process views of the 4+1 Views (Table 1.4). For example, the subsystem dependency view maps to the Logical View. None of the viewpoints described in this book fit in the Implementation View.

Table 1.4 Approximate Mapping to 4+1 Views

4+1 View	Our Viewpoints
Logical View	Subsystem Interface Dependency, Layered Subsystem, Component, Component Interaction, Component State, Logical Data
Process View	Process, Process State
Deployment View	Deployment and Physical Data
Implementation View	None – see box
Use Case View	None – see box
No Equivalent in 4+1	Context and Analysis

1.4.2 RM-ODP viewpoints

The Reference Model for Open Distributed Processing (RM-ODP) is an ISO standard that provides a framework for the development of standards-related distributed processing. RM-ODP defines the important properties of distributed systems to be openness, integration, flexibility, modularity, federation, manageability, provisioning of quality of service, security, and transparency. In addition, a set of viewpoints are also defined. The RM-ODP viewpoint definition roughly corresponds to the IEEE 1471 definition. The five viewpoints described by RM-ODP are:

- **Enterprise viewpoint** – looks at the system in the context of such factors as the business requirements and policies as well as the scope and purpose of the system. RM-ODP deals with enterprise-related information, such as organizational structure, that may affect the system.

- **Information viewpoint** – refers to the structure of the information, how it changes, how it flows, and the logical divisions between independent functions.

- **Computational viewpoint** – focuses on the decomposition of the system into entities and their interfaces.

- **Engineering viewpoint** – deals with the interaction between distributed system objects and how this interaction is supported.

Table 1.5   Comparison to Bass architectural structures

Structure name	Description	Our viewpoints
Module Structure	Units of work that have associated products and are assigned to development teams.	No direct mapping, but subsystems are used for this purpose.
Conceptual	Abstractions of functional requirements used to understand the problem.	No direct mapping here. Analysis views perform a similar role, but not from using functional requirements.
Process	Physical process or threads in the system.	Process View.
Physical	A mapping of hardware to software.	Deployment View.
Uses	Defines dependencies between modules.	Subsystem Interface Dependency.
Calls	Specifies the invocation relationship between functional procedures or sub-procedures.	Component Interaction views provide similar information. However, we are more concerned with interactions between higher-level entities.
Data Flow	The sending of data between entities.	Not covered.
Control Flow	This indicates which program, module, or system states become active after another has completed some task.	Component State. Also similar is the Process State.
Class Structure	Traditional objected-oriented class structures.	Used in the Analysis and Logical Data.
No Mapping		Context, Layered Subsystem, Physical Data

- **Technology viewpoint** – defines the hardware and software components that make up the system.

Several of our viewpoints are similar to the Engineering, Technology, and Computational viewpoints, but our viewpoints have slightly different concerns and stakeholders.

1.4.3 Bass architectural structures

Bass *et al.* define several 'architectural structures' or views of the software architecture. Bass does not use the UML, but still has significant conceptual overlap with our viewpoints. For example, the ideas of process and deployment viewpoints are similar to the process and physical structures. Table 1.5 compares our set of viewpoints against those defined by Bass.

1.4.4 Hofmeister software architecture views

In a recent software architecture book, Hofmeister *et al.* utilize four UML-based views: the conceptual, module, execution, and code views. These views share some similar concepts and stereotypes with the views we define (Table 1.6). For example, there are similar uses of layering and subsystem modeling. Hofmeister provides an extremely detailed method for protocol development that goes beyond our technique.

1.5 Recommended Reading

IEEE 1471 (2000) describes a framework for the development of software architecture descriptions. This document defines many terms, including architecture and architecture description.

A good source of information on Enterprise architecture is the web site for Enterprise-Wide IT Architecture (EWITA).

Information on application/software architecture can be found on the Bredemeyer web site.

Definitions of technology/infrastructure architecture, business architecture, information/data architecture can be found on The Open Group Architectural Framework (TOGAF) web site. This site also contains description of architecture qualities.

The Army technical architecture (2000), also referred to as the Joint Technical Architecture – Army (JTA-Army), is available on the web.

Table 1.6 Comparison to Hofmeister views

View name	Description	Our viewpoints
Conceptual View	This contains the major design elements and their relationships to one another.	Our approach is different, employing actual components from the start and progressively adding the detail and refactoring as the architecture evolves.
Module View	In this view, the components and their interfaces are mapped to subsystems and modules.	Similar to the Layered Subsystem and Subsystem Interface Dependency.
Execution View	Describes how modules are mapped to threads of execution.	Process and Deployment views.
Code View	Mapping of build-time entities such as source files to components.	Not covered – see box.
No Mapping	There are several of our viewpoints that are not utilized in Hofmeister's approach.	Component, Component Interaction, Context and Analysis, Physical Data, Process State, Component State, Logical Data

David Parnas (1972) was one of the first to recognize the importance of software structure in his seminal paper on decomposing systems into modules.

Shaw and Garlan (1996) coined the term architectural style.

Hofmeister *et al.* (1999) and Bosch (2000) have good discussions of product-line and reference architectures.

The Reference Model for Open Distributed Processing (RM-ODP) is defined in ISO/IEC DIS 10746-1:1995. A book on the subject by Putman (2000) has a complete description of the structuring approaches, viewpoints, and transparencies.

The 4+1 Views of architecture are described in the paper by Philippe Kruchten (1995). There are later discussions in the book by Kruchten (1998) and in the UML User Guide (Booch *et al.*, 1999).

Robert Martin coined the terms 'Fragility' and 'Rigidity' to describe changeability aspects of software. A paper describing these terms can be found at the Object Mentor web site.

2

Roles of the Software Architect

This chapter will provide an understanding of the role of the software architect and how this role relates to other key roles on the development team. In addition, the skills required for the software architect, key approaches for leading the software architecture team, and traps and pitfalls associated with the software architect are discussed. In keeping with the philosophy of providing a practical guide, many of the detailed definitions and discussions are left to the recommended reading at the end of the chapter.

The importance of a good software architect should not be underestimated. There are plenty of examples of projects gone awry for lack of good leadership. Lack of someone filling the architect role is sometimes part of the story. Of course good architects can fail in a non-supportive environment. A poor architect that is out of touch, however, can quickly drive a project to ruin.

The software architect should be instrumental in the development of a 'shared vision' for the software. What is a shared vision? At a basic level the development team must have an idea in their minds about what the final product will be, the effect the software will have, and the goals of the organization. The architecture will reflect and define a large part of the vision.

The shared vision is influenced by many factors, many of them non-technical. However, it is in the technical aspects of the vision that the architect typically makes the largest contribution. The final architecture will necessarily balance the conflicting interests of the various stakeholders. The architect must always be prepared to communicate and interact with other team members about the overall vision.

Defining and communicating this technical vision includes the following activities:

- Analysis of the problem domain

- Risk management

- Requirements management

- Interface design

- Technology roadmap management

- Determination of implementation approaches

- Definition of an architecture that meets the system requirements

- Definition of an architecture that meets goals of the organization

- Definition of an architecture that meets the project budget and schedule

- Oversight of the mapping from the architecture to the design and implementation

- Communication of the software architecture to technical and non-technical audiences

- Maintenance of the software architecture throughout the project lifecycle

Although the exact roles and responsibilities vary somewhat by project and organization, the following are typical:

Requirements tend to be a topic that consumes much of the attention of the software architect. This is because the architect is typically responsible for understanding and managing the non-functional system requirements such as maintainability, performance, testability, reusability, reliability, and availability. In addition, the architect must often review and approve both the requirements provided by the system-level systems engineering organization and the designs produced by the development teams. The software architect participates in reviews of these development work products. Often the architect will work directly with customers, marketing, and support organizations as well on the formulation of requirements.

Technical risk assessment and management is another crucial role for the architect. The architect should use his or her experience to provide management and other stakeholders with information about the key technical risks of the proposed software. A risk reduction plan, either formal or informal, to address these risks is the responsibility of the architect. The architect needs to be capable of assessing the impact of requirements changes on the system as well as the risk of the proposed changes.

Analysis of the problem domain is an important role. This is especially true if the task is to create a product line, framework, or family of products. The architect needs to be able to dissect problems into component parts and structure solutions that can meet the needs of the organization.

Design of the overall software structure as well as critical components, interfaces, and policies is the direct responsibility of the architect. The software architect should also provide a set of design guidelines to the development team as well as input to the development of coding style guides. The software architect is the final authority on issues such as design/development style, interface negotiation and definition, and requirement modifications.

The software architect serves as a **reviewer and approver** of many different project deliverables. These including subsystem designs, interface definition documents, coding style guidelines, and system engineering work products. In addition to reviewing, the software architect also approves many of these documents. The software architect also reviews and approves software deliveries and associated documentation. Examples of these associated documents should include test reports and updated design documents that accompany the delivery.

Mentoring of designers and developers is another key role. Since the software architect is an expert developer and designer it is critical to share this knowledge and experience with other team members. This can be done in a number of different ways, including developing and teaching classes, individual help sessions, and brown-bag seminars. Participating in design sessions, peer reviews, and inspections are additional mentoring techniques. An occasional programming session will also be beneficial.

Integration and test support is another important role of the software architect. This includes defect prioritization and assignment, resolution of defect issues, definition of test scenarios, and participation in test execution.

Implementation is a role that may be played by an architect on a small project. In addition, an architect may be involved in initial prototyping efforts to defer major risks. However, on large-scale projects there are simply too many high-level issues for an architect to spend significant time in an implementation role. One caution for the architect on large-scale systems is to avoid getting tied up in the implementation details to the point that the architecture suffers. In spite of the fact that software architects usually have a strong development background, the architect should not be personally responsible for code deliverables as this involvement may end up as a bottleneck for other developers.

Finally, **team lead** is another critical role played by the architect. The architect is part of the leadership team and needs to work with that team. In addition, in large projects an architect may have a supporting staff, or at a minimum an architecture team. The architect needs to lead these teams and keep them focused on addressing the most critical project risks.

The software architect is also a key **liaison** to project management, other technical leaders, system engineering, and developers. The architect will need to translate and interpret technical information for other team members as well as helping a team member find appropriate contacts.

These roles and responsibilities will be emphasized or de-emphasized as the project evolves. As the systems engineers begin requirements definition, the software architect will be focused on understanding the domain, preparation and review of the requirements. As requirements are becoming more defined, the focus will shift to staffing the senior technical team members, and process definition. During the development of the top-level architecture, the focus will shift to architecture definition.

As subsystem teams start design, the role of reviewer and approver will be the focus. As the software deliveries to the integration and test organization begin, the role of integration and test support may be the focus. In addition, the software architect must start the architecture definition tasks for the next increment of the software during the development of the current increment, or the architecture definition will not be complete when the next set of subsystem design activities begin.

2.1   Relationship to Other Key Roles in Development Organization

The following roles are usually found in large-scale software development. Each role has an associated relationship with the software architect. Note that no organization will necessarily have all these roles, nor will each role be assigned to separate individuals. Often in smaller organizations, two or more of the roles can be combined and assigned to one person. In addition, there will often be more overlap of individuals focused on architecture and those focused on development in smaller projects. On large projects, these kinds of overlap will occur less frequently. The relationships between the role of software architect and other roles in the organization are described below:

Role: project management

Description: This includes the top-level project manager, and the immediate staff associated with that role. This could include program planning, sub-contract management, supplier management, software estimation, release management, and operations management.

Relationship to Software Architect: The program management must understand how the software architecture maps to internal development teams, subcontracted development teams, COTS tools, hardware, network architecture, and external organizations/entities with whom the software must interface. In addition, the architect will work with project management in the definition of release content as well as prioritization of features included or omitted from a release.

Role: development team managers

Description: These are the managers for each individual development team. These may be internal or subcontracted teams. These leads may also have a small staff with whom the software architect must communicate.

Relationship to Software Architect: These development team managers should clearly understand the interfaces they provide and consume with respect to other development teams and external entities. This includes the high-level technical aspects, such as COTS tools involved in the interface, as well as the complexity involved in the development or modification of each of these interfaces. In addition, the managers should understand the key interfaces that may be a potential performance problem. Finally, the software architect will need to assist the development team managers in the addition of features or reduction of functionality.

Role: system architect/chief engineer

Description: Many organizations have a top-level technical lead responsible for the overall system design and delivery. This is frequently the case when significant hardware components are to be delivered along with software. The responsibilities associated with this role often include technical leadership of the systems engineering, software development, hardware design, network (LAN and WAN) design, and even test organizations.

Relationship to Software Architect: The software architect must communicate the overall software design to the system architect. This includes interfaces between development teams, external interfaces, requirements-related issues, and dependencies from other organizations that may impact the software development. In addition, the software architect will work closely with the chief engineer to identify and resolve significant technical issues.

Role: chief software engineer

Description: In some organizations, a role of chief software engineer (CSE) is separate from the software architect. In smaller organizations, these roles may be merged. The role of the chief software engineer is usually tied more closely to the development process than the details of the software architecture. This means the CSE should not only play a key role in the definition of the process, but should ensure the process is followed throughout the development life-cycle. The CSE works closely with the technical lead and build manager for each release.

Relationship to Software Architect: The software architect and CSE work closely together not only to make sure the delivered software meets the requirements, but also to ensure that the interface and port definitions match those defined by the software architecture team. In addition, the CSE will consult the software architect on many process definition issues, especially those related to requirements, architecture definition, and design.

Role: hardware architect

Description: The hardware architect is responsible for the selection and configuration of the hardware on which the software must execute. This requires a careful analysis of several types of requirements. These include requirements related to performance, input/output, data storage, COTS products, software sizing, and the user interface.

Relationship to Software Architect: The software architect will provide detailed information on the low-level requirements the software will levy on the hardware. These estimates will often vary widely early in the architecture definition process and less widely as the architecture becomes well understood. The hardware architect will also communicate to the software architect the restrictions that are imposed by the hardware that will be used. Often the selection of hardware is mandated by the customer or prior installations of the system and the software architect must make sure the software architecture is defined within the constraints of this hardware. In addition, the software architect must participate in the hardware selection and the specification of configuration information, making sure all key requirements are considered.

Role: network architect

Description: The network architect is responsible for defining the LAN and WAN design and configuration. In addition, the network architect must make sure the installation of the network hardware is performed to meet the network design. This role is sometimes combined with the hardware architect, primarily because knowledge of the various hardware components and how these components are interconnected are closely related.

Relationship to Software Architect: As with the hardware architect, the software architect must communicate network requirements to the network architect and participate in the selection and configuration of the network. In addition, once the network configuration is defined, the network architect must communicate the constraints implied by the network back to the software architect.

Role: technical leads of each release

Description: One effective approach we have seen is to have a manager and technical lead work together to deliver each major release of the software. Each individual can then focus on what they do best, leaving the release management tasks to the manager and the technical issues to be worked out by the technical lead. This lead is responsible for technical aspects of the interfaces, defects, building, testing, and delivery of the software. These technical leads will often participate in the definition of and modifications to the software architecture.

Relationship to Software Architect: First, the software architect must deliver a set of architecture views to the technical lead that clearly communicates the system under development and test for that release. This will enable the technical lead to quickly detect and remedy issues with the software. In addition, the software architect should work with the technical lead to change representations in the architecture that do not accurately represent the software that was delivered.

Role: data architect

Description: The data architect is responsible for the definition, development, and documentation of the data architecture. This includes both the logical and physical data architecture. When specific aspects of the physical data architecture are the responsibility of the subsystem development teams, the data architect will review and approve the team's data architecture.

Relationship to Software Architect: The data architect will usually be one of the members of the software architecture team. It is important that the data architect work closely with the software architect and that the software architect have insight into and final approval of the data architecture.

Role: systems engineering leads

Description: The systems engineering leads are responsible for delivering the system requirements that have been allocated to software, to the development organization.

Relationship to Software Architect: The software architect must review these requirements to make sure they can be developed, given the project constraints, and provide feedback to the systems engineering leads when a mismatch occurs. In addition, the software architect must communicate the software architecture to the systems engineering leads to make sure the requirements have been correctly understood and translated into the architecture.

Role: software systems engineering lead

Description: Many development organizations create a software systems engineering (SSE) group that translates and maps the requirements from the higher-level systems group into lower-level requirements, which can be assigned to individual development teams. This often means that the higher-level 'shall statements' which are used at the top level must be translated into use cases and other artifacts that more clearly communicate the requirements to the software development teams. In addition, the requirements associated with each interface may also be specified by this team.

Relationship to Software Architect: The software architect should participate in many of the use case and interface definition activities with the SSE team. The preliminary software architecture will often be provided to this organization, and the resulting activities of the SSE team will evolve the software architecture as the system is better understood.

2.2 Skills and Background for the Architect

A software architect should have most or all of the following skills, background, and attributes.

Extensive software design and development experience is required to create an effective overall design, and the software architect must understand and explain how this will map to the implementation. In order to do this, the software architect should have significant development experience.

Technical leadership is key to making timely and effective decisions. The management and development leads need to be convinced the decisions being made by the software architect are good ones, based on current information. The software architect should be a recognized technical leader and, as a result, instill this confidence in the program managers, development managers, and development leads.

Team facilitation skills are essential. The software architect should be effective in leading both the architecture team and the development teams. The architecture team usually consists of individuals with strong technical backgrounds and who often have strong opinions. The architect should be able to handle the dynamics of this team as well as be the final decision maker when there are technical disagreements.

Communication skills are vital to the job of architect. The software architect should be able to handle hundreds of emails a day, provide clear direction to the architecture team and technical leadership, and make the architecture and related issues clearly understood by both technical and non-technical stakeholders. The software architect should also be able to clearly communicate needs and concerns related to the architecture to these stakeholders.

The architect will spend a great deal of time **building consensus** among technical leaders and managers. This is often required in advance of technical meetings, so the meetings will run smoothly. However, the amount of consensus building should not increase to the extent that the project stops progressing. There is an appropriate time to make a decision and move on, preparing those on the opposing side in advance, if possible.

Technical skills of the software architect should be broad, deep and up to date. In addition, based on a wide knowledge of technology, the architect should have the ability to make technology selections that can facilitate development within the project schedule, budget, and developer skill set. Technical leaders in the development organization that try to push their own favorite technology should be dealt with carefully by the architect. In addition, the architect must avoid the tendency to select one technology and apply it to all situations. Finally, the architect needs to keep **up-to-date technical skills** on new software design and development technologies and should always be researching new techniques that are more effective. Development languages, modeling techniques, and platforms continue to evolve rapidly. The architect needs to assimilate the relevant aspects of these new technologies for their applicability to the system or systems.

One facet of the architect's technical skill set is **knowledge of component communication mechanisms**. In order to select the correct implementation approaches and tools, the software architect should have experience with and knowledge of several mechanisms. Examples include remote procedure call (RPC), Java Remote Method Invocation (RMI), Common Object Request Broker Architecture (CORBA), other standards-based communication protocols, directory services, web services, and relational as well as object-oriented databases.

In addition, **knowledge of the domain** is also important. The software architect must be able to develop an architecture that meets the needs of the customers and end users of the system. In order to meet these needs, the approaches and techniques applied by the end users in performing their day-to-day tasks must be clearly understood by the architect. This can frequently be achieved by spending on-site time with existing or potential customers. There is no substitute for actual hands-on experience, or at least discussions with and observations of end users of the system under design. Good architects tend to be quick learners and keen observers because of the need to quickly acquire new domain understanding.

Finally, the software architect must possess very good **abstraction skills**. This is critical to the definition of views that communicate the appropriate information. Many developers will not be good software architects, as they are not able to focus at the right level of abstraction and quickly become overwhelmed by the low-level aspects of the software design and implementation.

2.3   Injecting Architecture Experience

Frequently an organization may not have a person with the necessary experience to be the software architect when embarking on a major project. In this case, a contracted specialist can be brought in to perform the responsibilities of the software architect or assist the individual selected from within the organization to be the software architect. Contract architects have the distinct advantage of a broader range of systems experience than can typically be obtained by employees. However, contract architects often lack specific experience with existing team members and organizational norms. As a result, a good compromise is to use contract architects to guide and assist the project software architect. In this way, the diverse experience of the contract architect can be leveraged within the confines of the existing culture of the development organization.

In addition, a contracted specialist in software architecture can be used to reduce the workload on the software architect. Contract architects can be used for assisting in the development of the software architecture, support of the development of subsystem designs, and for assessments or reviews of both the top-level architecture and subsystem-level design.

Several other approaches can be used to inject architecture experience.

These include mentoring of select individuals by members of the architecture team or contract architects, purchased or developed training courses for architects and designers, attendance at software architecture and design conferences and workshops, brown-bag seminars, and participation in reviews and inspections of architecture and design work products.

2.4   Structuring the Architecture Team

In order to function effectively, the software architect must not become detached from the other technical leadership. This includes the chief software engineer, the software systems engineering lead, and the development team leads. The approach that works best for communication of both the top level and subsystem level of the software architecture is to create a small software architecture team made up of the key technical individuals on the development team. The size of this team should usually be limited to no more than seven individuals. If the development is geographically distributed, then a weekly meeting via network-connected meeting software and teleconference can work well. If the travel budget permits, it is good to have the software architect and a few key individuals travel to the different sites occasionally for some of the meetings. This can be done in conjunction with periodic technical interchange meetings with the development teams.

The architecture team is composed of team **members, not representatives**. When the team meets, the team members should be representing the best interests of the system architecture, not the individual groups they may feel the need to represent. These team members should report to project management personnel, not to the software architect. This will allow the software architect to focus on the technical aspects of the system and not on the management tasks, such as performance reviews and other personnel management activities. However, a large project may require a small group of people that report to the software architect to support such activities as preparation of the top-level architecture document or definition/negotiation of interfaces between the software subsystems or processes.

The architecture team should take **ownership of the overall software architecture and design**. In addition, they are responsible for **defining the design and coding guidelines**. The software architecture team should be the group of individuals that makes the key design and implementation decisions. They are responsible for making the architecture and design as effective as possible, given project constraints. In addition, both requirements and design changes to the system should be approved by this team.

The architecture team is a working group that **approves all design reviews, documents, deliveries,** and makes sure the software delivery and the architecture defined for that delivery are consistent. Members of this team should be invited to all key reviews. In addition, they should participate in many of the peer reviews and inspections of the design artifacts and code. Many of the members of the software architecture team will be development leads, since these are usually the senior technical members of the development team. This will also facilitate acceptance of decisions made by the team among the development team members.

It is important this team be composed only of technical design and development leads that are responsible for the software architecture, not just individuals who are interested in or who may need to review the architecture. One exception to this rule is that a technical lead from the test team is sometimes a good addition to the architecture team to ensure the testability aspects have been considered.

While project management support is important for the success of the software architecture team and managers should be used to facilitate the team activities, **a manager should never lead the team nor should any managers be members of the team.** These managers should not be making or guiding the technical decisions made by the software architecture team, other than to provide input on the budget and schedule aspects of architectural decisions.

In order to facilitate communication, **presentations** should be scheduled for the **sole purpose of communicating the latest architecture** and related issues to the managers and other development team members. These presentations are effective communication and training sessions and will be effective in minimizing the number of requests to add interested individuals to the architecture team.

2.5 Traps and Pitfalls Associated with the Role of Software Architect

Many organizational issues can have a significant impact on the ability of the software architect to function effectively. As much as possible, the architect should focus on the definition of an effective architecture that meets the requirements. Distractions caused by a poorly defined or misaligned development organization can detract from this focus. A few of these issues and their potential remedies are discussed below.

2.5.1 Clear definition of leadership

Description: In the organization, the definition of clear leads is critical in many key areas. These include software systems engineering, development leads, test leads, and potentially the software architect or chief software engineer. Often, especially if there are two diverse geographical development centers, management will create two or more co-leads with equal roles and responsibilities. The degenerate case of this is the 'self-managed team.' This is a clear sign of trouble on the horizon, as these two leads will seldom be able to act as one and an inevitable set of conflicts will occur.

Remedy: Encourage management to establish a clear leader and offer an equitable solution. For example, the lead of one type of team (for example, the test team) could be established at one site and the lead of another team (for example, the process team) at another site. Another approach we have seen to be successful is to clearly define the roles and responsibilities of the two individuals so that there is no overlap and to have a common manager or technical leader that arbitrates conflicts. Of course, this approach works best when the two individuals are located at the same site and can easily coordinate with one another.

2.5.2 Reporting structure for the software architect

Description: The software architect should report directly to the overall software development manager. Any attempt to create a software architect from one of the lower level technical leads and leave that lead reporting to the same manager will fail. In order to garner the respect required for the job of software architect and to effect change and arbitrate management disagreements, the reporting level of the software architect must be at the appropriate level. In addition, a software architect reporting to a manager at too high a level is often seen as an outsider by the entire development organization.

Remedy: Key individuals should usually report to the top-level software development manager. These individuals include the software architect, chief software engineer, software systems engineering lead, and data architect. The network architect and hardware architect often report to a project hardware management lead. An example of an organization chart based on this approach is shown in Figure 2.1. The key technical positions are shown as staff positions reporting to a manager. Another approach we have seen to be

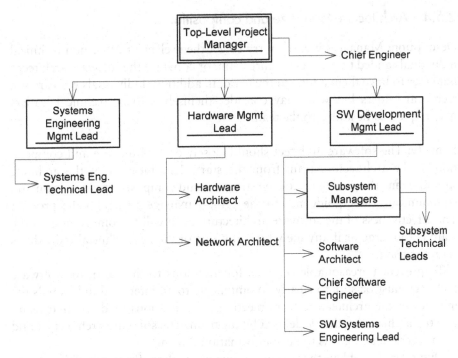

Figure 2.1   Organization chart example

effective is to have all these key technical individuals, with the exception of the subsystem technical leads, report to the chief engineer.

2.5.3   Geographical location of software architect and technical leads

Description: In geographically distributed development organizations, the software architect must either be located with the majority of the development leads, or plan on commuting frequently to the other site in order to communicate with these leads.

Remedy: The technical focus will shift early in the program to one primary site, usually the one where the top-level development manager spends most of his or her time. Select the software architect from the qualified technical leads at the site where technical focus will most likely result, or plan on having the software architect travel for a significant amount of the time.

2.5.4 Architecture team size and composition

Description: Managers will often try to get themselves or other non-technical individuals added to the architecture team, or convince the software architect's manager to have them added to the team. In addition, individuals who are not technical leaders but who may consider themselves to be technical leaders may request to be added to the team.

Remedy: The software architect should closely control the size and composition of the architecture team from the start. This means that the architect should define the guidelines for the structure and composition of the team and communicate these guidelines to the project managers early in the process. The effectiveness of the software architecture team will be compromised if the team is too large or if anyone who is not one of the key technical individuals is on the team.

To prevent unreasonable requests for additions to the team, the software architect must be sure to clearly communicate to all interested individuals the minutes of the architecture team meetings, the decisions made by that team, and the architecture that is defined by the team. The software architect should keep several mailing lists to keep information flowing.

One related problem that occurs frequently is that effective individuals are often overlooked when the team is first structured and individuals might be added who are not effective. One approach for adding to the team is to start very small (3–4 key individuals) and then determine if others have emerged as technical leaders in the organization. Removing people from the team is very difficult, so the initial selection must be done carefully.

2.5.5 Software architect lifecycle participation

Description: The software architect is frequently moved on to the next project in advance of the final delivery of the system. This may be due to the perception that the software architecture task ends before the final build or due to the needs of the new project. This should be avoided, as the architect will not be able to evaluate the true effectiveness of the architecture and will not learn from architecture flaws that existed in the system, but were not noticed until the end users interacted with the software over an extended period. This could potentially introduce the same flaws in the software architecture of the new system.

Remedy: The software architect should participate in the development effort, either in the role of software architect or as the technical lead of the final software build. If the architect remains in the architecture role, this will have the added benefit of ensuring the documentation of the software architecture accurately represents the final state of the software. If the architect is filling the technical lead role, then this will result in a closer involvement with the end users and a better understanding of the weaknesses in the architecture.

2.6 Recommended Reading

McCarthy (1995) describes the nuances of the development of a shared team vision in great detail.

Hofmeister *et al.* (1999) and Bass *et al.* (1998) have good discussions on the role and skills of the software architect. The book by Sewell and Sewell (2001) also has a good discussion of the overall role of the software architect.

Organizational issues affecting the software architect are discussed in the book on organizational practices by Dikel *et al.* (2000). The manager's perspective and use of the software architecture can be found in the book by Paulish (2001). The topics in this book include an approach for defining the software organization based on the architecture as well as how to extract project planning and management information from the architecture.

Jim Coplien and Neil Harrison are building a pattern language that includes several patterns related to the software architect and architecture team. Links to this information can be found on Jim Coplien's web page under the links to the organizational pattern language effort.

Kruchten (1999) describes some of the roles discussed in this chapter and Brown (1998) discusses several of the software architecture pitfalls in the Anti-Patterns book.

The Worldwide Institute of Software Architects (WWISA) has a good description on their web page of the role of the software architect and how it changes throughout the phases of software design and development.

There are several good descriptions of the role of the software architect and links to papers and to other sites containing similar information on the Bredemeyer web site. Additional information can be found on the HP software architecture web site. Another good description of the role of the software architect can be found at the IconProcess web site.

3

Software Architecture and the Development Process

This chapter provides an overview of the development process and its relationship to the definition of the software architecture. This discussion is included to provide an overall context for the discussions that follow, not to mandate a specific development process. Our architecture definition approach can fit within the context of most development processes. Included in this chapter is a brief description of an iterative development process, deliverables and artifacts that relate to software architecture, use case driven approaches for architecture development, technology roadmap definition, development process traps and pitfalls, and a discussion of case tools.

3.1 Overview of Iterative Development

The Rational Unified Process (RUP) is a widely used framework for defining and managing the development process. The RUP process framework provides some key terms that will be used throughout this book when process phases and lifecycle stages are discussed. While RUP is not a requirement for applying the viewpoints, we use elements of RUP to describe software process in general. In a RUP-based process, viewpoints are artifacts associated with a particular milestone in the process.

3.1.1 Overall process phases

While some managers may prefer to look at development as a waterfall for project planning purposes, large software development projects will always be an iterative process. There are many reasons for the iterative nature of software development. These include the inability to completely specify requirements, modifications to requirements, and the need to maintain systems over a long lifecycle. The only decision, then, is whether or not to take control of the iterations.

The phases defined in the RUP process are organized over time in the order shown below:

- Inception – This phase is where the vision of the final software product is defined. In addition, the business case and scope of the work to be done are specified in this phase. In order to perform inception-related tasks, the higher-level requirements must be analyzed and understood. These requirements are often incomplete when the preliminary analysis is performed. Assumptions must be made for missing requirements. These assumptions can be refined in later phases.

- Elaboration – In this phase, a plan for the development activities is prepared. In addition, the bulk of the requirements and top-level architecture definition is performed in this phase. This architecture definition will evolve from a very preliminary version to the architecture definition that allows the development teams to begin to design their own architecture and begin development. The architecture will continue to evolve throughout the subsequent phases, due to requirements changes and project re-scoping.

- Construction – This phase is where the actual software product is built. This software will evolve from preliminary versions that have limited functionality, but allow the development team to get through the development/delivery/integration/test cycle, to the final version that is delivered to the users.

- Transition – In this phase, the product is transitioned to the users. This includes delivery, training, support, and maintenance. The end of this phase is the product release.

Within each phase, one or more iterations may be defined. These iterations further divide the work and the deliverables for that phase. One of the key tenets of RUP is to get deliveries as early in the development process as possible to avoid the 'big bang' integration and test phenomenon that occurs on so many software development projects. In addition, high-risk functionality and interfaces are moved to early iterations to help mitigate risk and drive out issues as early as possible. This is a change for most development team members, since the natural tendency for developers and managers is to put off the high-risk work until late in the development cycle. The software architect should assist the product management and release management leadership in defining the functionality for each of the iterations.

The architecture team will go through a process of refinement of the top-level software architecture. This process will normally be done over several iterations. The software architecture will evolve as the development process identifies necessary changes. This is delivered to the development teams as a specification for them to use when doing their own level of design. While the types of artifacts produced at each level are similar, the content and level of detail will change. In addition, some artifacts from the software architecture description can be used as-is by the development teams and do not require further elaboration.

3.1.2 Lifecycle stages

The lifecycle stages, called process workflows in RUP, define the activities that occur within each phase. Not all of the workflows occur in every phase. Which workflows apply in a particular phase is part of the planning process for the project. The software architect will primarily be involved in the analysis and design workflow, but will be involved in all workflows. We don't make a clear distinction between analysis and design, nor does RUP. The definitions of these activities can often blur, especially when several levels of software architecture are defined. The analysis and design activities for the top-level architecture can be quite different from those done by each individual development team.

The core process workflows and software architect responsibilities are:

- Business Modeling – This workflow is not necessarily needed for all development efforts. This modeling is useful for understanding the business domain, usually before the development effort begins. Business modeling usually consists of end-user-centric use case development, along with a business domain model of the key entities. The software architect can play a key role here in the selection of use cases, definition of use cases, and in developing the business domain model. Individuals with knowledge of the business aspects of the system often don't have modeling experience. As a result, the architect may play the role of facilitator while learning the business aspects of the system.

- Requirements – In large-scale projects, the higher-level systems engineering organization, in conjunction with marketing organizations and target users, often provides the functional requirements for the software. The software architect and other members of the architecture team should participate in this activity. Some of the architecture team members are often assigned to the system engineering team in the early project stages. In addition, the software architect is the customer of these requirements and should review them carefully. The requirements will become the basis for the architecture definition. Another set of requirements is often generated for the development teams, often by a software systems engineering team. The software architect should participate in this process as well, working in conjunction with the software systems engineering team to define the top-level architecture.

- Analysis and Design – This workflow occurs at two levels. First, the software architecture team performs analysis and design, using the software system engineering work products, and produces the top-level architecture. Second, each development team performs analysis and design under the review and approval of the architecture team. The software architect must make sure the subsystem-level analysis and design meets the specification from the top-level architecture. In addition, the subsystem-level effort will undoubtedly uncover problems or even mistakes in the top-level architecture.

- Implementation – The top-level architecture and subsystem-level architectures are input to the implementation workflow. The software architect must ensure the resulting implementation matches the top-level and subsystem-level architecture for each of the iterations. Implementation will also uncover areas of the software architecture that need to be modified.

- Test – The software architect should be an active participant in testing of the resulting software. This includes providing a top-level architecture description that can be used by the test organization to understand the software, and in the identification of implementations that have strayed from the guidelines in the top-level architecture. The test workflow will also drive out problems with the architecture that will result in modifications to the original architecture.

- Deployment – This workflow involves delivery of the software to the end users. The software architect at this point is involved in communicating the architecture to the end users, and potentially to the sales staff, so that the benefits of this architecture over others can be easily seen.

Figure 3.1 shows an example of the relative level of effort for each workflow over a series of three example iterations. In addition, it shows some typical architecture-related artifacts that would be produced by the workflows in each iteration. In this diagram, we have shown top-level architecture development as a separate workflow from subsystem design. This sort of tailoring is often needed in RUP to deal with multiple levels of architecture and design.

3.1.3 Architecture and agile processes

A recent movement is the rise of agile processes such as Extreme Programming (XP) and Scrum. These processes have some of the following characteristics:

- Rapid and frequent delivery of useful, working software

- Responsive to rapid requirements changes

- Architectures that emerge from self-organizing teams

- Teams regularly self-examine processes to make them more efficient

We see little conflict between agile processes and the techniques and viewpoints we recommend. Agile teams may tend to maintain and create fewer of the views than teams with a more traditional process. However, larger projects inherently have larger numbers of developers, and an increased need for training and communication of the architecture. Even teams using agile processes will need a reasonable number of architecture views to communicate a common understanding of the architecture and to coordinate development effectively. Having all team members reading the code to understand the

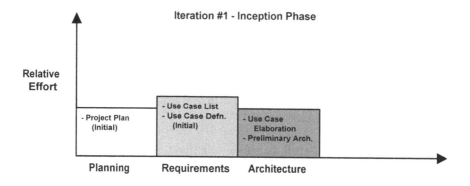

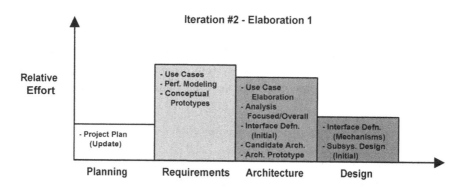

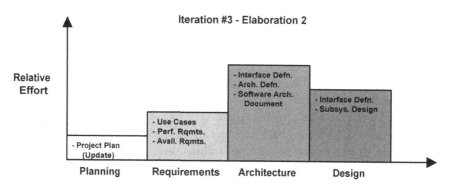

Figure 3.1   Workflow level of effort and artifact summary example

architecture is neither feasible nor effective as a means to communicate the overall design.

We fully agree with the philosophy that prefers the production of code to secondary artifacts. So for each artifact or document that is produced, the software team and architect need to ask the question, 'Who will look at this?' If a large document is produced which has no stakeholders, then it should be scrapped. While this book recommends several views and diagrams to capture the software architecture effectively, we do not suggest they all be used for every development project. It is the responsibility of the software architect and the teams to select the important views that convey the appropriate information to the stakeholders for the current system.

In our experience with large projects, a good architecture will not emerge without a focal point for communication. The tendency is for individual teams to reinvent infrastructure code, use different development standards, and to be focused on limited objectives rather than the overall goals. An architecture team nicely focuses the communication among development teams and provides a conduit for setting architectural standards and for focusing the development of reusable infrastructure libraries.

Some might suggest that there is conflict between the software architects, who want to spend time designing the system, and the programmers, who want to start writing code. This can result in proposed approaches that reduce or eliminate the need for analysis and design. But the best architects are usually also developers and understand how to limit their efforts to the development and maintenance of the primary system viewpoints. Experienced software architects can successfully avoid this pitfall.

Extreme programming (XP) advocates performing design before coding. Designs are typically sketched on a whiteboard and documentation is not maintained. In our experience this approach will not scale up to large development, due to the lack of an architectural focal point. XP advocates acknowledge that XP has not been utilized on many large projects. Of course individual development teams within a larger development team might utilize XP practices using the architect and other team members as a source of design input and constraints. In the end, most of the XP practices are compatible with an organized architecture effort. However, for this approach to work the system must be divided into smaller chunks that smaller teams can address in a relatively independent fashion. Moreover, dependencies between these chunks require additional coordination between teams.

An Experience Combining Architecture and Agile Processes

A few years ago we worked on a project that successfully combined architecture with agile development techniques. In this project, a large development team used a Scrum-like iterative development process to cope with a very dynamic requirements environment and to support rapidly evolving project goals. The nature of the subsystem being developed was fairly novel and, as a result, even domain experts had difficulty writing good requirements. The subsystem team peaked at about 40 developers and the project team peaked at about 250 developers.

The project was far from perfect, but without a focal point for architectural decisions the result would have been utter chaos and potentially project failure. In fact, the project started without an architect. The appointment of a full-time architect emerged as a result of a need for better coordination of cross-team issues. While there were many experienced and motivated developers that attempted to address architectural concerns, they were not successful. This was due, at least in part, to these developers lacking the authority to make decisions and partially because there wasn't total agreement. Appointment of an architect and architecture team to mediate and drive these issues to resolution solved the problem. Unfortunately, the late recognition of the architecture role meant that the architect and the architecture team had to play catch-up.

From the development team perspective, the appointment of an architect to help mediate architectural issues was critical and had little impact on the process. Architectural issues and concerns brought up at daily team meetings would now finally get the attention needed to resolve them. The movement of reusable assets into a common infrastructure group was helpful in reducing the team workload. Finally, the additional effort to participate in the development of a top-level architecture document and architecture team meetings was a relatively minor investment of time and paid many dividends in helping teams to communicate and to understand the system.

The 'stories' used by XP practitioners are very much like use cases. If the traps and pitfalls of use cases we describe below can be avoided, the two concepts of use cases and stories are very similar. The need to do more development and less documentation can be met from two aspects. First, the approach advocated in RUP is to start implementation iterations as early as possible, put high-risk items early in the development cycles, and evolve the system iteratively. This should get coding going sooner. However, the top-level architecture is required to provide guidance to that evolving development. The approach we recommend is one of cautious moderation.

Finally, some XP practices can create issues in the deployment. Specifically, merciless refactoring of the data schema is usually not usually practical due to the testing and transition costs. Attempts to do this can result in deployment nightmares. We discuss the reasons for this in detail in Chapter 9.

3.1.4   Start early, refine constantly

In order to have a successful software development project, several activities must be started as early as possible. One key activity we have seen that must be started early is the development of software infrastructure. This infrastructure includes frameworks and utility classes that will be used by multiple development teams. These include debug and logging capabilities, wrappers around COTS products, component frameworks, process startup/shutdown utilities, and network management interfaces. These products must be available when developers start development, and may also be needed for development teams to complete their design. To make these available in a timely fashion, the design and development of the infrastructure must be started in advance of subsystem-level analysis and design. The catch, however, is that the requirements for this infrastructure often come out of the development activities. The approach we have used is to design and build a preliminary set of infrastructure products, based on experience, and modify/add to this set of infrastructure quickly as new requirements arise.

Another effective approach is to start the design as soon as any descriptions of the system become available. This design will be preliminary and should be clearly marked accordingly. This 'straw man' approach to doing top-level architecture has the benefit of getting a design out early so input can be obtained from systems engineers and development teams. One drawback is that some managers may forget that this is preliminary and start to build a development organization around the preliminary design. The only remedy for this is to constantly remind them that the architecture is preliminary, and to indicate which aspects of the architecture may be well defined enough to devote one or more dedicated development teams to them.

Another aspect of starting early on the architecture is to look for other sources in the absence of requirements. For example, in some telecommunications domains, standards exist which go a long way in describing the behavior and functionality of certain aspects of telecommunications systems. This information should be used whenever possible to get a jump on the top-level architecture definition.

The definition and deployment of a set of key prototypes is also a task that should be done early. These prototypes may be developed in the inception or elaboration phase. The definition and management of an effective prototyping plan is one of the key responsibilities of the software architect.

Determination of the appropriate views and artifacts to produce can vary depending on the needs of the project. For example, a set of preliminary deployment views may need to be created if the purchase process requires the hardware architect to budget or even purchase hardware early in the project lifecycle. In a different scenario where the hardware is more flexible or even predetermined, these views may be done much later in the development of the system.

3.2 Requirements Management

3.2.1 Use cases and requirements engineering

Use cases can be an effective tool in the identification of key software requirements. They can also be used as a means to translate higher-level systems engineering requirements and functional artifacts to a meaningful set of information for software developers. In this way, the 'shall' statements in the higher-level requirements can be mapped to use cases as a simple means to show traceability. The elaboration of these use cases can provide the necessary information on how the software subsystems and components will communicate.

If a software systems engineering organization exists, then this group should be focused on use cases and related artifacts, such as sequence and collaboration diagrams. Use cases can also be effective as one means to drive out the software system partitioning. This approach is described in Chapter 12.

However, caution must be exercised when use cases are applied. Use cases cannot be expected to form a complete specification for the system. Use cases are usually not effective for the specification of system characteristics such as performance and availability. Use cases often need to be supplemented to capture this type of information.

The misapplication of use cases can cause unnecessary effort to be expended. This wasted effort is sometimes called 'analysis paralysis' and has led to use cases being referred to as 'useless cases' or 'abuse cases'. The application of use cases should be limited to driving out the key interfaces and interactions, and their application to form a complete specification should be avoided. In addition, use case misapplication can include creating too many use cases, when separate interaction views that all map to a particular use case would have been a better approach.

3.2.2   Additional requirements that impact architecture

One set of requirements that impact the software architecture can be described as the 'ilities': reliability, maintainability, testability, and usability. Some others include fault tolerance, error handling, security, portability, and performance. These are requirements that impact the attributes of software architecture as described in Chapter 1. The architecture team needs to ensure that these requirements are as clearly stated as feasible.

Complicating the clear statement of these requirements is the fact that some overall requirements may not apply to all components. For example, it might be vital for a database engine to sustain an availability of 99.999 per cent while a monitoring tool might only need 90 per cent. Engineering the monitoring tool for the higher availability can dramatically increase the cost of development and testing. It is important to sort out how various components fit into the overall system strategy so that these requirements can be interpreted properly.

From a process perspective the architect and the architecture team should play devil's advocate with the trade-offs represented by the architecture-impacting requirements. Questions, such as the following, need to be answered:

- What would happen if a particular component were not really fault tolerant?

- Is portability really a hard requirement or just nice to have?

- Do all processes need to be highly available, or just certain ones?

- Is a quick restart of a process a better option than a complicated checkpointing scheme?

3.2.3   Requirements tracing

There may also be a large number of 'shall' statements that apply to the basic functionality of the system, and duplicate the information captured by the use case process. The software system engineering team should map the use cases to these functional requirements. In addition, requirements, such as performance, should be mapped to key interactions and interfaces. In this way, the test team can verify that the higher-level requirements have been met.

As described above, key requirements should be traced to the appropriate entity functionality and interfaces. Conventional functional requirements, on the other hand, can be mapped to key use cases and scenarios. These key use cases can then be mapped to specific test cases. This mapping is usually best maintained in tabular form in a spreadsheet application, for example. The generation of mapping information can often be automated if requirements databases are utilized by the top-level systems engineering team.

3.3   Management of the Technology Roadmap

One of the key responsibilities of the software architect is to manage the selection of technologies and software products used in the current product, and to develop a plan for evolving these technologies as the product evolves. Similarly, the software architect will be tasked to identify key technologies and products on which the development organization as a whole should focus. This section focuses first on identification, selection, and management of the technology roadmap for a development project.

3.3.1   External software products

For the software architect, the primary objective of managing the technology roadmap is to control the infusion of commercial software products, open source software, and freeware. We will refer to the collection of these categories of technology products as commercial-off-the-shelf or COTS. This responsibility should be considered at the same level of importance as that of controlling the design and development of software from scratch. The final software product will often be impacted as much by the COTS as by the software developed by the development team. A poor choice of a COTS product can have major consequences to project cost and can even result in project failure. If the organization does not have experience with a particular COTS technology or product, the risk of making a poor choice is magnified.

Complicating the acquisition process is that COTS selections typically involve trading off multiple variables. For example, there may be trade-offs between time to market and functionality. A COTS product that provides a 70 per cent solution may be superior to a homegrown solution that provides

90 per cent due to the cost and time required to develop the homegrown solution.

The other reason to control the selection of COTS products is to prevent uncontrolled introduction of open source and freeware products that may potentially conflict with each other. In addition, the versions of COTS products must be kept consistent across the development teams and in the integration and test facilities. This will minimize the impact to development teams that would need to retest their software because their entire development and test were done with an older version of a COTS product.

One approach for controlling COTS selection that we have seen to be effective is the creation of a COTS selection and approval team. The responsibility of this team is to approve COTS products that are both evaluated and selected for the project. This team is best facilitated by a key development manager and populated with technical leads from each of the development teams, the software architect or other members of the architecture team, the chief engineer, one or more of the technical leads from the test organization, and a member of the configuration management team. This team meets regularly, usually once a week, and approves all requests to evaluate COTS products as well as requests to adopt a product at the conclusion of a successful evaluation.

The COTS evaluation process should include a technical evaluation of competing products, followed by a down-select to a few products. The selected set of products should be included in a pathfinding activity to make sure there are no compatibility issues with the existing system and that the product meets the project needs. This development evaluation should include as many of the COTS products that will be in the final system and interact with the product being evaluated as possible. These prototyping efforts should be included in the schedules for the early process iterations. One exception to this process may be the selection of a COTS product on which the development team has significant experience or a product that has gone through a similar selection process on a previous project. Examples of this type of product include a configuration management tool or a relational database product. If most of the development team has significant experience with one product, the evaluation may not require pathfinding or development of a prototype.

In addition to management of COTS products, this team may be tasked with the selection of design tools, operating system version, compilers, other development tools, and test tools. However, a clear distinction must be made between tools and technologies used for design, development, and test, and those that are delivered with the software. Caution must be taken to avoid unnecessarily delivering to the end user software used only in the development and test phases.

Different projects and organizations will have different overall philosophies about the use of COTS products. On one extreme is the approach where the goal is to buy as much of the software architecture as possible. The advantage of this approach is that the amount of hand-crafted software is minimized and, with the proper selection of technologies, the parts of the system that are not hand crafted are much more stable and thoroughly tested. One disadvantage with this approach is the potential for conflicts among the products and the inability to resolve these conflicts without requesting changes by the supplier. A second disadvantage is the lack of flexibility to change the product to match the needs of the project. Commercial products must be changed by the vendor, and custom changes to open source products will cause problems when upgrading to a newer and better version of the open source product.

Another disadvantage of using primarily COTS products is that they will not have consistent approaches for configuration, startup, shutdown, logging, and monitoring. A final disadvantage to using a large number of COTS products is the cost of licensing and maintaining the COTS products. Large-scale systems are often characterized by a large number of computer nodes, developers, development workstations, and operators. Products that are licensed by individual developers, users, or workstations can be very costly to purchase. In addition, maintenance contract costs can often be 15 to 25 per cent of the product cost and can greatly increase the maintenance costs for a large system.

The other extreme for utilizing COTS is to minimize its use and craft as much of the functionality required for the project as possible. This approach is often referred to as the 'not invented here' technique. This term applies to the fact that certain developers or development teams are reluctant to use any software they did not develop themselves. The advantages of this approach include reduced COTS licensing and maintenance costs, more control over functionality of the components, the ability to make changes directly in the code without concern for upgrade, and smaller total code size (COTS code size plus crafted code size) due to the focused nature of the final software. There are many problems with this approach. One is that the large amount of crafted software will have a much higher defect rate than COTS products. In addition, the development time will be much greater than if COTS products had been utilized. Finally, overall system costs may actually be higher, depending on the complexity of the components that were developed for the system, due to the higher number of developers required and the recurring maintenance costs for a larger developed code base. In addition, features may need to be reduced in the developed version of a COTS tool due to project budget limitations.

The ideal solution is somewhere between the two extremes. Purchase as much COTS as practical for the project and produce internal versions of COTS where it makes sense. Trade-offs may need to be made where costs are not within project limitations, where functionality is much more than required and the necessary functionality can be developed, or where COTS products cannot integrate or place an unnecessary burden on the end user for configuration or management.

A third option is to identify a supplier that specializes in custom modifications to the specific open source product and contract them to make the necessary changes. These changes can first be introduced in the project's version of the open source and then included in the open source distribution. In this way, the open source community can enhance and identify defects in the modifications made for the project.

One way to reduce the licensing and maintenance fees of a COTS product is to have a team of negotiators who can strike compromises with COTS vendors whose licensing schemes don't make sense on a large project. If the project is one being developed in a large corporation, corporate licensing fees with the costs spread out over several development teams are often the answer. In addition, licensing and maintenance costs must be included in the criteria for selection of a COTS product. A competing product that has fewer features may be selected, if the cost of the fully featured product is prohibitive.

3.3.2 Software technology management traps and pitfalls

Several pitfalls should be avoided while managing the technologies selected for a project. Caution should be used when using technologies that are on the leading edge, sometimes called the 'bleeding edge'. Products tied to these technologies usually lack maturity and functionality. These products will also be less fully tested than more mature products.

A similar caution is to be wary of features that are new to the current release of a software product. The probability of defects in these new features is usually much higher than features that have been in the product for some time. Dependency on these features can cause catastrophic design changes when the software must be modified to eliminate the use of the feature. A related pitfall is to base the architecture or design on vendor claims of a feature in the next release of the product and to design the software to depend on this feature. In addition to the high risk associated with new features, the overzealous sales person may actually be pushing functionality that will be moved to a later release of the product.

Another trap to avoid is the excitement some members of the development team experience when they read about a new technology or have some initial experience using products aligned with the technology. Certain personality types are easily enamored with new technologies and see them as the solution to many problem areas, ignoring the lack of maturity of the technology. While these new technologies should not be ignored, caution must be taken and a careful analysis performed before adopting them. The inclusion of technology for technology's sake could cause a large redesign or increase maintenance costs by introducing significant defects in the product under development.

Open source products can alleviate many of the cost problems for purchased COTS products, but bring a few problems of their own. One of these problems is that new releases of open source products often have many defects that have not yet been uncovered by the users of the product. While many popular open source products have an adequate test suite, the complete testing of these products occurs as users adopt the product. In addition, open source products with a small user base may not be as well tested as those with a large user base. It is a good idea to test an open source product thoroughly prior to adoption or upgrade to a new release. Monitoring of the user's groups and primary web site for the open source product is also required to identify potential problems that have been uncovered by the user community.

A final problem with open source products is that inevitably a defect will need to be fixed in the project version prior to getting the fix in the online version of the product. This could be due to the fact that no one in the open source community is working on the specific problem, or that the problem is fixed in a newer version, which the project has not yet adopted. These fixes should be carefully monitored and identified so they can be applied to the new version of the open source product, if necessary. A recommended approach for dealing with open source products is to identify a vendor who supports the product, for a fee, and will provide quick turnaround on fixes. These vendors often add value in several areas. These include getting new features into the product, quick turnaround of fixes, additional testing prior to release, improved documentation, training, and consulting on proper use of the product.

3.3.3   Organizational technology roadmap

Developing the organizational technology roadmap is a somewhat different process from developing a project technology roadmap. This activity should involve, at a minimum, the software architecture teams from the various projects and other technical leaders in the organization. This process should include identification of potential technologies that impact all products developed by the organization.

A small team should then be put in place to become knowledgeable in these technologies, evaluate related products, perform prototyping related to these products, and communicate the results to the rest of the organization. In-process communication to the software architects and other key technical leaders should be included to keep these leaders aware of potential technologies for their particular projects. Included in the evaluation activities of this small team should be the potential users of the technology under evaluation. In this way, a core group of developers will emerge from the evaluation with the necessary skills to begin using the technology immediately.

3.4 Effective Technical Meetings

The software architect will attend and lead many different types of technical meetings. These include informal technical meetings, peer reviews, inspections, and design reviews. These meetings should be limited to technical team members. Attendance by managers should be minimized. This allows the technical teams to focus on key technical issues and minimizes taking extra time at these meetings to educate non-technical team members. To help managers and other team members to better understand the overall architecture, key interfaces, design issues, and risks, the software architecture team members should provide regularly scheduled presentations that focus on the key areas and help keep the other team members informed.

3.4.1 Informal technical meetings

The first types of technical meetings that usually occur are informal meetings held with a group of designers from the development teams and the software architecture team. The purpose of these meetings is to determine, prior to or in lieu of any sort of more formal review, the status of a particular design or development effort. These meetings will occur first in the development process with the framework or software infrastructure development teams, as these products will lead the subsystem development teams significantly. The goal of these meetings is to determine the status of the design and to identify any issues that need the attention and focus of the architecture team to resolve.

The best approach for these meetings is to schedule them at regular intervals during the design aspects of the development process. With each of the iterations of the development process comes a new round of design activities that require the input of the software architecture team. In addition, these meetings may be held as needed to discuss relevant technical issues such as the status of prototyping, technology evaluation status, or to select a particular software or hardware product to be used on the project. The topics to be covered at these technical meetings include:

- Subsystem views for each subsystem or framework

- Component design for all components owned by the subsystem team

- Process views for all processes and threads in which the components execute

- Subsystem-level design of significant analysis classes or interface classes

- Requirements overview, including a discussion of key subsystem-level use cases and interactions

- Interface and port details, including interface implementation mechanisms

- New functionality and changes since last meeting or review

- Performance-related information, including memory and CPU utilization estimates

- Approach used for reliability, availability

- Configuration information

- Technical concerns

- Development environment concerns

3.4.2   Peer reviews and inspections

Peer reviews and inspections are closely related, but not quite the same. Peer reviews are held with a relatively small group of technical representatives to review the status of a work product that is under development, but nearing an initial stage of completion. These reviews not only determine the feasibility of a certain approach, but also allow a certain amount of discussion on alternatives. Action items are captured and tracked, but formal defect metrics are not normally tracked. Inspections, on the other hand, are a detailed evaluation of a work product with a small team (no more than six, usually) with the goal to identify and track defects. In these meetings, discussions of design alternatives are not allowed. Action items are captured where decisions or discussion of alternatives needs to occur.

3.4.3 Design reviews

Design reviews are formal reviews held with a larger group of representatives from the software architecture team, the development teams, integration and test team members, and others. The purpose of these reviews is to validate and approve a design prior to initiating a more detailed design or a development stage in the process. If the software architecture team has been attending the appropriate number of informal technical meetings and participating in peer reviews of the design work products, there should be few surprises in the design reviews. These meetings may be followed by a formal inspection of the design documentation. With an effective process of regularly scheduled informal technical meetings, along with peer reviews and inspections of the design documentation in which the appropriate stakeholders are included, the formal review may be omitted.

3.4.4 Design communication meetings

Design communication meetings are targeted at explaining the software architecture to managers, system engineers, developers, customers, or other team members. These meetings are held based on a need for a particular group to understand an existing design or modifications to a design. These meetings might be focused on the top-level architecture or the subsystem-level architecture of one or more specific subsystems.

3.4.5 Management meetings

While the software architect and architecture team members may be invited to many management meetings, attendance should be limited to meetings where the software architect will be required to discuss key technical issues or where an understanding of key schedule or budget issues is communicated to the software architect to help shape the decision-making process. The daily or weekly management meetings should be replaced with regularly scheduled technical issue meetings. One example of this type of meeting is a daily defect review, during the development or test stage. The software architecture team members can provide insight into how a defect impacts other facets of the software being developed or tested. In addition, the architecture team members can assist in determination of ownership for a particular defect due to their understanding of the overall software architecture.

3.4.6 Vendor presentations

Another type of meeting the software architect will be required to attend will be vendor presentations. For a large-scale development project, many vendors will need to be evaluated if the project has a strategy to utilize COTS products. These meetings must focus on the technical aspects of the software and not on the history of the company or other non-technical issues. Otherwise, much time will be wasted listening to non-technical discussions that are not relevant to the selection of the COTS product. While a brief discussion of the status and size of the company, along with similar projects where the product has been used, is very useful, the real effectiveness of the presentations lies in communicating the detailed design and usage aspects of the product. One approach we have seen to be successful is to request that the vendor send only technical representatives and that the sales personnel attend another meeting with the vendor contract management team members, if needed.

3.4.7 Distributed technical meetings

One final recommendation for holding effective meetings, given that nearly all large-scale development efforts are geographically distributed, is to become very effective in network-based meeting software. This technology can be useful for all technical meetings, especially since the architecture team will be geographically distributed and may not all be able to travel for all meetings. The combination of a network connection to review or discuss technical material and a good teleconference connection can quickly become the preferred means to hold a technical meeting. This technology has proven to be more effective than teleconferencing alone or video conferencing because real-time updates to documents can be seen immediately on the screens of all meeting participants.

One caution is that individuals who haven't worked in a distributed mode often run meetings like there is no one on the phone. This includes use of transparencies and whiteboards that can't be seen by the remote team members, use of inexpensive speaker phones, not repeating questions, allowing discussions which can't be heard at the other end of the phone, etc. These habits should start to subside as the networking software is introduced into the teleconferences.

In addition to using network meeting software, several techniques can be used to make the meetings more effective. These include purchasing telephone headsets and emailing all the materials before the meeting. If these techniques are used effectively, meeting rooms don't even need to be scheduled; the meeting can be held using only online software for viewing, a headset for listening/speaking, and a teleconference service to set up the call in advance.

3.5 Traps and Pitfalls of the Software Architecture Process Activities

The software architect must exercise caution in several areas with respect to the design and development process. The pitfalls we discuss here are based on our own experience as software architects on large development projects.

The out-of-touch architect

One of the primary areas of concern relates to the difference that always occurs between those that prefer to design and those that prefer to write code. The software architect must make sure that communication of a proposed design precedes development activities. In the case of prototype development this design need not be formal, nor a formal review be held, prior to development. However, for most other development, an effective set of technical meetings, peer reviews, design reviews, and design inspections should occur prior to the start of formal development. Quite often in many development projects, the software architect is informed that a design flaw detected in a design review cannot be changed because the code is already written. The problem of coding going on without involvement of the software architect and the architecture team in the design is even more of a problem for remote development teams. The software architect should plan regular on-site technical meetings with these development teams to track design progress and assess whether or not coding has started. As described earlier, this technique may be used as a replacement for formal design reviews.

Analysis paralysis

A problem that occurs on the opposite end of the design versus code spectrum is that of spending too much time on the analysis and design, and not starting the coding on time. This problem occurs when inexperienced development leads get stuck discussing abstract concepts. Just as the software architecture team is responsible for providing the top-level architecture in a timely manner to the development teams, the development design teams should provide the design to their developers on time. This problem has traditionally been called 'analysis paralysis'.

Design for reuse

Similarly, while design for reuse is a good goal, it must not drive the overall approach of the project. Spending too much time on designing for reuse, or other design activities that are even less productive, can also severely limit the amount of time left for development and test of the product. The software architecture team must ensure that all analysis and design activities are producing work products that will prove useful in the downstream project activities or in the development of a family of related software products.

Use cases

As described in the discussion of use cases above, caution should be exercised when utilizing this technique. These use cases can quickly become abuse cases, where every low-level aspect and every possible scenario involving the system is being described in a use case. This abuse will also prevent the start of coding, or even the start of lower-level design activities.

Schedule

While the software architecture team should be focused on technical issues, they cannot lose sight of schedule issues and should make sure the analysis activities, design reviews, and design inspections are held in a timely manner to meet the overall project schedule.

3.6   Computer-Aided Software Engineering (CASE) Tools

Despite the fact that the diagrams in the book comply with the UML specification, it does not mean that the available design tools can be used to create them. Most of the current design tools are not extensible in that they don't allow for extension of the existing set of icons and behavior required to define all the key views of the system. While most of these tools have support for detailed design and code generation, they cannot be easily extended for capturing the types of diagrams and notations shown in this book.

There are two classifications of tools: those built to model the UML and drawing tools. Most of the UML tools support an underlying model independent of the graphical representation. Having support for an underlying model is critical to maintaining a consistent model, much like a compiler checks the syntax of a programmer. For example, if the name of a class is changed on one diagram, all the other diagrams should be automatically updated to reflect the change. The internal model is essential if the project intends to create a large number of diagrams that need to be consistent.

The general conundrum of UML tools is that those supplying a rich underlying model tend to be poorer in their ability to render complex drawings. In addition, they also will want to enforce consistency. Sometimes the model consistency gets in the way. For example, if you want to create two versions of model so that you can see two different design approaches side by side, it is usually difficult. Usually these tools will require an entire copy of the model repository for each variant.

Finally, tools do not necessarily support all variations of the UML specification. Most tools have been tuned to support basic class modeling and lower-level design. This is frequently troublesome because the project cannot easily employ desired architecture modeling techniques with the selected tool.

In practice, the result is that often both types of tools are employed. A drawing tool might be employed by the architecture team to render some diagrams that are not possible in the project design tools. Top-level diagrams are usually one-of-a-kind and there aren't a lot of them, so a good drawing tool is often sufficient.

Once developers start using CASE tools, they may resist generating design documents. The usual response is that the design is in the CASE tool and doesn't need to be documented anywhere else. The architecture and design products for a large system need to be highly accessible by a large number of team members. Design tools have complex interfaces that make it difficult for non-experts to find information easily. In addition, there are usually limited numbers of licenses available and installation is usually a long process. The major architecture and design documents should ultimately be rendered in a common format such as HTML that can be viewed without the original tools. As much as possible, these documents should be generated from the CASE tool, but there may be some mixture of hand-generated information and auto-generated information in the final set of design documents.

3.7   Recommended Reading

The Rational Unified Process is well described in the book by Kruchten. The phases, lifecycle states, and iterations are well defined. Rational also provides a software product, which includes extensive web pages and document templates, for RUP. The software product is confusingly also called RUP. In addition, Fowler and Scott (1997) has a good and brief outline of the software development process. This description has a lot in common with RUP, and even references Kruchten's book. In addition, the Jacobson (1999) book on process has more detail on the UML process. These should all be used as a guide or, at best, a framework as all these processes will need to be tailored to meet the needs of your project.

The Agile Manifesto web page provides a clearinghouse of information about agile processes.

The Scrum process is described in Rising and Janoff (2000).

There are many papers and web sites providing information on process. One recent article by Vaughan (2001) discusses effective approaches for utilizing use cases and a discussion of 'abuse cases'. In addition, the first Antipatterns book by Brown *et al.* (1998) has several process-related Anti-patterns. More information may also be found in Brown's project management Antipatterns book (2000).

Lakos (1996) provides tools for extracting and analyzing dependencies for C++ projects.

The book by Meyers and Oberndorf (2001) covers the areas of COTS and open source software selection and management. The paper by Anthony *et al.* (1999) discusses the advantages and disadvantages of using frameworks.

An interesting article by Jackson and Chapin describes some of the issues with the lack of high-level system documentation in the redesign of an air traffic control system.

Foote and Yoder (2000) have described the result of coding for a long time without a design as the Big Ball of Mud Pattern.

4

Example System Overview

The following example system will be used throughout the book in order to illustrate various concepts and views of a large-scale system. We have decided to use a banking system because most people are familiar with the concepts involved in this type of system. In addition, the banking system includes an ATM, a design example that has been the choice of most texts on object-oriented software design for the past 10–12 years. For that reason, we concluded it was only proper to include an ATM in our example system.

We will often select some part of the overall example system to illustrate certain concepts and may add elements to the example in order to illustrate an architectural view. The inclusion of a legacy system in the example will be used to illustrate how to define the software architecture for a large-scale system that includes legacy elements. However, we may not make a distinction between the legacy elements and the new elements of the banking system if the diagram or discussion is not illustrating how to deal with legacy elements. Remember that this example is for illustration only, and it is not intended to show a specific, or even meaningful, architecture of a banking system.

The next few pages could be considered a 'typical' summary of concepts that serve as the initial input to a large system. There is a wealth of interesting conceptual and requirements information in the material. The information is incomplete, steeped in undefined terminology, and yet contains basic implementation constraints. There are broad and over-generalized statements like 'build quality software' that must be transformed into principles that guide the software development.

4.1   System Overview

The example system is intended to show a complete banking system. The legacy part of the system will support traditional checking, savings, and loan services. This includes customer record keeping, transaction history, and transaction management, as well as bank personnel and customer query support. Legacy interfaces include those to external banks, other instances of this system in other major bank branches, traditional ATMs, banking personnel, and customer phone queries.

The new system will support web-based customer interfaces, two-way pager and cell-phone web browser access, enhanced ATMs, and enhanced interfaces to other branches. The new web-based customer and cell-phone browser interface will not only support traditional account queries but will also support stock portfolio management, electronic funds transfer, bill payment, and account transfers. Teller, account manager, and loan officer interfaces will gradually be converted to new intranet web-based interfaces and migrate away from the legacy interfaces. In addition, ATMs will eventually be converted over to the new interfaces, which will also be web-based and touch screen, and will include voice and facial recognition.

Figure 4.1 is a typical conceptual diagram that would be provided by the top-level systems engineering or marketing group. Notice that this diagram includes elements that are logical ones, such as the external banking systems, in addition to physical elements, such as the edge router and firewall. This is a common occurrence in top-level conceptual diagrams and we included them here for that reason. In addition, this diagram makes use of 'network clouds' that do not display element interfaces, but leave the diagram reader to guess how the elements actually interface to one another. In addition, several key interfaces are omitted. These include the interface to the customer service organization and to the network operations personnel. This was intentional, especially since the network management interface to a system is often the last one considered when doing top-level requirements.

4.2   Overview of System Interfaces

The following interface elements will be supported by the example banking system:

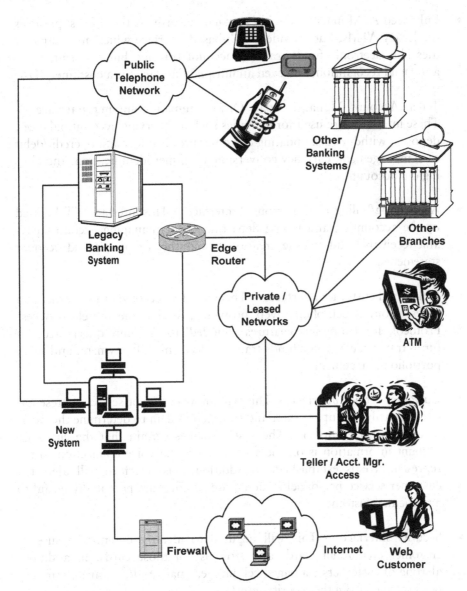

Figure 4.1 Conceptual diagram of the example banking system

- Legacy remote ATM machines – These allow the traditional support for viewing balances, getting cash, and updating customer account information. There are hundreds of these networked to each instance of a legacy banking system.

- Enhanced ATM machines – These machines provide the same support as the legacy ATMs, but provide a web-based interface which adds capabilities like electronic funds transfer, account transfer, bill payment, voice and facial recognition, and even an infrared interface for a customer PDA.

- Teller, Account Manager, Loan Officer human–computer interfaces – These interfaces are used for activities such as querying account balances, deposits, withdrawals, updating customer profile information, credit/debit card management, currency conversion, customer identification, and closing out accounts.

- Accounting/Billing bank personnel interface – This interface will be used by the accounting and billing departments for managing accounts payable/receivable and for the creation of monthly or on-demand account statements.

- Web-based customer interfaces – This includes access via the Internet and access from a cell-phone web browser (running the Wireless Access Protocol, for example). Features included are account query, account funds transfer, electronic funds transfer, electronic bill payment, and stock portfolio management.

- Customer service interface – This will allow customer service representatives to easily pull up account and transaction data to determine the cause of a customer complaint. The system makes certain that the customer account information is on the screen before the voice connection to the representative is established. In addition, this interface will alert the customer service personnel to new products that are potentially useful to a particular customer.

- Security interface – This will be used to identify potential misuse of customer credit/debit cards and stop use of those cards. In addition, alerting of customers via pager, cell phone, email, and/or home phone can be performed from the security interface.

- Interfaces to other banking systems – These will be used for ATM transaction data exchange, electronic funds transfers, and electronic bill payment.

- Interface to other branch systems – This assumes the banking system is more decentralized, with major banking centers in several major cities. As a side effect of this, separate backup facilities could be established or the multiple sites could back up one another.

- Interface to network operations personnel – This includes access by both the network operations personnel and system management personnel. This interface is critical to the effective operations of the banking center, but is often overlooked when requirements are being written.

4.3 Constraints

The following constraints apply to the example banking system:

- Legacy interfaces (graphical user interfaces and external interfaces) must still be supported. Some of these will be supported only by the legacy system, while others will be supported by both the new and the legacy system.

- The legacy ATM types must be supported, in addition to the new ATM type and new ATM interface types. The new system will provide an integrated interface to both new and legacy ATM types.

- Conventional telephone interface must be supported, in addition to access from a cell-phone web browser. The may require a WAP server.

4.4 Major Operational Requirements and Software Requirements

The following major requirements must be met by the banking system:

- System must be up 24 hours per day, 7 days per week, 365 days per year, with no downtime for software upgrades

- Server systems will be located at multiple sites for disaster purposes

- A backup facility will be in place, located at a remote site. One option for the back up capability is for major installations of the banking system to back up each other.

- Network operations team must be able to detect and respond quickly to any failures

- Fault zones will be utilized within the software to provide for software/hardware recovery without operator involvement, unless necessary.

Some of the major software requirements include:

- All software will be built to be both robust and maintainable
- Software will be of the highest quality
- All software will be implemented in either C++ or Java

5

UML Quick Tour

5.1   UML Diagram Summary

The UML defines nine kinds of diagrams. These include the class diagram, object diagram, component diagram, deployment diagram, use case diagram, sequence diagram, collaboration diagram, statechart diagram, and activity diagram. All of these except for the object diagram and use case diagram are useful for describing the software architecture. This chapter will briefly describe the subset of diagrams useful for architecture description.

All UML diagrams in this book use features available in the UML 1.4 specification. Current UML 2.0 candidate specifications have nothing that would invalidate any of the diagrams shown here. Subsequent versions of the UML should also not invalidate any of the notation we utilize.

One complex aspect of understanding the UML semantics is the dichotomy between design/build-time and runtime. The dichotomy provides for the modeling of snapshots of the running system as well as the elements used only during design. Most of the UML diagrams depict either a build-time or a runtime perspective. Somewhat confusingly, some modeling elements are used in both build-time and runtime diagrams. This is discussed more below.

Table 5.1 describes the diagram types we utilize for software architecture description. The table summarizes their design/build or runtime context, the UML constructs used in the diagram, and a brief description of each. Examples of these diagrams will be provided later in this chapter.

Interaction diagrams, which include sequence and collaboration diagrams, are logically equivalent and will be grouped together for purposes of our

Table 5.1   UML diagram types and their build/run lifetime

Diagram type	Build versus run time	Elements	Description
Class	Build-time	Classes, Packages, Subsystems, Interfaces, Database Tables, Database Entities, Relationships	A set of classes, packages, subsystems, interfaces, and relationships. Illustrates the static design view of the system, which should map directly to build-time entities. For defining software architecture, the subsystems and interfaces are used most often.
Component	Runtime	Components, Interfaces, Ports, Relationships	A set of components and their relationships. Included are the interfaces and ports that apply to each component. The component diagrams that are key for software architecture are the component instance diagrams. Build-time components will not be used. Subsystem diagrams will be used to illustrate build-time grouping and relationships.
State Diagram	Runtime	States, Sub-states, Transitions, events, activities	Illustrates the dynamic view of a class, component, or process. This diagram shows the states and the means by which state changes occur.
Activity Diagram	Runtime	Activities, Objects, Processes	A variant of a state diagram that shows the flow from activity to activity. Swimlanes can also be used to show the objects, threads, components, or processes involved.
Interaction (Sequence & Collaboration)	Runtime	Objects, Components, Messages	These diagrams show an ordered set of specific communications, generally among a set of objects. For software architecture, components or processes can be used.
Deployment	Runtime	Nodes, Processes, Components, Threads	Shows a set of nodes, the processes or components on those nodes, and their relationships to other nodes, processes, and/or components.

discussion. When a sequence diagram is used, a collaboration diagram may be substituted. While an activity diagram is a variant of a statechart, they have not been merged because there are somewhat different semantics and elements involved. Activity diagrams can be very effective in communicating parallel activities and in showing the flow of control among objects.

As mentioned earlier, model elements have limitations about whether they can be utilized during build-time or runtime diagrams. For example, packages and subsystems are only relevant in design/build-time. They have no direct

Table 5.2   Modeling elements and build/run lifetime

Modeling element	Lifetime	Description
Object	Runtime	An object is an instance of a class. The instance exists only at runtime.
Class	Build-time & Runtime	A class is the build-time view of a corresponding object. Classes will only have runtime semantics in systems that support reflection or where there is class-level data and behavior.
Package	Build-time	A package contains a set of model elements.
Subsystem	Build-time	A subsystem is a part of the system. It is represented as a stereotyped package. A subsystem is a group of build-time constructs that are as independent as possible from the other subsystems. A subsystem can be thought of as building one or more components.
Layer	Build-time	A stereotyped package that groups a set of subsystems.
Component	Runtime	A component is a physical part of the system. The UML also defines build-time components – these are avoided for clarity. Each component executes within a process.
Interface	Build-time and Runtime	A stereotyped class that provides the means by which subsystems or components communicate. Interface instances are used for runtime diagrams.
Ports	Build-time and Runtime	A port is a stereotyped class that is used for communication of a particular category of messages. Port instances are used in runtime diagrams.
Process	Runtime	A stereotyped object that provides corresponds to an operating system process in deployment diagrams. A process contains one or more components.

existence in the executing system. Some model elements exist in both the build-time and the runtime system. These include components, interfaces, and ports. The runtime aspect of these is usually called an instance. Other elements exist only in the runtime system. These include objects and processes. However, there is a mapping between many build-time entities and runtime entities. Table 5.2 describes this mapping for the key architectural entities.

These distinctions are important because they are used to keep the models consistent and provide clarity. Diagrams that mix model elements that have different lifetimes should be avoided. For example, diagrams showing subsystems that contain components would mix build-time and runtime semantics. Diagrams that have this characteristic should be avoided.

5.2 General Diagramming Conventions

Figure 5.1 provides an example of a simple UML diagram. The diagrams will frequently be annotated with descriptive information to help highlight the meaning and purposes of the various diagram elements. The annotations are distinguished from the UML notation by enclosing the text in gray round-edged boxes with italic font. For example, in Figure 5.1 the round box with the words 'UML Comment' is an annotation for the comment that is part of the diagram.

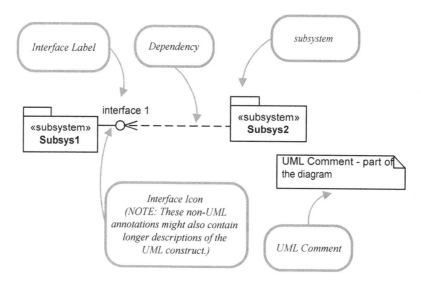

Figure 5.1 Notational conventions

5.2.1   General UML features: stereotypes, tagged values, multi-instance

One feature of the UML that is used heavily is the 'stereotype'. A stereotype is an extension mechanism that allows new specialized element types to be defined from the core element types. The stereotype often implies semantics, constraints, or properties beyond the core element type. Figure 5.2 provides an illustration of a stereotyped class and a stereotyped relationship. The stereotype name is contained between the '≪ ≫'.

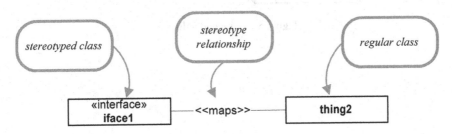

Figure 5.2   Stereotype example

In addition to the bracket notation, stereotypes can be associated with an icon or specialized visual representation. The UML provides some standard icons associated with standard stereotypes such as 'interfaces'. We utilize this feature to distinguish some elements such as data stores. Note that while subsystems can be shown with a multi-compartment package icon and a specific icon in the top of the package, subsystems can also be shown as stereotyped packages. We will use the stereotyped package. Either notation is allowed in the UML.

Another frequently used UML mechanism is the tagged value. The tagged value provides the ability to associate a list of properties with a modeling element. Tagged values can be used for nearly any UML model element. For software architectural views, tagged values are most useful for components, processes, threads, interfaces, nodes, associations, and dependencies. Figure 5.3 shows an example of tagged values in a deployment diagram. The tagged value name and value are surrounded by '{ }'. In the figure the node contains a tag named 'platform' with the value 'Linux' and a tag named 'memory' with a value '512K'.

Multi-instance notation is a mechanism to compactly depict multiple instances of runtime elements. In this convention, a 'shadow line' is drawn behind the modeling element to indicate that there is more than one of the given elements. Figure 5.4 illustrates the use of this convention with components, nodes, and processes elements.

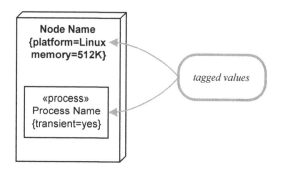

Figure 5.3   Tagged values

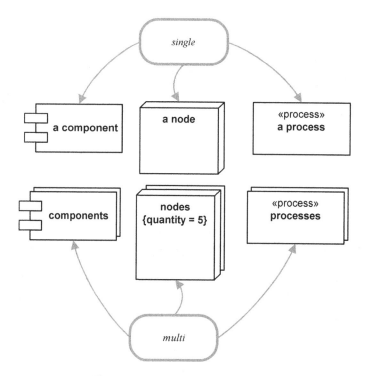

Figure 5.4   Multi-instance notation

5.2.2   View labels

A useful technique for managing the large number of views produced in large-system development is to provide context labels. This small bit of rigor requires only seconds when producing a view. However, it provides useful information later in understanding if the view is current. In addition, to manage complexity in large systems some views are frequently focused on a specific perspective. In order to capture the significant information relevant to the view, these basic attributes should be provided:

- Title: One line description of view

- Type: The view type, based on the viewpoint name

- Date: Last date updated. Helps users decide if the view is up to date with current architecture.

- Responsible: Person(s) responsible for creating the view. This provides a contact person to help explain the view.

Additional information, such as the subsystem of interest and the use case represented by the view, should also be indicated. Figure 5.5 shows an example of this type of annotation using a standard UML note. Examples of this notation can be seen in all the view examples throughout the book.

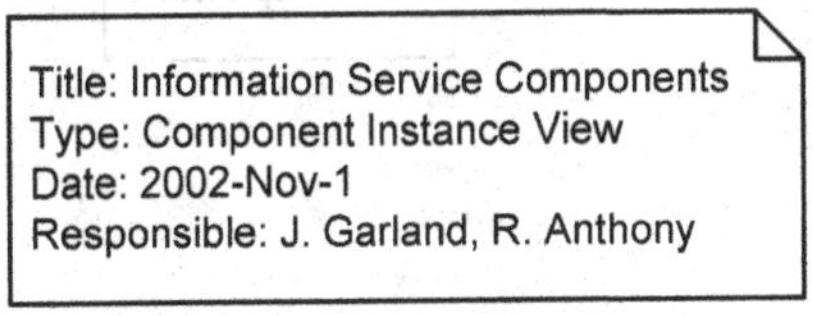

```
Title: Information Service Components
Type: Component Instance View
Date: 2002-Nov-1
Responsible: J. Garland, R. Anthony
```

Figure 5.5 View annotation

5.3 The Diagrams

The following sections describe the various UML diagrams from which the software architectural views, described in Chapters 6–10, can be developed. Each view will be developed using one of the UML diagrams below.

5.3.1 Component instance diagrams

Component instance diagrams describe the runtime components as well as their relationships, interfaces, and ports. As described above, we have found the use of build-time components and creation of diagrams containing build-time components to be often confusing. For that reason, we prefer to use subsystem diagrams to communicate design-time and build-time information and use component instance diagrams to communicate the runtime information about a set of components. For the remainder of this book, the term component diagram will refer only to component instance diagrams. In addition, unless the term 'component' is prefixed by 'build-time', it will refer to a component instance. Figure 5.6 shows an example of one of these component diagrams.

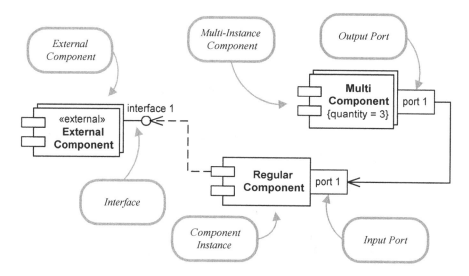

Figure 5.6 Component instance diagram

5.3.2 Class and subsystem diagrams

Class diagrams are usually focused on a particular type of model element. This includes class diagrams where the primary focus is a group of classes, packages, subsystems, database entities, or database tables. Of these categories, diagrams that focus on classes are useful for defining certain key concepts related to the software architecture. Since these diagrams are the most common UML diagrams and are covered in nearly all books on the UML, an example here is not needed. Package diagrams are most effective when the focus is on a particular stereotyped package, the subsystem. The UML considers process diagrams to be a type of class diagram. Once again, we have found process instances to be the most useful construct and have included them in the deployment diagrams.

The subsystem diagram (Figure 5.7) shows a group of subsystems and indicates how they provide and consume interfaces. As shown in this diagram, it is often useful to include key classes contained within a subsystem in the diagram. It can also be useful to include a system with which the subsystems interface in a subsystem diagram.

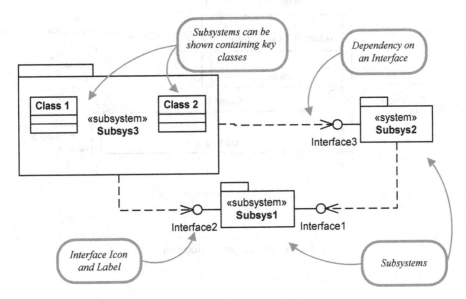

Figure 5.7   Subsystem diagram

5.3.3   Interaction (sequence and collaboration) diagrams

The UML provides two types of interaction diagrams, sequence diagrams and collaboration diagrams. Interaction diagrams are useful for capturing a set of instances and the messages that flow among them. While these diagrams traditionally have used objects, other instances can be used as well. When defining the software architecture, interaction diagrams focused on component and process instances are particularly effective. We show an example of each type of interaction diagram in Figures 5.8 and 5.9.

Sequence diagrams have instances as the labels above each vertical dashed line. The arrows from one line to another represent the messages from one instance to another. These messages may be synchronous, as in a method call,

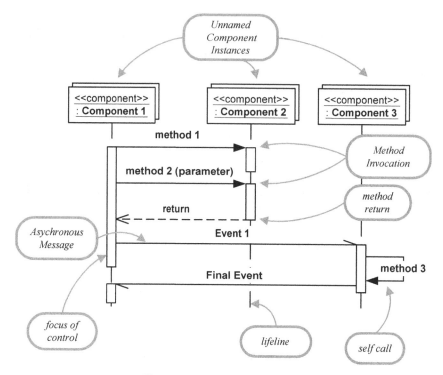

Figure 5.8   Sequence diagram

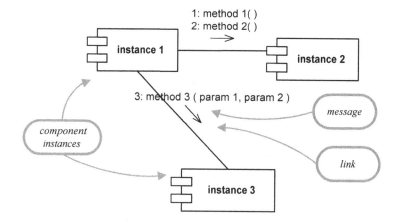

Figure 5.9   Collaboration diagrams

or asynchronous, as in an event. The instances in this diagram are component instances but process instances are also useful in some circumstances.

A collaboration diagram is logically the same as a sequence diagram, but may communicate the instance interactions more clearly. Collaboration diagrams work best when the communicating entities fit easily on one page, and the number of interactions is not too large, usually less than about 10.

5.3.4 Deployment diagrams

Deployment diagrams show the runtime relationships between the processing nodes, the components that reside on the nodes, and the processes. In addition, threads can be shown for multi-threaded processes. Since deployment diagrams also show the process communication, we consider a diagram that shows only processes to be a type of deployment diagram, one without

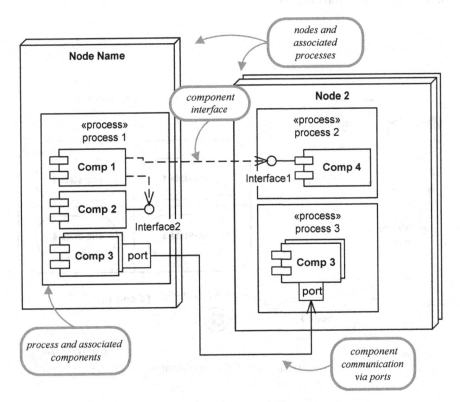

Figure 5.10   Deployment diagram

nodes or components. The diagrams that communicate the most information are those that include nodes, processes, and components (Figure 5.10). However, the system size or complexity may force higher levels of abstraction where not all elements can be included.

5.3.5 Statechart diagrams

Statechart diagrams, also referred as state diagrams or state transition diagrams, show the dynamic behavior of an element of the system. The most effective use of statechart diagrams for capturing the software architecture is to define the state of components, threads, and processes. State diagrams for key classes can also be valuable. For example, if the system is sending or receiving hardware alarms, the state transitions of an alarm may be critical to understanding the overall system behavior. Figure 5.11 shows the basic notation for a statechart diagram.

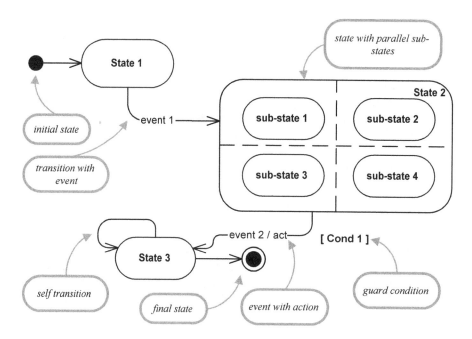

Figure 5.11   Statechart diagram

5.3.6 Activity diagrams

Activity diagrams are a kind of state diagram that focuses on the flow of activities within a system. While designed to deal with objects, these diagrams can capture the activity flow among a set of components, processes, or threads. Figure 5.12 shows an example of a process-to-process activity diagram.

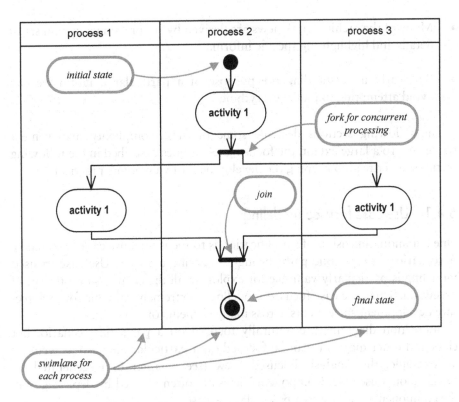

Figure 5.12   Activity diagram

5.4 Managing Complexity

In a large-scale development, reduction of complexity is critical to success. To be effective, software architects must focus on small pieces of the problem. This is due to the inability of humans to deal with many facets of a problem simultaneously. Frequently architects will simplify in an inconsistent and disorganized fashion. Explicit simplification is always preferred. That is, diagrams and other artifacts should describe clearly the simplifications made while creating the artifact. For example:

- By focusing a diagram on a particular system aspect (static structure, sunny day of a specific use case, in a specific subsystem) architects can attack manageable problems

- Many of the architectural views are derived by suppressing a certain set of details and highlighting specific information

- By clearly understanding the purpose of a particular diagram we can avoid attempting to model everything

The following sections describe some of these complexity management strategies. To a large extent, the focusing techniques described in the following sections are critical to keeping the development of viewpoints practical.

5.4.1   Use case focused modeling

One common dimension of simplification is to focus on a use case or scenario. A scenario is simply one path through a specific use case. Use case focused modeling is particularly valuable for exploring all the elements of a thread of execution. Thus, use case focused modeling is extremely valuable for architecture development since it cuts across many elements of a system.

Interaction diagrams are naturally focused on a particular scenario, but class and other diagrams can be focused on a particular scenario as well. As an example, the Analysis Focused View (see Chapter 6) is generated by focusing on a use case. Component Views are often focused by depicting only the components relevant to a particular use case.

5.4.2   Element focused modeling

Another dimension of simplification involves creating views from the perspective of a particular model element. For example, a view may be drawn to represent only the dependencies of a particular subsystem. The view should generally show the subsystem of interest in the center of the view with all related subsystems around the edges. In another approach, dependencies may be filtered into two separate views, one focusing on incoming dependencies, the other focusing on outgoing dependencies. Finally, the dependencies may be focused to a particular subset of other subsystems such as a particular system layer. This group would be central to the view, with the other subsystems surrounding them.

A view could also be created that explains the key relationships of a particular set of model elements. This allows the architect to focus on a particular set of entities that are of interest. This view could involve a set of subsystems, a set of components, or a set of objects.

5.4.3 Level of detail

Another dimension of simplification is the level of detail represented on a view. For example, a Subsystem Interface Dependency View (Chapter 8) may include interface information, or it may just indicate a dependency exists. For some systems and some purposes, the inclusion of additional detail only distracts from the purpose of the view. For example, analysis views strive to ignore aspects of the software solution in an attempt to model only the problem domain. For analysis, a typical approach is to exclude details such as method parameters. These details are only required in implementing software.

Another key aspect of level of detail is the clear definition of the level of entities for a particular type of view. For example, when doing system-level use cases the text of the use case may only discuss the system as a whole. However, the associated scenarios will usually be one level lower, for example at the subsystem level. It is critical that the use case writer not include discussions of the subsystem-level entities, or a change to the subsystem-level design will cause many use cases to be affected.

In other views the level of detail may be somewhat mixed. For example, when creating a sequence diagram, interactions with external components can show the external components as a single component. However, the entities of focus would be shown as objects in full detail. This provides a detailed focus on the internal design while ignoring the detail of the external elements. In fact, this is an example of combining element focused modeling with level of detail.

5.4.4 Controlling the number of models

Because it is possible to create hundreds or thousands of models to represent a large system, it is unrealistic to maintain or create them all by hand. Just as with software testing, the amount of modeling grows exponentially with the size of the system. Therefore, it is best to prioritize, because some modeling just won't be done. In addition, except for a few of these models, the models themselves are not the end goal. What is really needed is the deployed software system.

There are many different reasons to create models in the development of software architecture. Two critical reasons for modeling include design exploration and documentation. Exploration is a process of understanding existing or creating new parts of the system. Documentation is intended to communicate to other team members some aspect of the system. These different uses deserve different kinds of strategies in their creation and maintenance.

Exploratory models are primarily tactical in nature. That is, there is little expectation that these models will be maintained for the life of the project. It is simply impossible to expect, with current technology, that every model created will be maintained and consistent with every other aspect of a large software system. Since the purpose of the model was to explore some aspect of the system, that information will often be discarded. The most dramatic variation of this principle is whiteboard design sessions where the exploratory models are erased at the end of the discussion.

Documentation models, on the other hand, are strategic in nature. They are frequently created to assist new team members in understanding the structure, principles, and vision of the software system. These models need to be maintained as the software evolves. Because of the effort that is required to maintain these models, it is important to select a set of the most useful models. So, for example, sequence diagrams that represent detailed interactions are usually not maintained. However, a key set of abstracted diagrams may be provided to illustrate basic system interactions. These diagrams will be maintained for training purposes.

A major danger in the business of software architecture is working with incorrect models. By nature, almost all models that make up the software architecture will be incorrect in some fashion. As Coplien points out: 'It's dangerous to depend on a design notation alone, since notational artifacts are often limited in their expressive power and don't track product evolution well unless they are tied into the code-generation process.' For this reason, we recommended that detailed documentation models be reverse engineered from code where possible. This can be done as part of the build process to ensure the model is current. The model and the code must be made consistent with each delivery of the software to the integration and test team.

5.4.5 Use supplemental textual information

Sometimes a diagram does not provide the best mechanism for conveying a complex set of information. Consider using a textual table or other approach for organization of system information. The viewpoints described in the following chapters typically provide a table of descriptions along with the UML diagram. Examples of information that lends itself to tabular or other forms of textual descriptions include:

- Descriptions of subsystems, components, interfaces, actors

- Performance or availability information for each component, node, or interface

- Detailed descriptions of sequences or collaborations

- Detailed UML Object Constraint Language (OCL) or other formats for specifications of preconditions, postconditions, or guards for interfaces

- Descriptions of the states in a state transition diagram

Another example of non-UML techniques is to use code analysis to facilitate an understanding of subsystem, component, and other dependencies. Build tools can provide powerful mechanisms for managing and verifying the system dependencies. These build tools can also be used to generate custom reports that will ensure the integrity of the architecture is maintained in the face of the massive amount of daily change that occurs on a large-scale project.

Another type of example is performance reports generated from automated test tools. This type of report is easier to scan in simple tabular form than attached to a series of diagrams. Information about hardware characteristics or configurations is also a candidate for information best represented in a tabular form. This includes aspects of the hardware such as make, model, memory, disk space, and peripheral devices attached to the hardware. Finally, web-based documentation generated from code can provide a form of reference documentation that is far superior to that which can be maintained.

5.5 Recommended Reading

Details on the types of UML diagrams can be found in the UML specification, available from the OMG web site. The definition of OCL can also be found in the UML specification. Good sources for UML diagram types and examples include the UML Users Guide (Booch *et al.*, 1999), and Fowler and Scott's book on the UML (1997).

Coplien (1998) describes many interesting aspects of software design and modeling.

6

System Context and Domain Analysis

In this chapter, we will cover how to produce several overall representations of the top-level architecture. These include the Context View, conceptual diagrams, and the Analysis Overall View. Also included in this chapter is a discussion of an approach that takes advantage of use cases to produce the Analysis Overall View. The Analysis Overall View can be used to produce the Layered Subsystem View and the Subsystem Interface Dependency View described in subsequent chapters. The conceptual diagram and the Analysis Overall View will most likely not be part of the final software architecture package. Conceptual diagrams should be included in non-architecture documents, such as systems engineering documents, and may be referenced but should not be included in the software architecture description. The Analysis Overall View is primarily used to gain understanding of the key entities in the system. Except for use in product families, the Analysis Overall View is used only to produce other artifacts and is usually not maintained.

6.1 Conceptual Diagrams

The conceptual diagram in Chapter 4 illustrates some of the elements of the system and relationships to external entities. Conceptual diagrams are often very similar to Context Views, in that they capture the system and its interfaces. However, conceptual diagrams are less formal and may focus on diverse aspects of the system. Due to the lack of formality, variability in the stakeholders, and lack of specific modeling conventions, a viewpoint cannot be written for conceptual diagrams. For that reason, we will use the term conceptual diagram rather than conceptual view. While our goal in this book is to use UML for all views, the consumers of system information are not always familiar with UML notation or concepts. In this case, conceptual diagrams may be a better way to communicate with these individuals.

Conceptual diagrams can come in many flavors, depending on the intended audience. Systems engineering organizations often produce these views to illustrate a proposed functional breakdown of the system along with some key hardware they expect to be included in the final system. Marketing organizations use conceptual diagrams to communicate the functionality of the system to prospective clients of the product. Technical leaders on the project may use conceptual diagrams to prepare a technical white paper intended for readers who may not know UML. These views are also very critical in preparation of a proposal, where the evaluators of the proposals do not necessarily understand UML. Other examples include a view of the network connectivity and hardware that will be utilized in the network design, a view of protocol usage on key interfaces, or a graphical view of the hardware vendor and model selected for the system hardware elements.

The software architect or members of the architecture team are frequently asked to develop or support development of a conceptual diagram. Some guidelines should be followed when creating this type of diagram. The first consideration is to identify who are the stakeholders and what information the view is intended to convey. The next step is to analyze the level of information that must be communicated to the intended consumer. For example, if the purpose is to communicate types of hardware, then including specific vendors and models may not be necessary. If the intent is to identify point-to-point interfaces, then a network cloud should not be used, as this masks interfaces. However, if the communication of which elements are on which network is what is needed, then several network clouds may be used to show which elements are on a specific network without showing point-to-point interfaces.

As much as possible, the use of conceptual diagrams should be limited to communications with individuals external to the software development team. In general, these views should be prepared and owned by non-development teams such as marketing, systems engineering, network design, and hardware engineering. Occasionally, the software architects may be asked to prepare a technical paper for marketing purposes that will need to include conceptual diagrams. This is the only time the development team owns and maintains conceptual diagrams. However, communication of the architecture within the software development team should not depend on these ad-hoc diagram types. This includes communication with support teams, test organizations, and project management. These groups need to learn the basic concepts of UML notation in order to communicate effectively with the technical team members.

Several cautions are in order with respect to management of conceptual diagrams. As mentioned above, managers and others not directly involved in software architecture or implementation should learn basic UML syntax. Internal technical presentations or training should use UML diagrams and not conceptual diagrams. One exception might be to use a conceptual diagram owned by the systems engineering or marketing organization to give newly hired employees an overview of the system scope beyond the software being developed. However, architecture and design documents should not use these views, but instead refer to external documents that may use them.

The software architect should discourage the use of informal conceptual diagrams by members of the project team. The software development team requires the additional rigor described by the architectural views contained in this book to form a consistent basis for communication. This includes managers, integration and test leads, subsystem designers, and others who may feel the need to supplement the software architecture with conceptual diagrams for their own use.

Finally, before generating a conceptual diagram, be sure that a UML view won't work just as well. For example, a Context View or Subsystem Interface Dependency View with a few icons for key stereotyped actors may be just as meaningful and easy to understand as a conceptual diagram that contains the same basic information.

6.2 Context Viewpoint

The Context Viewpoint contains only the system, the external entities with which it interfaces, and the system's interfaces with these external entities. The goal should be to create only one view from this viewpoint that captures all external entities and their interfaces. We will refer to this single view as 'the Context View'. This single Context View is often the first view of the system the architecture team will create. This viewpoint can be based on information provided by the systems engineering, marketing or other sources that describe the system at a high level. The external entities along with the roles they perform are referred to as actors. This viewpoint includes the interfaces between the system and external systems as well as those between the system and human actors. The Context Viewpoint is summarized in Table 6.1.

Table 6.1   Context Viewpoint

Context Viewpoint	
Purpose	Model the set of actors with which the system interacts and the interfaces between the system and these entities.
When Applicable	Throughout project lifecycle. Primarily prepared during the first stages of design and analysis, but is updated as information about external interfaces changes.
Stakeholders	Software Architecture Team, Software Systems Engineering Team, Subsystem Design Leads, Developers, Testers, Systems Engineers, Marketing, or others who are interested in or negotiate external interfaces.
Scalability	The system should always be located in the middle of the view. The external actors should be surrounding the system. If the number of actors becomes too large, they may need to be grouped into higher-level actors. Multiple Context Views should only be used as a last resort.
Relation to Other Views	Should be consistent with other static views that show external interfaces. For example, the subsystem interface, component, process, or deployment views.

The view created from the Context Viewpoint can be very effective as the start of a discussion of the entire system. For example, a Context View can be useful as the starting point for a top-level design review or for a training session on the system. The Context View is also very useful for communicating external interfaces to managers that are on the project as well as higher-level managers that may be above the project team. Since the negotiation of the external interfaces can often be more political than technical, the support of project management will be needed to make sure the interfaces are well defined. For large projects, often one or more team members are dedicated to negotiating these interfaces. The Context View can be useful for discussions with these external groups.

An example of the Context View for the banking system described in Chapter 4 is shown in Figure 6.1. In this view, the interfaces from the banking system to the external systems and users are shown. As the view illustrates, other icons can be substituted for actors where this may provide clarity. These

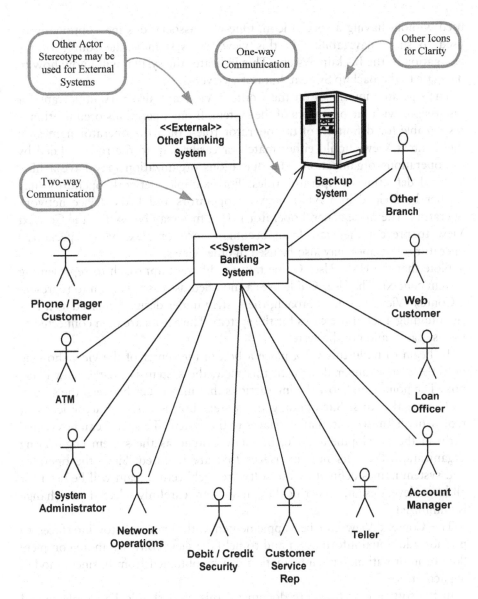

Figure 6.1   Banking system Context View

icons can even be added in a CASE tool if the CASE tool supports the definition of new icons mapped to stereotypes. These icons should be used sparingly, so the Context View does not become overly cluttered. In addition, as the view shows with the other banking system actor, stereotypes can be used without having a special icon. One-way associations may optionally be used to show navigability. In this view, the system is the source of the navigation to the Backup System. This indicates the system will know how to navigate to the Backup System, but not vice versa.

The operator interfaces on the Context View are also very important for discussions with the operators of the system. If one operations organization is responsible for definition of the operator roles, then the operator names on the Context View should either match or easily map to the roles defined by the operations organization. The operations organization may have a hierarchical definition of operator roles. For example, network operators may further be divided into ATM network operators and LAN device network operators. The more general operator role names may be used in the Context View to prevent the view from becoming too complex. More specialized operator role names may also be used in other views.

Note that the UML User Guide takes a different approach to representing system context. The User Guide uses a modified use case diagram to represent a Context View. In this approach, the system under design is placed as a box surrounding a set of use cases for the system. The actors are then connected to the use cases, and not the system.

To begin to build this view, place a box in the center of the view showing only the system under design. In this view, the system is treated as a black box. The point is to show the interactions that may occur between the system and external actors. Surrounding the system box is a set of actor icons to represent all known external interfaces to the system. This view can be created early in the development cycle, but may change as the system engineering organization discovers new interfaces that are required. Since the operator and system names defined by the software architecture team will be used for all lower-level design, it is critical the names are carefully selected and change is minimized.

The Context View can be supplemented with actor-to-actor interfaces to provide additional information and to help the view convey a more complete flow of information. This information can be obtained from business modeling activities.

In the software architecture document, this view should be supplemented with a table to provide a brief description of each actor and interface. Additional columns can be added to the table to indicate performance, data throughput, redundant connections, protocols utilized, potential interface mechanisms, or other information that is known about the system. An example of this type of table is shown in Table 6.2. A column has been added for estimated data throughput. With the initial iterations of the architecture, it

Table 6.2   Actor descriptions for Context View

Actor	Interface description	Estimated data throughput
ATM	The Automated Teller Machine handles customer interactions both at the bank and at remote sites, such as a grocery store or at an airport. Transactions such as deposits, withdrawals, account queries, account transfer, and stamp purchases are handled.	Given the large number of ATMs the system will support, this interface can total as much as 3 Mbps sustained data rate, although late at night, this rate can drop to as low as 200 Kbps.
Backup System	Data from the system will be continually sent to a set of replicated databases at the backup system. This will be done over a dedicated network connection. The backup system will handle all systems for a geographical region. This is not a hot backup system, in that its sole purpose is to maintain an extra copy of the data for purposes of restoration should data in the main system be lost or corrupted.	The amount of data will vary with the activities in the main system, ranging from 500 Kbps to 1 Mbps for each main system connection.
Network Operations	The Network Operations personnel perform tasks such as monitoring the system status, configuring the system hardware and software, and adding or removing hardware. They monitor alarms coming from the system and react accordingly. They differ from the system administrators in that they do not startup or shutdown hardware, nor do they physically install or connect the hardware.	This interface will have low data throughput needs, except in the case of software downloads. However, the internal LAN will be over-provisioned to handle this scenario.
Other Banking System	The system interacts with other banking systems for the purposes of electronic funds transfers, ATM transaction information exchange, credit history processing, or loan transfer.	This interface will range from 50 Kbps to 100 Kbps for each connection to an external bank.

(continued overleaf)

Table 6.2   (*continued*)

Actor	Interface description	Estimated data throughput
Phone/Pager Customer	The Phone/Pager customer will interact with the system to query account status, or transfer funds.	This interface will be very low bandwidth, due to the limitations of the telephone network. The peak rate will be 100 Kbps when the maximum number of phones is connected to the system.
. . .		

may be enough to identify the throughput as high, medium, or low. Eventually, specific numbers and other information (like critical time periods) should be captured in this table.

Context views can be used at several levels in doing the system architecture and design. A subsystem development team may also want to start their understanding of the subsystem by capturing the interfaces in a subsystem-level Context View. In this view, the actors will not only be the external systems and operators with which the subsystem interacts, but will also include other subsystems with which the subsystem interacts. These interactions could be via an interface provided by the subsystem central to the Context View, or those that are consumed. In addition, as described earlier, operator roles may be more specialized in the subsystem-level Context Views. For example, the stock management subsystem may interact only with operators that monitor the hardware and software dedicated to stock management.

6.3   Domain Analysis Techniques

Domain analysis is the process of identifying entities and abstractions related to the problem domain. The following describes several related viewpoints and approaches for developing the analysis views. There are three viewpoints used for domain analysis – the Analysis Overall Viewpoint, the Analysis Focused Viewpoint, and the Analysis Interaction Viewpoint.

It should be emphasized that the viewpoints in this chapter do not require a formal domain analysis process. However, for large complex systems using analysis to refine domain terminology and find abstractions, a bit of formality often pays dividends.

6.3.1 A formal analysis technique

One of the more structured approaches for creating the Analysis Overall View, and subsequent related views of the architecture, is to take advantage of use cases and use case elaboration. Use case elaboration is a means of capturing entities involved in a particular use case. Jacobson originally created this process as the Object Oriented Software Engineering or OOSE process. This process has now been incorporated into the Rational Unified Process.

The process begins with a list of use cases. This list should be kept to the core set of use cases that will help identify the key domain elements. These use cases should then be prioritized so that the process can produce valuable results even with a limited schedule for this activity. Use cases that are only a slight variant of one already in the list should be placed at a lower priority, along with use cases that are not anticipated to drive out a significant number of key entities, attributes, or behaviors.

For each use case, an Analysis Focused View and a set of Analysis Interaction Views are created, as illustrated in Figure 6.2. An Analysis Overall View can be derived by adding all the classes defined in the focused views for each of the use cases onto an overall view.

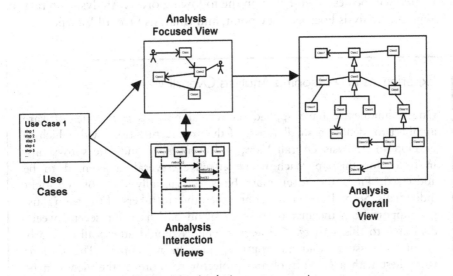

Figure 6.2   Analysis process overview

There is nearly always only one Analysis Overall View for the system under design. This Analysis Overall View is generally derived from a series of focused views. These focused views will be valuable for communicating various aspects of the problem domain and may provide additional context material for the software architecture document. One common technique for focusing Analysis Overall Views is to base each view on a specific use case. However, these views may also be focused on an interesting set of interacting classes. The complete set of interactions may take several use cases to describe.

This process works best when both the problem domain and the subsystems and components are not well understood. If the software architecture is based on significant previous experience, standardized design elements, or another well-understood partitioning, this approach may not work as well.

This process should only be done with a good CASE tool. The central data store provided by a CASE tool provides ease of renaming entities, attributes, and operations. The modified names are then updated on all diagrams in which the name appears. The complexity of making these changes on all related diagrams with a drawing tool can prevent the overall process from completing in a timely manner.

In the same way that the Analysis Overall View can be generated from a set of focused views, these focused views are often created in conjunction with a set of Analysis Interaction Views. The viewpoints from which these views are generated will be described below in the following order: Analysis Interaction Viewpoint, Analysis Focused Viewpoint, and Analysis Overall Viewpoint.

Experiences in Developing Analysis Overall Views

One technique we have applied on several projects is for the software architect to identify a small subset of the architecture team with which to develop an Analysis Overall View, and eventually candidate subsystems. In order for this approach to be effective, several areas need to be addressed. First, the team must be small, usually 3–5 of the right individuals. Second, the architect and the other members of the team must get support from the management to spend half days for several weeks dedicated to this activity. The team members should attend all or nearly all of the sessions, and interruptions must be minimized. The sessions work best with a CASE tool and projector so more of the view can be seen on a large screen.

This team begins by identifying the top 10 or so use cases, and from that set follows the process described above for developing Analysis Focused Views, Analysis Interaction Views, and the Analysis Overall View. From the Analysis Overall View, the team can then identify the initial candidate architecture. This is usually best done by doing some preliminary grouping in the drawing tool, then printing the Analysis Overall View on plotter paper. This paper version is then used for marking the candidate groups by circling them in pencil. Once the candidate subsystems are identified and documented, this team can then communicate a common vision of the candidate architecture among the other software designers. This will help validate the architecture and bring the technical leaders of the development team to a common understanding of the system to be developed.

The only danger with this approach is that the development organization should not yet be formed around this candidate architecture. However, several of the candidate subsystems will often be identified as potential subsystems in the final architecture and staffing of the leaders of these subsystems can begin in relative safety.

In addition, this team should have a clearer understanding of potential software infrastructure products that may be needed, based both on the analysis activity and on their experience. These infrastructure teams can also be staffed and begin design.

To provide clarification, we will show an example of a simple use case that may apply to the banking system. It is important to note that there is no real standard for use cases, so we will use a tabular representation here.

When the use case text is written, a set of guidelines for format and level of detail needs to be identified and followed. There should be no mention in the text of the use case of any entities internal to the software system. Producing the use cases at this level of detail will result in significant rework as the entity names are modified and new entities are created or deleted. The use case text should be from the perspective of actors that interact with the system. These actors may be humans or other systems. Alternates to the nominal flow through the use case steps should be identified and captured with each use case. These alternates usually include optional branches within the use cases or a failure that occurs during processing. Cockburn provides some good recommendations on handling use cases.

Several additions would help provide a better use case. These include a specification of preconditions, postconditions, a list of actors involved, and any other information relevant to this particular use case. There may also be additional sections for alternate flows and specific performance or availability requirements related to the use case. Table 6.3 shows a simple use case for adding new customer information.

The elaboration usually begins by developing an Analysis Interaction View

Table 6.3 Use case for collecting new customer contact data

Use case name: collect customer contact data	
Step	Description
1	The Customer Agent identifies that a new customer entry needs to be created.
2	The Customer Agent begins a session for creating the customer entry and entering the data.
3	A customer ID is allocated and the associated customer entry is created.
4	The relevant customer information, such as name and date of birth, is added.
5	The location information for that customer is added.
. . .	

or by developing a preliminary Analysis Focused View. The objects involved in the interactions are instances of the classes that appear in the Analysis Focused View for that use case. The Analysis Interaction Views identify the methods that belong to the Analysis Focused View classes. These should be consistent. Often changes to the Analysis Interaction View will propagate to the Analysis Focused View and vice versa. For example, if the name of a method is changed in an Analysis Focused View, the Analysis Interaction View needs to be updated to match.

Attributes are added to the object as needed for clarification. However, during use case elaboration, access methods for these attributes are generally not specified. In addition, data types for attributes are usually not specified. Parameters and return values for functions are not critical to the Analysis Focused View, but can be added as needed for clarification. Multiplicity and role names are added to nearly all the associations to provide a clear set of information for the person reading the Analysis Focused View. As with the Analysis Overall View, implementation details should be omitted from these views.

6.3.2 Other techniques for finding domain entities

There are many ways to capture an Analysis Overall View, ranging from ad hoc to well structured, but nearly all of the approaches will work best if a small but knowledgeable group participates in the process. In addition, using a group of this kind will produce a larger consensus that this is an accurate representation of the problem domain and wider acceptance of the terminology used in the view. This consensus acceptance of terminology will be valuable later on in the design process.

The most ad-hoc approach for capturing the Analysis Overall View is simply to brainstorm the view with a group of individuals. The first step is to brainstorm an initial list of candidate entities. Once there is some agreement on the initial list, begin to place the entities on an Analysis Overall View and connect the entities with the various UML relationships. Add operations and attributes as they are discussed. Do this for a few hours at a time over several weeks to allow some time to elapse so the team members can think about and refine the view. The hardest part of this process will be reaching agreement. It is the job of the software architect to arbitrate disagreements. When the small group has produced an initial Analysis Overall View, bring in a slightly larger group to analyze the view, using either a projector or a printed version of the Analysis Overall View.

Another approach to capturing the Analysis Overall View is to start with a set of documents that describe the problem domain and scan them for key entities to include in the view. These documents could come from standards bodies (like ANSI, ETSI, ITU, 3GPP, etc.), from marketing documents, or from systems engineering overviews. From this point, the preparation of the Analysis Overall View is much like the brainstorming approach.

Another, slightly less ad-hoc approach, is to prepare a set of Analysis Interaction Views in order to identify the key classes in the problem domain. These views can be prepared by identifying the primary scenarios in which the system being designed will participate. From this list, prepare one or more Analysis Interaction Views. This process will identify the problem domain classes and their operations. A process similar to the first two described above will be required to identify attributes and relationships.

An alternative to using Analysis Interaction Views would be to start with a set of system interactions produced by a standards organization or by a systems engineering group. For example, many telecommunications standards organizations produce message sequence charts to describe system behavior. From these interactions, the goal is to identify domain classes and operations. Be aware that the labels used in this representation may not map directly to domain view entities.

One effective technique for capturing key entities for many of these approaches is the use of CRC cards. The use of CRC cards was originated by Ward Cunningham in the late 1980s. This technique can be used to quickly evaluate analysis and design alternatives and is especially useful in the early stages of software analysis and design. CRC stands for Class, Responsibility, and Collaboration. The technique uses index cards to identify the class names, their responsibilities, and their collaborations with other classes. The index cards usually have the class name at the top, with the responsibilities and collaborations in two columns on the face of the card. More formalized techniques use colored cards to indicate different types of classes. These would be stereotypes, using the UML nomenclature. As with the brainstorming approach discussed above, use of CRC cards works best with a small group. Using use cases, product documentation, or knowledge of the problem domain, the group doing the design works to identify the classes, a description of their responsibilities, and other classes with which they collaborate. Approaches with CRC cards usually involve a group of people laying the cards on a table and moving cards into or out of the group to indicate how they are involved in the use case or functional area being designed. This type of collaboration to produce design elements may more easily performed with a laptop, CASE or drawing tool, and a projector.

6.3.3   Analysis shortcuts

There are many reasons to take short cuts in the generation of the Analysis Overall View. This is primarily because most projects come with real deadlines and constraints and projects that analyze endlessly are eventually canceled. Even more important, the initial iteration in which some initial parts of the system are developed will have a 'back-draft' effect on requirements. That is, using a part of the system will make users recognize missing functions. Therefore, it is important to get users looking at finished products as early as possible.

In addition to the inherent cycle time reductions in the less formal approaches described above, several techniques can be used to keep the analysis process minimal, yet effective. One approach discussed earlier is the prioritization of use cases. This is a good way to focus on a subset of system operations and yet realize most of the critical elements of the architecture before starting to design.

In addition, for many sorts of business interaction there will be a series of standard use cases based on the old data mantra: create, read, update, and delete. The question is, will creating an Analysis Focused View for each of these cases yield more information? Usually update and delete are not terribly interesting as separate views. They don't typically add significantly to the model in a way that can't easily be extended later. Finding specific data entities from these use cases may seem worthwhile, but often identification of specific data should be delayed until database design begins in earnest.

Another good way to reduce the analysis effort is to use analysis patterns or predefined views. These provide good guidance on recurring types of views that come up in many domains. These views may provide a starting point for an Analysis Overall View. Many of these views are available if a similar project has been done previously by the development team and object-oriented methods were used. Additionally, the information for these views may be available from standards documents that apply to the domain. These standards documents may also prove valuable for providing an initial set of use cases or interactions from which the Analysis Focused Views can be developed.

These approaches are bound to be controversial, especially to those who insist on following each step in the process. In addition, over-application of any simplification approach may prevent the production of a software architecture with the quality provided by a more formal approach. However, once rework is accepted as an essential part of the development process, the objective becomes to organize and manage for the iterations. It is also important to understand that talented designers experienced in the domain may be able to utilize analysis shortcuts and still produce a quality design.

6.4   Analysis Viewpoints

The following sections describe the viewpoints utilized by the techniques described in the earlier sections of this chapter.

6.4.1   Analysis Interaction Viewpoint

The Analysis Interaction Viewpoint identifies the class-to-class and class-to-actor interactions involved in a specific scenario or path through a use case. The views associated with this viewpoint will be grouped to identify a collection of classes that will be placed in an Analysis Focused View. The interaction views are especially useful as the basis for test case development. The fact that these views are identified early in the design process allows the test group to get an early start on writing test cases. This viewpoint is summarized in Table 6.4.

The Analysis Interaction View in Figure 6.3 is derived from the Collect Customer Contact Data use case. One use case may have several associated Analysis Interaction Views, each representing a different path through the use case. The class names used in the Analysis Interaction View will also appear in the Analysis Focused View. In addition, the methods and parameters may also be identified in the Analysis Interaction View. The early Analysis Interaction Views will provide a great deal of information to the Analysis Focused View.

Table 6.4 Analysis Interaction Viewpoint

Analysis Interaction Viewpoint	
Purpose	Illustrate a set of classes, attributes, methods, and associations for a specific path through a use case.
When Applicable	Prepared during analysis, along with use case development. Generally not maintained.
Stakeholders	Software Architecture Team, Software Systems Engineering Team, Subsystem Design Leads, Developers, Testers.
Scalability	The Analysis Interaction Views will be used to produce a focused view for that use case.
Relation to Other Views	Should be consistent with the initial focused views, but will most likely not be maintained as the focused views evolve.

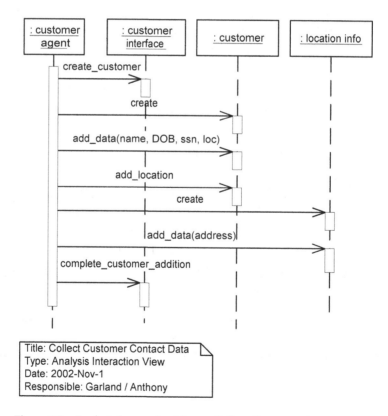

Figure 6.3   Analysis Interaction View – Collect Customer Contact Data

As more of these views are created, more of the information in the Analysis Interaction View will already have been placed in the Analysis Focused View. At the point that very little information is being added for each Analysis Interaction View, the use case should be considered fully elaborated.

6.4.2 Analysis Focused Viewpoint

The Analysis Focused Viewpoint defines a set of associated classes that participate in a specific use case or set of use cases. Prior to the development of the overall view, the focus is on only the actors, classes, attributes, methods, and interfaces that apply to that specific use case or set of use cases. After the Analysis Overall View has been developed, other focused views may be produced to capture subsets of the information in the overall view. The Analysis Focused Viewpoint is described in Table 6.5.

Table 6.5   Analysis Focused Viewpoint

Analysis Focused Viewpoint	
Purpose	Illustrate a set of actors, classes, attributes, methods, and associations for a specific use case, set of use cases, or subset of an Analysis Overall View.
When Applicable	Primarily prepared during analysis, along with use case development. Generally not maintained, unless a product family is being developed.
Stakeholders	Software Architecture Team, Software Systems Engineering Team, Subsystem Design Leads, Developers, Testers.
Scalability	The focused views will be used to produce an overall view that can be used to drive the software architecture definition.
Relation to Other Views	Should be consistent with the initial overall views, but will most likely not be maintained as the overall views evolve.

Prior to UML, Jacobson documented an object-oriented software engineering approach that took advantage of what were called Views of Participating Objects (VOPO). In UML, these came to be known as Views of Participating Classes (VOPC). We refer to these views as Analysis Focused Views. These views are generated in the process of use case elaboration. Each use case generates one Analysis Focused View. The view only displays the attributes and functions needed to satisfy the associated use case. The set of all Analysis Focused Views for the use cases is used to create the Analysis Overall View.

While these views are important for generating the Analysis Overall View, they are generally not maintained during the rest of the architecture development process. One exception is if the domain analysis is central to the development of a reference architecture or the development of a product family.

The view in Figure 6.4 provides an example Analysis Focused View for the Add New Customer use case. In this view, several stereotypes are used. First, the actor generally interacts with a boundary class. These provide a means to focus the external communications with the system. Generally one boundary class will be used for each actor type, but if several actors are utilizing the same methods, one boundary class may work for several actors. Second, the entity classes are used to identify key constructs of the domain. These entities will generally include data and behavior. To simplify view construction, access methods for the attributes are not usually included. Finally, controller classes are used to encapsulate a complex collaboration

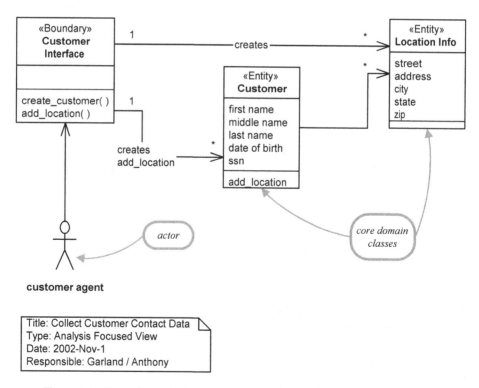

Figure 6.4 Example Analysis Focused View – Collect Customer Contact Data

among several entities that does not logically reside with any of the entities. We did not include controller classes in Figure 6.4 for simplicity reasons. The actor, indicated by the stick figure, is the external entity that interacts with the system. Refer to the recommended reading for a more detailed discussion of use case elaboration.

6.4.3 Analysis Overall Viewpoint

The Analysis Overall Viewpoint is used to provide an agreed-upon understanding of the problem domain, independent of any implementation details. This viewpoint provides a common representation for the set of entities in the problem domain along with their relationships, attributes, and behavior. The views that result from the Analysis Overall Viewpoint are often used to capture an agreed-upon definition of the problem space as well as how the system to be designed will interact with the external entities. The Analysis Overall Viewpoint is described in Table 6.6.

Table 6.6   Analysis Overall Viewpoint

Analysis Overall Viewpoint	
Purpose	Illustrate the set of key actors, classes, attributes, methods, and associations for a system. This viewpoint should not contain implementation details.
When Applicable	Primarily prepared during analysis, along with use case development. Generally not maintained, unless a product family is being developed.
Stakeholders	Software Architecture Team, Software Systems Engineering Team, Subsystem Design Leads, Developers, Testers.
Scalability	The overall view is seldom small enough to fit onto a single sheet of paper. Subsets of the classes, actors, and associated information can be extracted to produce focused views that convey a key concept or set of concepts.
Relation to Other Views	Should be consistent with the initial Analysis Focused and Analysis Interaction Views, but generally evolves to contain additional information.

As described earlier, there is usually only one overall view for the system. This Analysis Overall View can provide a common vocabulary to be used for further analysis and architecture definition. In addition, the Analysis Overall

View can produce a set of focused views that can be used to explain various facets of the problem domain.

What we refer to in this book as the Analysis Overall View was originally called the domain object model by Jacobson. This view is simply called the

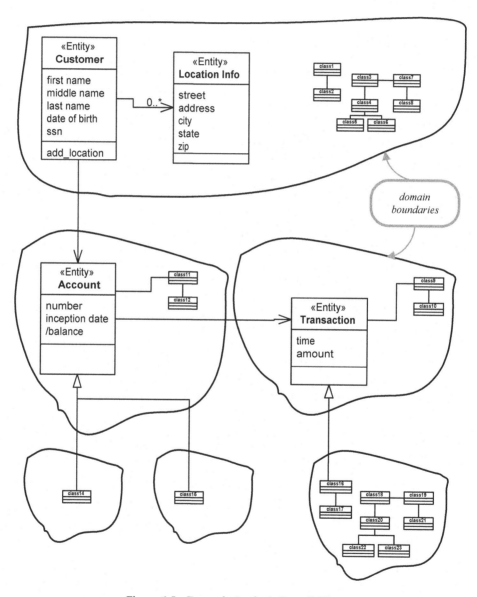

Figure 6.5 Example Analysis Overall View

domain model in the UML process book. Bringing together all the classes from the individually focused views creates the Analysis Overall View. Without good tool support, creating this view correctly is extremely difficult. The goal of this view is to be able to look at all the entities in the system as a whole, assess the coupling and cohesion, and divide the classes into subsystems for design. This view can also be used as a basis for data modeling and other design activities.

The Analysis Overall View is one of the few views that need not fit on standard paper. To simplify the view somewhat, the controller or actor classes are often omitted, showing only the entity classes. Even with this simplification, this view will often require a plotter to print, and as a result will most likely not be included in architecture documents. Because of the extreme size of these views, the example in Figure 6.5 shows only a perspective of the Analysis Overall View. Many classes are obscured due to the space constraints. In addition, we have drawn domain boundaries as a first cut at grouping the analysis classes. These groups correspond to a set of candidate subsystems as described in the following section.

However, putting the view on a web site where scroll bars can be used to find various parts of the view can be very useful to make the view accessible to as many architects and developers as possible. Due to the complexity of the problem domain view, it also may not be maintained throughout the development lifecycle. One case where the Analysis Overall View should be maintained is for use in product families or for a starting point to develop a new design for an existing product.

One pitfall to avoid when preparing the Analysis Overall View is the temptation to include implementation mechanisms and technologies. All of the participants in the creation of the Analysis Overall View need to resist the urge to include any implementation details. This should be viewed as an activity to produce a view that describes only the problem domain. That is, the view is implementation technology neutral.

6.4.4 Candidate subsystem identification

Extracting a set of candidate subsystems from the Analysis Overall View is the process of transitioning from a sketchy Analysis Overall View into something that forms the basis for implementation. Evaluation of the cohesion and coupling of the various domains allows division of the problem into a preliminary set of subsystems that can be evolved. What is produced in this process is a Subsystem Interface Dependency View, which will be described in more detail in Chapter 8. Additional information about how candidate subsystems fit into various architecture development tasks is described in Chapter 12.

The simplest technique for identifying the candidate subsystems is to use the domain boundaries identified in the analysis as the starting point. However, while this view can be useful in producing an initial grouping of subsystems for development purposes, it is important to remember that this is a description of the problem domain. The actual subsystems used for development may be somewhat different, due to the addition of implementation details.

One approach to obtain this implementation information is to follow through a similar elaboration process, but add implementation classes to the Analysis Focused Views and Analysis Overall View. In addition, some of the classes related to the common software infrastructure can also be added. This final view produced can then be divided into subsystems that will more easily evolve into the subsystems to be assigned to development teams. As usual, iterative approaches should be used for developing the Analysis Overall View and the version of the view that includes implementation classes.

6.5 Recommended Reading

The Context View originally came from Yourdon's Structured Analysis and Design approach. A good source for this discussion is his book on analysis (1991). The Context View in SASD showed the system as a box, external entities in boxes, and data flows from the external entities in and out of the system. Most UML practitioners refer to the Context View as the highest-level view of the system. The UML User Guide by Booch *et al.* (1999) shows a Context View as a use case view with the set of all top-level use cases and actors in a view with a box around the use case names. The box is labeled with the system name, making it very close to the context view shown here.

Analysis Focused Views or VOPCs were initially done as object diagrams and were called Views of Participating Objects (VOPO) in Jacobson's initial book on software engineering (1992). The term VOPC is described in the Unified Software Development Process book (1999).

Domain analysis views were discussed in Jacobson's initial book (1992). These are effectively the same as Analysis Overall Views. The domain model and other aspects of the use case driven approach to building the domain model are described in the book on UML process (1999). A more detailed description of the process of evolving use cases into the software architectural elements can be found in the paper by Lawrence *et al.* (1999).

Kent Beck and Ward Cunningham (1989) discussed CRC cards in a paper accepted to the OOPSLA conference that year. In this paper, Ward Cunningham is credited with the invention of CRC cards. A book was later released on CRC cards by David Bellin and Susan Suchman Simone (1997).

The International Telecommunication Union (ITU) Telecommunication Standardization Sector (ITU-T) defined the specification for Message Sequence Charts (1999). This is the notation used by systems engineers and software designers who use the Specification and Design Language (SDL), which is the ITU-T Z.100 specification (1999). Since many telecommunications organizations use these standards, it may be necessary for the software architecture and software systems engineering teams to be able to understand requirements and systems specifications done by systems engineering using this approach.

Cockburn (2000) describes techniques for the writing of effective use cases.

Czarnecki and Esenecker (2000) describe a system of domain analysis to support product line engineering using Feature Modeling. This much more sophisticated method provides a technique for modeling commonality and variability between members of a product family. In addition, they describe some of the practical limits of the simpler techniques described here.

7

Component Design and Modeling

7.1 Overview

This chapter describes some of the fundamental architectural viewpoints for a large-scale system. Component structure, interfaces, dependencies, and dynamics are the topics addressed by the viewpoints in this chapter. The views produced from these viewpoints are especially critical to the implementation teams, as they document the runtime component structures and interactions.

Component development often occurs in the context of **distributed system development**. However, the views in this section are focused on the logical interactions of the components. The Process and Deployment Views, described in Chapter 10, are focused on the exploration of the distribution of components in a system.

7.1.1 Component-based development

Component-based development is a major trend in the construction of large-scale software systems. Component-based development facilitates reduced development times and increases system functionality. Components also enable developers to utilize off-the-shelf software. In addition, designing with components enables development teams to build and test parts of the system independently. Delivery of a software component to the integration and test team typically includes up-to-date documentation, test drivers, and communication specifications for that component.

Component development is nothing new. For many years, Unix systems have had a command line or scripted development environment that facilitates the rapid creation of novel applications by chaining together executable components. For example, to build an application to perform a count of the statements in a source code file requires the following shell code:

$$\% \text{ cat }^*\text{.cpp} \mid \text{grep ';'} \mid \text{wc } -1$$

Here the commands shell, cat (catalog), grep (find), and wc (word count) are executable components that are connected together by data pipes (the '|') as created by the shell program. This program simply counts the number of lines with one or more semi-colons in the C++ files in the current directory. Note that the cat, grep, and word count programs have no dependencies on each other except the ability to read and write character data from the operating system pipe. This operating system pipe provides a data port for the executable components to use for communication.

Today, there are many different **component implementation models** available. COM, CORBA, and Java Beans all provide component implementation models. All of these component implementation models vary in the details of required interfaces, allowed programming languages, and required environments. Many of these implementation models provide the capability to use the same interface definition for co-located components and distributed components. This allows the component location to be more flexible, co-locating performance critical interfaces and moving less critical interfaces to separate processes. These mechanisms optimize these interfaces when co-located to take advantage of communication within the process.

Very large systems may utilize multiple component implementation models simultaneously for system implementation. Projects that have the option of selecting a single implementation model for components should do so early. This enables teams to begin training, experimentation, and other development activities utilizing the target component implementation infrastructure.

7.1.2 Terminology

In order to accurately model the entities and relationships at the component level, the terminology must be well understood. In addition, the relationship between UML concepts and real-world runtime software development concepts must be clearly defined. Given that there is much confusion in the modeling community, it is appropriate to provide clarification here.

As described in Chapter 5, the UML defines three types of components – compile-time components, link-time components, and runtime components. Examples of compile- and link-time components include object code libraries and executable files. Runtime components are the in-memory instantiation of these build-time constructs. We only define views that describe the runtime aspects of components. For our purposes, the **definition of a component** is a physical set of object-based or functional constructs that provides system functionality through well-defined communication mechanisms. A component definition includes a set of ports and/or interfaces that provide for interaction with other system components. Often they are deployed as an executable, dynamic library, or via another runtime packaging technology.

Understanding component properties helps the software architect determine if the potential component will facilitate effective design and execution of the system. A component always has the following properties:

- Provides services through well-defined interfaces, ports, and interaction protocols

- Encapsulates both state and behavior

- Depends only on a component framework or operating system to provide startup and communication to other components

A component frequently has the following properties:

- Obtained by purchasing rather than developing
- Operates in an independent process or thread of execution
- Utilizes transparent distribution location via naming service or other location techniques
- Has many configuration options, that may impact component behavior
- Is developed, tested, and delivered independently of other components
- Is developed using object-oriented concepts

- Is language independent, thus providing binary compatibility

Each component has a subsystem of origin. The result of the build process for that subsystem is one or more components. However, the component built by a particular subsystem may also include entities from other subsystems. These other subsystems merely provide the build-time entities so that the component can be built. They are not the subsystem of origin. An interface on a component is an instance of an interface on the subsystem of origin for the component. This is described in more detail in Chapter 8.

Composite components group a set of components together into a single 'logical component'. Composite components are a form of abstraction that allows modeling of large sets of components at a higher level of abstraction. In essence, the composite component represents the 'union' of all the functions and interfaces of the grouped components. Composite components are very useful for simplifying complex views. However, care should be taken not to consider these composite components to be first-class elements of the architecture and produce a complete set of work products as are required for conventional components. For example, an interface specification at this level is not useful and produces additional documentation maintenance and opportunities for inconsistencies.

Frequently, the component is the **physical unit of replacement** for the system. Replacement of components is important for system evolution. If a component supports replacement, it limits the impact for software upgrades to only the modified components. The key to successful architecture definition using components is that each component has well-defined configurations and communication mechanisms that can be used to combine a set of components to achieve a set of system functions.

During **initial system design**, some components may be nothing more than a list of required functions and a rough set of interfaces. These components should be classified as 'preliminary'. As the design progresses, the component definitions are expected to change. However, some components may be completely understood because they are either products (e.g., web server) or parts of an existing legacy system. Eventually, however, the preliminary components should be evolved into the actual components to be delivered. Others have used the term 'conceptual components' to refer to something similar to preliminary components. We prefer to use the term 'preliminary' to indicate that the component definition will evolve and the architecture team should not spend a great deal of time documenting these components at a lower level of detail.

7.1.3 Communication and interfaces

Three other key terms will be used throughout this chapter. These terms are interface, messaging, and port. In the UML, an **interface** is a stereotyped class that provides the means by which external components communicate with the component that provides the interface. Interfaces are generally implemented as methods on a class that has been provided to an external client. The interface may be implemented using mechanisms such as CORBA, COM/ DCOM, Java Remote Method Invocation, as well as a native language function or class method invoked by the client.

Messaging is another form of communication between components. While the UML doesn't provide specific stereotypes for static representation of messaging-based communication, we have found the distinction between messaging and interfaces to be significant. Interfaces are focused on defining a set of methods to be invoked by a client, while messaging provides a set of message types to be transmitted. As a result, interfaces specify a method-based form of communication, while messaging specifies a data schema and a protocol. A protocol defines constraints on appropriate message ordering and content.

To facilitate the discussion of messaging, the concept of **ports** is useful. A port is a stereotyped class that is used to denote communication of a particular category of messages. Ports are used to identify incoming messages accepted and outgoing messages generated by a component.

7.1.4 Finding components

One issue for the architect in using component-based modeling is partitioning system functionality into components. If the design is for an existing system, a system utilizing a standards-based architecture, or a system based on a reference architecture, there will be a set of well-established candidate components. The determination of the actual components can be straightforward since the current as-is structure or predefined architectural elements can guide the modeling. For systems without such a clear architectural basis, for example a new system with no precedence upon which to base the architecture, components can be identified using a number of approaches. Several of these approaches for finding components are discussed in Chapters 11 and 12. One of these techniques is simply to decompose the major functional domains as a preliminary set of composite components. The composite components provide a starting point for modeling and design activities.

7.1.5 Qualities of component design

Several aspects of a component design should be analyzed to determine if the component design will produce effective component behavior and interactions at runtime. The software architect should carefully analyze the component dependencies to make sure they will be effective. Co-dependency of components is one example of a potential problem. For example, if two components depend on one another at startup a deadlock may occur.

Another aspect of determining the effectiveness of the component design is the assignment of system state to components. For example, if system state information is duplicated among several components, keeping this information consistent may be a problem. Similarly, if the system state is too widely distributed, and several components need access to this information, communication overhead may severely impact performance. The nature and usage of each category of system state data must be analyzed to determine which of these two approaches best applies.

Since components are independently developed sets of functionality, they are an ideal way to break down large software architectures into smaller elements. The architectural effort then focuses on making sure the objects that are in the components are cohesive and that the interfaces between components are specified to minimize coupling between components. In addition, dependencies between components must be managed so that classes that are used in multiple components are provided in a timely manner to all component development teams.

7.2 Component Viewpoint

The Component Viewpoint provides a set of **static views of component runtime structures and their relationships**. This viewpoint ignores the issues of component distribution and threads of execution. Instead, the Component Viewpoint is focused on the partitioning of functionality among components, the interfaces between components, and any global state that must be shared among the components.

The goal of component modeling is to describe the runtime system, often before much of the software has been designed. A Component View provides a mechanism to divide a large set of functions into a coherent set of runtime components and illustrate the interactions between them. During the initial software architecture development, component modeling can provide a useful tool for understanding the system.

A Component View provides a different perspective on the software system than analysis or subsystem views. Component Views illustrate how various runtime entities will communicate. This is similar to using an object diagram to show how class instances interact, but the Component Viewpoint is at a higher level of granularity. Table 7.1 summarizes the Component Viewpoint.

Table 7.1   Component Viewpoint

	Component Viewpoint
Purpose	Describe runtime component connectivity and communication. Can be applied to performance analysis and later the process interaction design.
When Applicable	During system design and development, as analysis views and subsystems are identified.
Stakeholders	Architecture Team, Subsystem Developers, Test Team, Software System Engineering Team, Systems Engineering Team, Project and Development Managers (to a lesser degree)
Scalability	Drawn with scenario or component focus. Can make use of composite components.
Relation to Other Views	The Component Views should be consistent with components shown in the Process and Deployment Views.

7.2.1 Component communication

As described above, components can communicate either using an interface or via messaging. At the lowest levels of the software, all types of network communication are built on a packet transmission protocol, much like messaging. However, if an application is built on a remote procedure call communication mechanism, the interface to the application appears to be that of normal method invocation, not that of packet-based communications. That is, all the packet exchange is at a level of abstraction below the level of the design concern. This is to be contrasted with applications that make direct use of messaging or publish/subscribe protocols to implement the system functionality. Thus for component modeling we only model communication as messaging when the component depends directly on this style of communication.

The best choice for a component communication style on a particular interface depends on the particular application interface under design. However, most large systems have combinations of both messaging and traditional interfaces. One way to think about the difference is to think of an interface as a data-pull approach and messaging as a data-push approach. Data-push is especially relevant when communications are asynchronous, such as when connecting systems to instruments that measure or produce events. Data-pull is especially relevant when querying for information, such as when accessing external process data in memory, data in shared memory, or large amounts of data stored in a database or in files.

The software architect should determine whether a particular component interaction should be based on messaging or on an interface. When the interface requires a large amount of data to be transmitted, messaging may not be the best choice. Messages normally carry smaller amounts of data. On the other hand, if the interaction is asynchronous, then a message may be the best way to implement the interface. Similarly, if the message sender and the message consumer need to be decoupled, then a message publication/ subscription approach is usually best. Normally, point-to-point communication requires interfaces. That is, if a message contains source and/or destination information, then the use of messages should be questioned. However, there are applications for point-to-point messaging. For example, many telecommunications protocols use this approach. In that case, we recommend this interaction be modeled and implemented as messaging.

7.2.2 Component interfaces

The view in Figure 7.1 shows an example Component View that is focused on the interactions between different system interfaces and the servers that provide customer information. The view succinctly provides an overview of the major runtime components that make up the system. In addition, it highlights the interfaces utilized for communication among the components.

Interestingly, the information for this system view is likely available well before system construction begins. For example, in the banking system there is a requirement to work with existing products such as the web server and voice response systems. Of course, other architectures for the backend systems are possible. For example, the session management may be combined with the customer information server. These are the types of trade-offs that Component Views are ideal for exploring and documenting.

The multi-instance components on the view indicate that there is expected to be more than one of these component types running in the system. That is, there is an expectation that the load from all the clients will be split across several component instances. The lines between components and interfaces illustrate a 'client–server' communication relationship between the

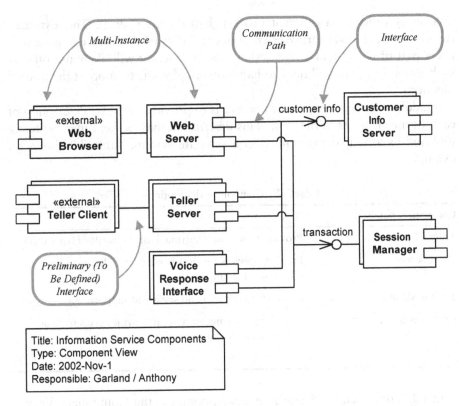

Figure 7.1   Component View with interfaces

components. The Teller Server, Voice Response Server, and Web Server all use the customer info and transaction interfaces. All the interfaces in this view represent traditional interfaces rather than messaging interfaces. These will be illustrated later in this chapter. Also shown in this view is that during preliminary design, interface definition may not have been completely determined. In this case, an association is drawn directly between the components without an interface icon to indicate that the details of the interface have not yet been defined.

It is important to note that this view does **not constrain** the process and thread structure of the solution. For example, to improve performance, the server implementation for customer information and session management may ultimately be delivered as a library that is linked directly into the same executable as the web server, teller interface, and voice response interface. However, one constraint of the architecture is that the web browser will necessarily reside in a different process than the web server. The 'external' stereotype on the web browser component indicates that this component is not a part of the system under design. The web server will likely use off-the-shelf technology, but will need to have custom plug-ins to support the desired functions.

In addition to the view, a best practice is to provide a tabular description of each of the elements in the view. This description may be kept in a modeling tool and exported or maintained in a separate system. Table 7.2 shows an example.

Table 7.2 Component descriptions

Component name	Role
Teller Client	Provide a user interface tuned for the needs of bank tellers.
Teller Server	Provides services for the use of tellers. This includes administrative functions.
Session Manager	Provides transaction and session id support.
Customer Info Server	Provides service interfaces that provide access to basic customer information.
. . .	

In addition, a table of interface descriptions for the Component View is valuable. Table 7.3 is an example of a component interface description table.

Table 7.3 Component interface descriptions

Interface name	Description	Provided by	Consumed by
Customer Info	Provides access to customer data.	Customer Info Server	Web Server, Teller Server, Voice Response Interface
Transaction	Provides transaction coordination for components.	Transaction Manager	Web Server, Teller Server, Voice Response Interface

Figure 7.1 is a rather manageable size. However, if we expand the scope of the Component View it may become unwieldy. One way to cope with the complexity is to abstract a set of components into a composite component. Figure 7.2 illustrates the combination of the Web Server, Teller Server, and Voice Response Server into a single composite component. In addition, the

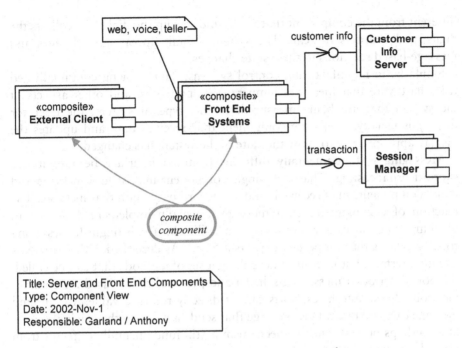

web, voice, teller

customer info

**Customer
Info
Server**

«composite»
External Client

«composite»
**Front End
Systems**

transaction

**Session
Manager**

*composite
component*

Title: Server and Front End Components
Type: Component View
Date: 2002-Nov-1
Responsible: Garland / Anthony

Figure 7.2   Composite component example

external client components are also abstracted into the 'External Clients' component. The composite components are labeled with the stereotype 'composite' in order to clearly distinguish them from actual components.

7.2.3 Message-based component modeling

In many types of systems, **interfaces may not accurately describe the component interactions.** These systems can be thought of as a collection of independent components that communicate via messaging protocols. The messages between components are typically asynchronous and may have highly variable transmission rates over time.

Often in these systems, external hardware or software pushes data or events into the system. The system must often handle some of the data in real time and do other processing over a more extended period. For example, consider the architecture of telephone central-office systems. When a telephone subscriber picks up the phone, this is detected by hardware. The software must then detect the state change and connect the phone to a dial tone. The software component scanning the telephone lines for state changes is typically different from the component that reacts and sets up the dial tone, collects the digits, and connects the call. The system is built up on state changes and message-based reactions to these state changes.

Similarly, in manufacturing control systems, data is being continually fed from hardware that measures temperatures, pressures, and other aspects of the system that are being measured. In this type of system, the operator display is usually a separate component that receives data and updates the display appropriately to show the state of the system has changed.

Messaging is fundamentally different from an interface because it can support broadcasting. That is, a single component may send a message and many components may receive it and act accordingly upon that message. The reaction of a component to a message is usually implemented as a non-blocking function call, referred to as a callback. To distinguish messaging from interfaces the component exports a 'port'. As described earlier, a port is like an interface, but instead of describing a set of methods that can be called, the port describes a messaging schema and protocol that is used for communication. Unlike interfaces, ports cannot directly return a value. An inbound message can generate a new message that sends a value to the original sender (and perhaps others), but the mechanism is still fundamentally different from a synchronous return to the sender.

From an architectural perspective, we are interested in answering several key questions concerning message-oriented component interactions. These include:

- What are the protocols in which a component participates?

- Is the component a sender or receiver for these protocols?

- What processing functionality does a component provide as a result of sending or receiving these messages?

- Is the information in the message sufficient for the component to act accordingly?

- What are the peak messaging rates?

Figure 7.3 illustrates a message-oriented component design. In this part of the banking system, a stock server component receives asynchronous messages that update the current prices for stocks. Simultaneously, a historical trending component receives the same data. The Stock Trade History component processes the events and stores summarized and raw data so that graphs and charts can be generated. The Stock Server, on the other hand, is only

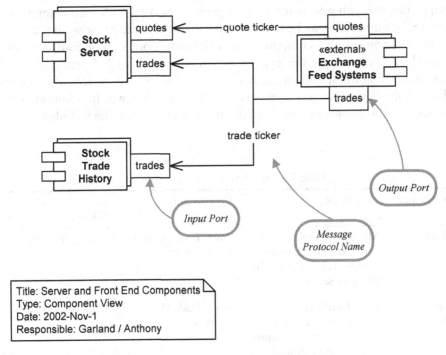

Figure 7.3   Component View with messaging

concerned with providing the latest information to other clients. The ports in the view illustrate a division between different messaging schemas. Ports are connected via associations, indicating navigability. The direction of the arrow indicates the port from which the message initiates. The arrowhead is placed on the receiving port, with no arrowhead on the sending port. This is similar to the use of arrows in use case diagrams.

Table 7.4 summarizes the components in Figure 7.3. This table could be

Table 7.4   Component descriptions

Component name	Role
Stock Server	Provide real-time collection point for latest trade and quote data.
Stock Trade History	Provide historical summaries of trade prices. Historical summaries include up-to-the-second daily summaries as well as monthly, quarterly, and yearly profiles.
Exchange Feed Systems	Provides raw real-time feed of market information.

supplemented with information about ports associated with each component, but this information may be better defined in the port table, shown later.

In addition to the component descriptions, port descriptions are also valuable. The ports in the system are shown in Table 7.5. An additional column, listing the specific messages associated with each port, is often useful later in the design process as the messages become known. In addition, a list of specific components expected to use these ports can also be included.

Table 7.5 Stock Server Port Descriptions

Port name	Description	Components – IN port	Components – OUT port
Trades	Messages containing periodic quotes for stocks identified to be tracked by the stock server.	Stock Trade History, Stock Server	Exchange Feed Systems
Quotes	Provides transaction coordination for stock trades to client components; usually this includes the stock server and the stock trade history components.	Stock Trade History, Stock Server	Exchange Feed Systems
. . .			

One important variation of this view excludes all details of ports and protocols. Thus, only components and connections are represented. This variation is useful during the initial design to identify a preliminary component set. Subsequent iterations of the view can add port and protocols details.

7.2.4 Combining interfaces and messaging

Large systems frequently have both client–server interfaces and messaging in combination. As an example, in the banking system, the requirement to keep a host of quote server components updated with the latest quote information uses messaging. The Exchange Feed Systems provide asynchronous updates constantly to the current quote prices. The number and nature of the servers that need to be updated are hard to predict until the system is scaled. In addition, the types of processing required may be very different for different applications. For example, one program may want to maintain the history of the stock price for the current day to perform statistical prediction analysis while another may simply provide the latest market prices to a web client. This example of combining messaging and interfaces in the same view is shown in Figure 7.4.

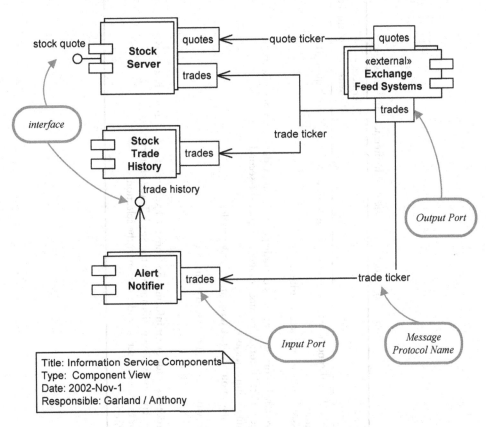

Figure 7.4   Component view with both interfaces and messaging

Table 7.6 shows the components in this view, along with a brief list of interfaces and components.

Table 7.6 Component View with interfaces and messaging

Component name	Role	Interfaces – (P)rovided (C)onsumed	Ports – (I)n (O)ut
Stock Server	Provide real-time collection point for latest trade and quote data associated with market securities.	stock quote (P)	quotes (I), trades (I)
Stock Trade History	Provide historical summaries of trade prices for individual securities. Historical summaries include up-to-the-second daily summaries as well as monthly, quarterly, and yearly profiles.	trade history (P)	trades (I)
Exchange Feed Systems	Provides raw real-time feed of market information.		trades (O) quotes (O)
Alert Notifier	Processes trade event information from the Exchange Feed Systems, providing notification to the Stock Trade History for the selected set of trades that meet the selection criteria.	trade history (C)	trades (I)

7.2.5   Comparison of interfaces and messaging

Messaging architectures have a different dependency structure than interface-based interactions. With messaging, both components depend on message data schema and protocol instead of an interface. Thus, messaging architectures tend to be more decoupled since data senders and receivers often do not depend directly on each other. Rather they depend on the **message protocol** and the messaging infrastructure, which may be purchased or developed by an infrastructure team.

The two different dependency structures of messaging and interface approaches are illustrated in the Figures 7.5 and 7.6. These figures are used to illustrate relationships between components, messages, and interfaces. These diagrams are for illustration and not suggested for use as actual architectural views.

In a message-oriented design, both components depend on the subsystems

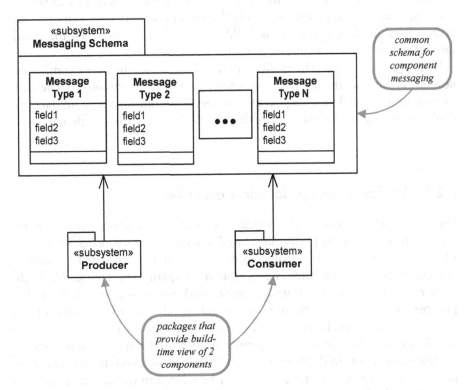

Figure 7.5   Build-time component dependency concept – message-oriented

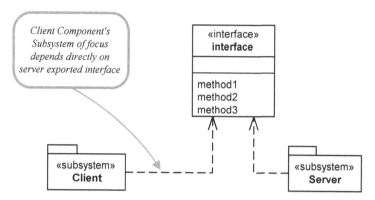

Figure 7.6 Build-time component dependency concept – interface-oriented

and classes that represent the message types to be exchanged. In Figures 7.5 and 7.6, a subsystem is used for the build-time representation of a component. Figure 7.5 illustrates that there is build-time dependence between the build-time aspects of a component and a specific set of messages.

In an interface approach, as illustrated in Figure 7.6, the client component depends directly on the interface exported by the server component. The clear impact of this is that changes to the server component will impact the deployment and testing issues more than in the message-oriented design.

7.2.6 Mechanism and performance annotations

One aspect of the system the architect would like to capture early in the development will be the **performance and scalability** requirements. In another variation of the view, the Component View can be annotated to include implementation mechanisms and performance quantities. Figure 7.7 is the same as Figure 7.1 redrawn with quantity and mechanism annotations. The purpose of these annotations is to document the relative scaling of the proposed system. As the view shows, it is expected that each web server can handle up to 200 (10000/50 assuming even load balancing) simultaneous browsers. Note that multiplicity is not used to represent quantities because the number of component instances may not be related to the interface relationships. Initially these quantities will likely be guesses based on experience, but

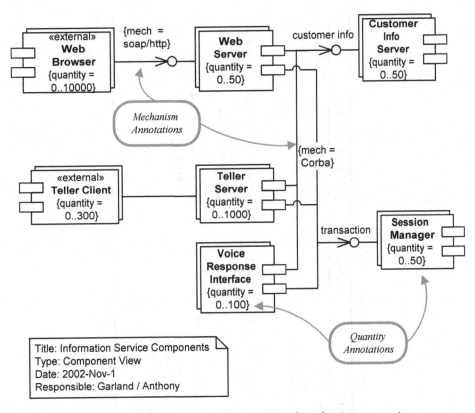

Figure 7.7   Component View with quantity and mechanism annotations

may be deemed critical enough to test in an architectural prototype or in early system tests.

Figure 7.7 also shows the expected implementation technologies for the various interfaces. If no mechanism is shown, then the mechanism has not been determined or is not of interest for this view.

Table 7.7 is an example of a table that might be produced to capture the key information on the interfaces shown in the Component View above. Another useful table for this type of view is a table that lists all the components in the view and has a description of each. Supplementary information, such as estimated memory footprint, can also be included in this type of table. Whenever possible, these types of supplementary tables should be generated in an automated manner from the CASE tool or a central database, such as a

Table 7.7 Component View interface table

Component	Interface provided	Description	Mechanism	Peak client load and throughput
Customer Info Server	customer info	Provides customer information such as address, account numbers, credit history.	RMI	Est. up to 1150 clients with total of 300 kbps during operational hours
Session Manager	transaction	Interface to begin, end, and cancel transaction.	CORBA	Est. up to 1150 clients with total of 400K requests per minute with < 256 bytes of data each.
Teller Server	client interface	Provides common server for teller terminals to query customer data, account data, or perform deposit/withdrawal.	TBD	Est. 300 clients with a total of 300 kbps per server.
...				

requirements database. In this way, information repeated in several tables can be kept consistent.

7.3   Component Interaction Viewpoint

The dynamic aspects of components are modeled in two ways. These are the Component Interaction and Component State Viewpoints. The Component Interaction Viewpoint utilizes component-level sequence or collaboration diagrams to show how specific components will interact. This viewpoint is summarized in Table 7.8.

Table 7.8   Component Interaction Viewpoint

Component Interaction Viewpoint	
Purpose	Validate structural design via exploration of the software dynamics.
When Applicable	Throughout project lifecycle. Primarily prepared during design and analysis, but can also be used and expanded during development.
Stakeholders	Software Architecture Team, Software Systems Engineering Team, Subsystem Design Leads, Developers.
Scalability	Based on scenarios, can be scaled to higher levels by using composite components.
Relation to Other Views	Should be consistent with Component, Process, and Deployment Views.

7.3.1   Component to Component Interactions

Figure 7.8 shows a Component Interaction View. This view illustrates the startup and login scenario for the Teller Interface component. The view also illustrates the protocol used to access an Authentication Server component. All the details of the individual object instances exported by the various components are elided so that an overall understanding of the component dynamics can be explored. Stereotypes are used to indicate that the instances in the view correspond to component instances.

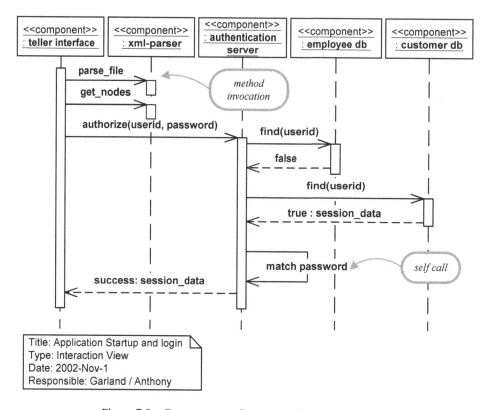

Figure 7.8 Component to Component Interaction View

Component Interaction Views scale better than object interaction diagrams since the details of the individual object instances are not shown. Component Interaction Views are also helpful when illustrating the use of off-the-shelf or legacy software. COTS can be represented as a component, thus hiding the detail of the interface and reducing the modeling demands.

The view shown in Figure 7.9 illustrates the use of an alternative interaction view using a component collaboration diagram. This type of view is logically equivalent to a sequence-based interaction view, but may communicate the component interactions more clearly. As described in Chapter 5, collaboration diagrams work best when the communicating entities fit easily on one page, and the number of interactions is not too large, usually less than 10.

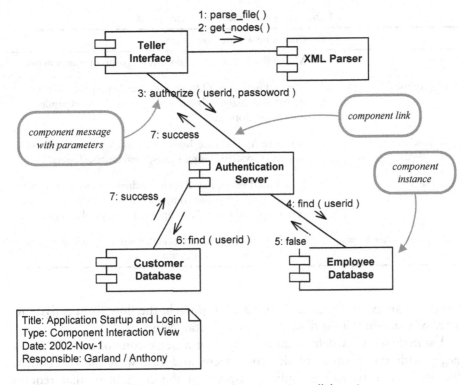

1: parse_file( )
2: get_nodes( )

Teller Interface

XML Parser

3: authorize (userid, passoword)

component link

component message with parameters

7: success

Authentication Server

component instance

7: success

4: find (userid)

6: find (userid)   5: false

Customer Database

Employee Database

Title: Application Startup and Login
Type: Component Interaction View
Date: 2002-Nov-1
Responsible: Garland / Anthony

Figure 7.9   Component interaction using collaborations

7.4 Component State Modeling

The Component State Viewpoint provides a means to communicate the internal states and activities for one or more components. The views specified by this viewpoint provide visibility into the overall behavior of the component(s). This behavior can be documented in two ways: by illustrating the potential states of a component along with the transitions among the states, or by illustrating the flow of control from one activity to another.

Table 7.9 summarizes the Component State Viewpoint.

A state is a part of the life of a component during which the component performs some set of activities. The component enters the state upon completion of another state or upon receipt of an event causing the transition from the other state. The component leaves the state upon completion or

Table 7.9   Component State Viewpoint

	Component State Viewpoint
Purpose	Model the state of a component or group of components.
When Applicable	Throughout project lifecycle. Primarily prepared during design and analysis, but can also be used and expanded during development.
Stakeholders	Software Architecture Team, Software Systems Engineering Team, Subsystem Design Leads, Developers, Testers.
Scalability	State-based views, based on individual components, can be scaled up to composite components. Activity-based views can be applied to single component or several components.
Relation to Other Views	Should be consistent with other dynamic views as well as interface and message definition.

receipt of an event. In the activity-based approach, the flow from activity to activity is shown. This is described in more detail below.

A state-based view defines state changes for a single component. The states begin with the creation of the component and end with the component lifespan. These transitions indicate aspects of the component that require some activities to occur. One common mistake among modelers is to model a transition as a state. Transitions are the short-lived occurrences in the life of a component, usually triggered by an event or the completion of a state. Within each state, entry and exit actions are defined. In addition, actions that occur within the state as well as internal transitions are listed as text inside the state.

Figure 7.10 shows a Component State View for the Stock Alert Notifier component shown in Figure 7.4. After loading, the component is initialized and, if successful, waits for updates. When an update is received the Notifier processes the update. When the Notifier receives a shutdown it is unloaded and terminates.

The information in nearly all Component State Views could also be represented in a tabular form. This form may be useful to provide better descriptions of the states or activities. However, this form of component state often makes it more difficult to follow the transitions from one state or activity to another. The good approach involves capturing the states or activities and supplementing with a table that describes the key information.

An activity-based variant of the Component State View is also useful. This approach shows a flow from activity to activity for a component. In this case,

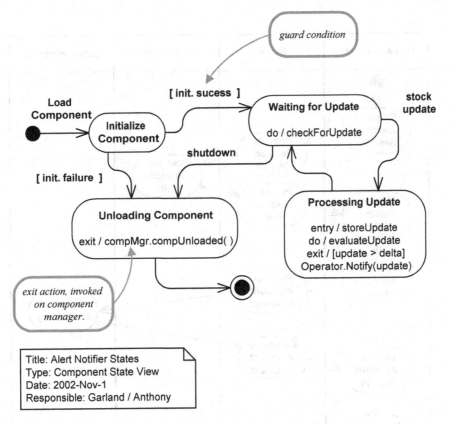

Figure 7.10   Alert Notifier Component States

an activity differs from a state-based view in that the states shown in the view usually include one activity and that the transitions in an activity-based view are normally triggered by the completion of a state. Any statechart notation can be used in this type of state view. These include branches, forks, joins, composite states, and nested states.

In addition to showing activity flow for one component, these activities can be for multiple components and can be grouped into structures referred to as swimlanes. One approach we recommend is to have each swimlane group the responsibility of one or more components. In this way, the flow among a set of activities can be illustrated across several components. An example of this approach is shown in Figure 7.11.

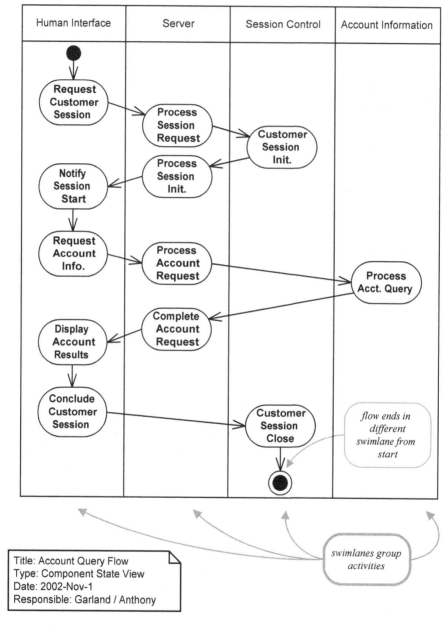

Figure 7.11   Activity-based state view

7.5 Modeling Highly Configurable Component Architectures

Standard UML modeling techniques model static architectures well, but are not as good at representing dynamic component architectures. That is, components that are made available dynamically as requests are made by the component infrastructure. This would include systems that dynamically load and unload components based on the needs of the system. These highly adaptable component architectures can be shown by using the creation and destruction semantics in Component Interaction Views. These views were discussed earlier in this section.

A similar problem is determining how to represent components that have many different configuration options. While the static view of the components does not necessarily change during these configurations, certain component interfaces may be more or less emphasized under different configurations. Options for different configurations include annotations to indicate interfaces emphasized or de-emphasized by each configuration. Utilizing well-known configuration names is useful to support these annotations. Another approach is to once again capture several views, one or more per configuration, each showing how different aspects of the static view are involved in each configuration. As the UML evolves, other approaches to solving the problems of dynamic and configurable components may be found.

7.6 Recommended Reading

Hofmeister *et al.* (1999) describe a conceptual architecture view for modeling components. Their system enables the description of components, connectors, ports, roles, and protocols. This is a more detailed sort of modeling that may be useful for message-based systems. However, Hofmeister *et al.* apply this to 'conceptual components' that are 'relatively independent of the particular hardware and software techniques'. The viewpoints described in this chapter can be considered a simplified version of the Hofmeister approach, but the components are not conceptual. We prefer to define 'preliminary' components and evolve them into the final component set. At that point, the preliminary components are no longer useful. At some point in the implementation, the actual components identified in the early design should be built and available for use. Of course, the assignment of functionality to components may shift over time, and unique combinations of components can be created.

The Jacobson paper (1995) discusses the system of systems approach. It is also discussed in the UML User Guide (1999).

Hofmeister *et al.* (1999) also discuss the concept of ports. However, they include both operations and messages in the port definition. We have found these to be fundamentally different, and therefore require separate modeling elements.

In his PHD thesis *Component Interaction in Distributed Systems*, Nat Pryce (2000) has defined an architecture description language for modeling components.

Kruchten's (1999) book on the Rational Unified Process has a good discussion of component-based development.

8

Subsystem Design

As Fowler suggests, 'Packages are a vital tool for large projects. Use packages whenever a class diagram that encompasses the whole system is no longer legible on a single letter-size (or A4) sheet of paper.' Fowler's standard would almost certainly guarantee the extensive use of packages for most system development, especially large-scale systems. Our recommendation is to focus on the subsystems, which are similar to packages but have a few additional constraints. As discussed in Chapters 11 and 12, the partitioning of classes into subsystems and managing the dependencies between these subsystems is a key focus of the software architect.

Subsystems define design/build-time system structure, interfaces, and dependencies. The subsystem viewpoints described in this chapter provide information on the system's build-time and organizational dependencies. These views are especially critical to the implementation teams, as they will document the static software structures.

8.1 Terminology

In order to accurately model the entities and relationships at subsystem level, the terminology must be well understood. In addition, the relationship between UML packages and subsystems, and the corresponding build-time software development concepts, must be clearly defined. These concepts include package, system, and subsystem.

The UML User's Guide defines a **package** as a collection of model elements.

All model elements, except for the top-level system package, must be contained within a package. These elements include classes, interfaces, components, nodes, collaborations, use cases, and other packages. These model elements are owned by the package. That is, they are deleted from the model if the package is removed. Packages can have model elements that are hidden from other packages and others that are visible. The visible model elements are usually the interface classes within the package.

A **system** is shown graphically as a stereotyped package, and is a representation of the entire scope of the development effort. A **subsystem** is a part of the system and, as with the system, is shown as a stereotyped package. The subsystem is important because this is the level at which design work products are to be assigned to development teams. Subsystems should map to the build-time directories that will be developed, tested, and delivered by the respective development teams. To ensure maintainability it is desirable to have subsystems that exhibit high cohesion and low coupling. If the coupling is inappropriate, the development teams will expend unnecessary time and effort negotiating, developing, and delivering interfaces between the highly coupled subsystems.

Subsystems are typically the lowest-level entity for which the software architecture team manages interfaces. In addition, a subsystem is the unit for which design documentation will be produced. This means that if a subsystem team identifies lower-level subsystems, that software development team, not the architecture team, will manage these interfaces. Conversely, multiple subsystems may be assigned to a development team, but should be designed, developed, and tested separately. In addition, each subsystem should have the subsystem-level interfaces and design managed and reviewed by the software architecture team.

Subsystems are also the unit at which testing is performed. Automated test suites are often developed at this level. As issues are isolated, defects are usually assigned to subsystem teams for resolution. Often integration teams use subsystems as the unit of delivery for documentation, source code, test reports, and other delivery products.

The UML User Guide also refers to modeling large development efforts as a system of systems. In this approach, each subsystem may be considered the system under design. This means that many of the architecture processes and techniques we describe can be applied at the subsystem level, given the subsystem is of sufficient complexity.

Another technique to help abstract a system design is the use of **layers**. Layers decompose the functions of a software system into clearly defined groups where functions of the higher layers depend on functions of the lower layers. There are many variations on layering, including strict layering, relaxed layers, and inheritance across layers. In all cases, however, the higher layers depend on the lower layers. Some of these semantics are detailed later in this chapter.

The practical implications of layers are many. For example, layering can enhance the portability of the architecture. To port a layered architecture from one platform to another is simplified because there is a natural division of effort and order inherent in the design. Layers also provide additional support for the minimization of software by skipping builds of lower layers when they have not changed. Finally, layers facilitate communication by allowing the suppression of detail.

8.2   Modeling Subsystems, Interfaces, and Layers

Subsystems and layers are two fundamental tools for structuring large-scale systems into smaller, more manageable parts. As described earlier, a subsystem groups related classes and other elements into an entity that can be independently designed, developed, managed, and tested. The decomposition of software naturally leads to the creation of dependencies between subsystems. The following sections will describe the modeling of subsystems, layers, and subsystem interfaces.

Dependency management and interface development are some of the fundamental tasks of architecture development. **Dependency management** is fundamental because it directly impacts the changeability and testability of the system. A system where many subsystems are co-dependent quickly becomes difficult to change because every modification potentially requires rebuilding and retesting of all the subsystems. In addition, the process for negotiating subsystem and component interface changes becomes insurmountable. This problem has been described in the Big Ball of Mud Pattern. Conversely, an architecture without codependent subsystems is much more changeable since the impact of a change is localized. In fact, moving classes and functions between different subsystems is probably the most critical task of the architect and architecture team.

8.2.1   Subsystem Interface Dependency Viewpoint

Often the visualization of dependencies is helpful in developing an understanding of the system structure. Subsystem Interface Dependency Views

(Table 8.1) provide the tools for recording, exploring, and managing the overall system dependencies.

Table 8.1 Subsystem Interface Dependency Viewpoint

Subsystem Interface Dependency Viewpoint	
Purpose	Describe subsystem dependencies and interfaces. Will most likely be one of these for overall system, potentially one for each top-level subsystem complex enough to require a view of its own.
When Applicable	During system design and development, as subsystems are identified.
Stakeholders	Project and Development Managers (primary stakeholders for top-level subsystem views), Architecture Team, Development Leads, Test Team.
Scalability	Can be focused on individual subsystems or scenarios. Layers also provide for hiding of detail.
Relation to Other Views	These views should be consistent with the Layered Subsystem View.

A common strategy in large systems is to provide one or several views for each major subsystem where the 'focus subsystem' is treated as the center of attention. Related subsystems are placed around the subsystem of focus. Figure 8.1 illustrates a basic Subsystem Interface Dependency View. The billing subsystem is the focus and the view is filtered such that only subsystems on which it depends are included. In this view, interface dependencies are not illustrated. That is, if a subsystem exports multiple interfaces, this detail is not shown.

A variation of the Subsystem Interface Dependency View includes the interfaces exported by a particular subsystem. As shown in Figure 8.2, the billing subsystem is still the focus and the dependencies to the interfaces of some of the related subsystems are illustrated. This clarifies that the actual dependencies between subsystems are only to specific interfaces. This distinction may be important if an interface would be better provided by a different subsystem.

Ports are usually not included in a Subsystem Interface Dependency View. This is because port usage does not necessarily imply a dependency between subsystems. The use of ports in component views is described in detail in Chapter 7.

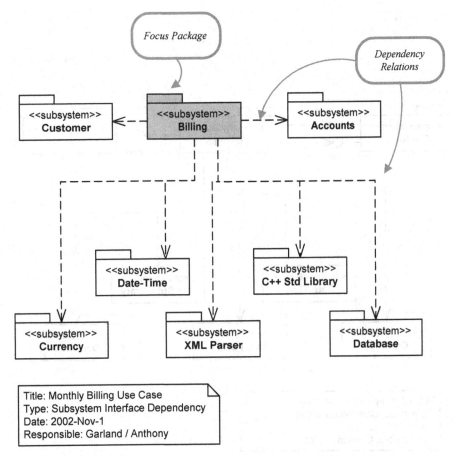

Figure 8.1   Subsystem Interface Dependency View – focused on billing

8.2.2 Enhancing the Subsystem Dependency Views with layers

Layering of software systems is a highly successful design strategy. Almost all modern software systems are composed of multiple layers, with most having several clearly identifiable layers. Including layering information can enhance the Subsystem Interface Dependency View. This provides additional information about the structure of the system as related to a particular subsystem. In Figure 8.3, the containing layers illustrate the structure of the subsystems upon which the billing subsystem depends.

Layers can also be used to suppress detail in complex views. In Figure 8.4, the focus is changed from a particular subsystem to a scenario. In addition,

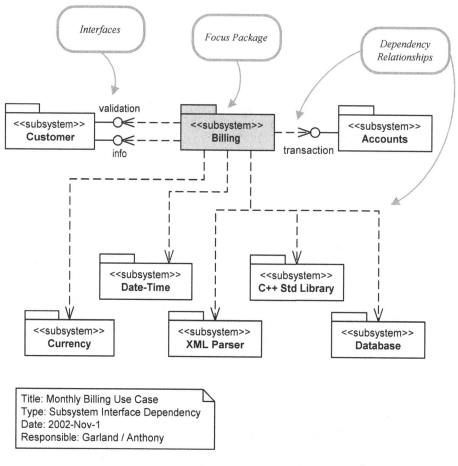

Figure 8.2   Subsystem Interface Dependency View – focused on billing

the 'information level' has been decreased by suppressing all interface dependencies and moving dependencies on lower layers up to the layer level. The view loses the detail of which lower-level subsystems are depended upon by the higher layer subsystems, but is simpler to create and maintain.

8.2.3 Top-level Dependencies

A top-level version of the Subsystem Interface Dependency View may be created by combining a set of subsystem centric views. The purpose of this variation is to describe the 'organizational interfaces'. This allows the

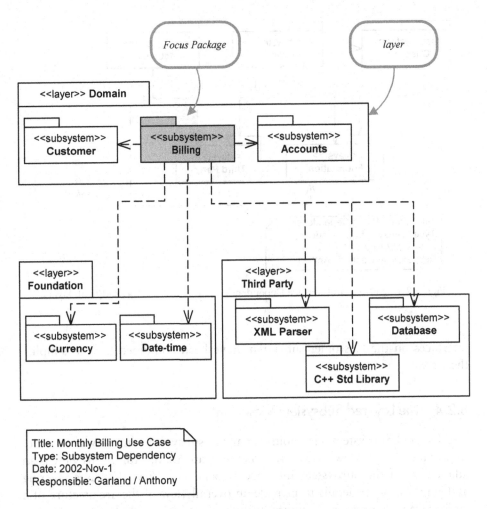

Figure 8.3   Subsystem Dependencies with layers

software architect to communicate development team boundaries, communicate and negotiate interfaces between development teams, and communicate with project management. Due to this focus, this variation of the view typically omits infrastructure and off-the-shelf subsystems.

Figure 8.5 illustrates a top-level view for the banking example. Notice that the subsystems from the foundation layer have been omitted. Interfaces that are shown in the detailed views of the system or in the subsystem-centric views can be collapsed in this top-level view. For example, the validation and query

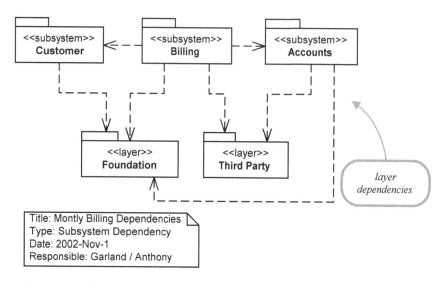

Figure 8.4   Subsystem Interface Dependency View – use case focused, with layers

interfaces on the Customer subsystem have been combined here to simplify the view.

8.2.4 The Layered Subsystem Viewpoint

The Layered Subsystem Viewpoint organizes subsystems into layers in order to provide a single view that represents the entire architecture. This view is an adaptation of the Subsystem Interface Dependency View that uses layering and suppression of details to provide an overall view of the architecture of a large system. Traditional architecture documents often include a layered view of the system. These are easy-to-understand views for non-software experts. However, these ad-hoc diagrams are not drawn consistently and therefore do not provide significant technical information about the architecture. The Layered Subsystem Viewpoint (Table 8.2) builds on this tradition by adding dependency semantics for the technical teams while maintaining the easy-to-understand form of traditional layer diagrams.

For the software developers the Layered Subsystem View concisely represents a critical aspect of the software architecture: build-time dependencies. Specifically, subsystems in higher layers depend on lower layers but not the other way around. The Layered Subsystem View is used as a fundamental representation of the software system design and build-time architecture.

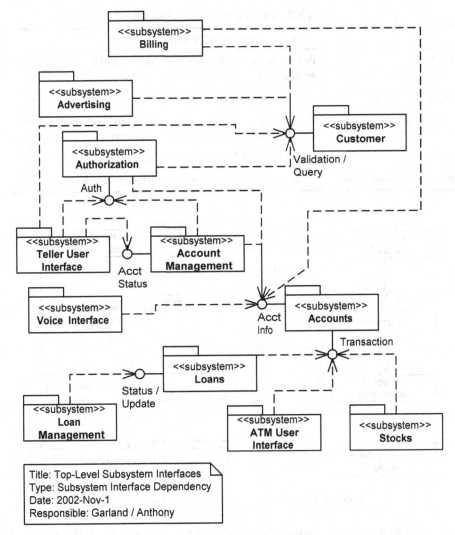

Figure 8.5   Top-level Subsystem Interface Dependency View

Extensions of this view can be used to communicate multiple system aspects to different project stakeholders.

Figure 8.6 shows some of the possible dependency semantics of the Layered Subsystem View. These semantics are important primarily for development teams and the architecture team. We include this diagram to illustrate the semantics of the Layered Subsystem View. It will not be part of any architecture or design documentation. For very large systems that share

Table 8.2   Layered Subsystem Viewpoint

Layered Subsystem Viewpoint	
Purpose	Provide top-level view of the subsystem and layer build-time architecture.
When Applicable	Throughout project lifecycle.
Stakeholders	Program and Project Managers, Software Architecture Team, Development Team, Test Team, Customers.
Scalability	Omits detailed dependency information.
Relation to other Views	Abstraction of the Subsystem Interface Dependency View.

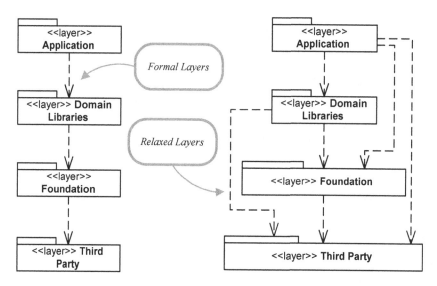

Figure 8.6   Layering semantics – formal and relaxed

common foundational components a relaxed layering approach is a practical arrangement. In small systems or within a restricted context, a formal layering semantic may also be achieved.

Figure 8.7 provides an example of the Layered Subsystem View. The lowest layer consists of third-party subsystems such as database and user interface libraries. The second layer represents subsystems maintained by the project to simplify common programming tasks. The third layer consists of subsystems that provide components specific to the problem domain. Finally, the top layer provides application subsystems realized by utilizing and often extending the functionality in the lower layers. This example does not represent the only

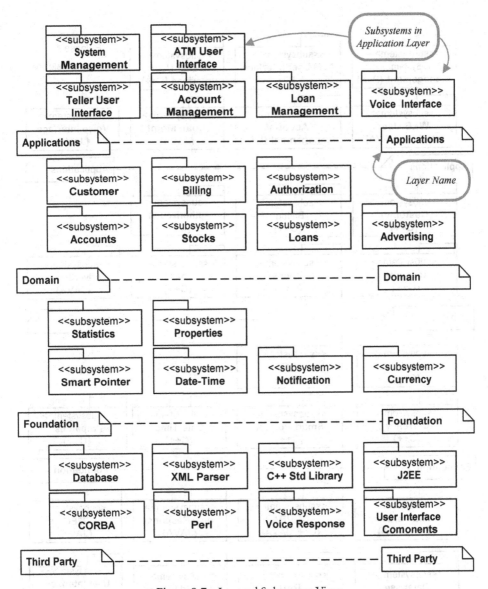

Figure 8.7 Layered Subsystem View

possible set of layers. A system may have a larger or smaller number of layers and may also have different logical relationships. The guiding principle, however, is that the upper layers should depend on the lower layers and not vice versa.

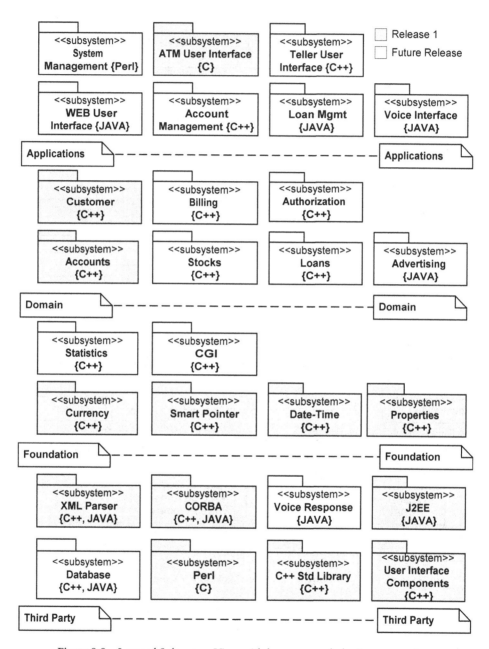

Figure 8.8   Layered Subsystem View with language and phasing annotation

One issue in the construction of the Layered Subsystem View is whether to allow dependencies within a layer. The resolution of this issue is really determined by how layers are defined. In some systems, it may be possible and desirable to create a totally ordered set of layers. In this case, dependencies between subsystems in a layer would not be allowed.

Supplementing the Layered Subsystem View with dependency tables or other subsystem-level dependency mechanisms is valuable so that the details of individual subsystems can be explored as needed. The Layered Subsystem View can be used as a starting point for more detailed dependency exploration.

Architects are frequently asked to provide managers and others with auxiliary information about the software. The Layered Subsystem View can provide a handy vehicle for communicating such information. For example, Figure 8.8 provides an example of the Layered Subsystem View annotated to describe the languages used to implement various elements of the system. In addition, shading is used to highlight subsystems that have deliveries as part of the first phase of development. Many types of information can be compactly represented using this view. As another example, highlighting of subsystems that will be developed internally versus those that will be purchased or subcontracted.

8.3   Mapping Subsystems and Layers to Implementation

The following sections describe some details of how to map subsystems, layers, and components to the final implementation.

8.3.1   Subsystems, layers, and build trees

In large projects, we recommend that layers and subsystems map directly to the build-time implementation structure of the project. A subsystem in the design is realized as a subdirectory of the same name in the source directory tree. A subsystem directory should contain a set of common subdirectories to manage the products of subsystem development, including source code, subsystem test suites, and documentation. Subsystems can also be composed of other subsystems as needed. If layers are used in the architecture, they are also reflected as a directory in the implementation. The layers serve as the top-level set of directories in the hierarchy.

Figure 8.9 illustrates a mapping of layers and subsystems to the

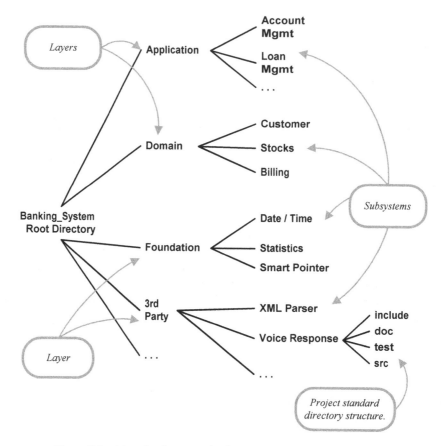

Figure 8.9   Mapping layers and subsystems to a directory structure

development directory structure. Note that the directories for third-party subsystems often do not physically reside within the directory tree, but may use linking to appear as though they reside there. In addition, some projects may find the use of multiple trees preferable. This diagram is used for illustration purposes only. It is not intended to become an actual architecture view.

We also recommend a direct reflection of the subsystem architecture in the source code. A best practice is to have 'include' paths that match the layer and subsystem structure. For example, in our example system for a C++ module to access the date class in the date-time subsystem of the 'foundation' layer the programmer would write:

#include "foundation/date-time/date.hpp"

The benefit of this approach is that the architecture of the system is directly reflected in the source code. This helps implementers learn and grasp the overall system organization.

The alternative is to remove these details from the source. In this case, the build system is used to manipulate the inclusion paths such that the programmer only writes:

#include "date.hpp"

While this is shorter, it conveys much less information. The downside of the explicit approach is that if the subsystem organization changes (say by renaming a package), much more source code is impacted. However, such changes are mechanical and can be easily automated with a script.

8.3.2 Subsystems and components

In the UML, it is technically possible to develop views with components and subsystems together. We recommend against this approach. The issue stems back to the definition of a component and the relationship between components and subsystems. In our definition, components are runtime instances while subsystems are a build-time structuring technique. Therefore, the only relationship that makes sense is that a subsystem 'builds' a component. As a result, each component has a corresponding subsystem, called the subsystem of origin. The component is not in the subsystem of origin, but rather is a result of building, installing, and executing that subsystem. To describe both the build and runtime aspects with components only, we would need to have 'build-time' components and runtime components with the same name. We prefer to avoid this entire issue with appropriate subsystem naming and comments that explain relationships.

Figure 8.10 illustrates the conceptual relationship between a subsystem and a component built by that subsystem. This diagram is here for illustration only and is not an architectural view. In addition to being built by a subsystem, a component also has an instance of an interface that was defined for its subsystem of origin. Similar to the naming conventions for subsystems and components, the interface on the subsystem and the one on the component will have the same name. It is important to note that a subsystem can build one or more components.

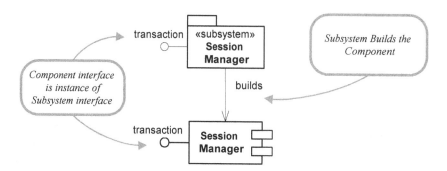

Figure 8.10 Subsystem and component conceptual relationship

8.4 Recommended Reading

Hofmeister *et al.* (1999) discuss modularization and layering design.

Buschmann (1996) describes Layers as an Architectural Pattern. He also describes the different variations of the semantics of layers, including strict layering, relaxed layers, and inheritance across layers.

This Layered Subsystem View is similar to the 'Tiers View' suggested by Doug Smith (2000), except that the layered subsystem view does not attempt to represent dependencies explicitly.

The Layered Subsystem View was initially presented as the Layered Package View by Garland (2001).

Lakos (1996) describes package groups, dependencies, and many other aspects of architectural structuring for large C++ implementations.

9

Transaction and Data Design

This chapter provides an overview of architectural issues and viewpoints surrounding the development of data models and transactions. Since this topic could consume an entire book we focus on the highlights here and provide suggestions in the recommended reading for further study. In this chapter we focus mostly on the logical aspects of the data design. Physical deployment topics such as data distribution and backup are discussed in Chapter 10.

9.1 Logical Data Architecture

The logical data architecture describes the form or structure of the entities, data relationships, and constraints used in the software. The logical data architecture is often referred to as the data schema or logical data model. We will use these terms interchangeably here and will shorten logical data model to data model for this chapter.

A data schema has two main applications: persistent storage and messaging. For modeling messaging, the data schema definition would define the individual messages and their relationships, primarily in a hierarchy of message types. In the case of modeling the data schema for persistent storage, the relationships between the data schema and their mapping to persistent storage mechanisms become more important.

The data schema may be modeled as a conventional object model or using entity-relationship (ER) models. In this book, we will focus on using a UML approach. We find the UML notation to be a sufficiently rich representation of the entities, their relationships, and constraints. The data schema will be represented as UML classes with attribution. Methods are generally not applicable for the data architecture.

An entity relationship model may be preferred if the project makes widespread use of relational databases and has a significant investment in and experience with ER modeling tools. However, ER models are not as effective for non-relational data, including storage schemes such as files and object databases. In addition, the wide use of technologies such as shared memory is another reason to use a technology-neutral approach such as the UML for modeling the data schemas. Finally, very complex object models are often quite difficult to implement using relational databases.

The logical data architecture can be developed by a dedicated group of data architects, by other members of the architecture team, or by the subsystem design teams with oversight by the architecture team. In large-scale systems, a combination of these approaches is often used. Aspects of the data architecture that cross subsystem boundaries should be defined by the architecture team and data used entirely within the subsystem should be defined by the subsystem team.

An Unhealthy Split

In our experience, there has been an unhealthy split of data modeling and object modeling with the widespread adoption of object-oriented design techniques. Object-oriented advocates suggest that data and behavior must always be combined. However, there are important aspects of large systems that are best designed viewing 'data as just data'. Similarly, database designers insist on ER modeling even though an object model will suffice. In addition, database designers often develop stored database procedures to achieve complex system behaviors when this functionality should be part of the application software. On the other hand, application designers hard-coding duplicate data integrity constraints into application code creates problems as well.

In the end, there is not one right answer. It is important to realize that redundant models, disjoint teams, and squabbling over turf won't move the project forward. Team members need to cross-train in the various techniques and technologies and keep an open mind. In addition, the architecture team should ensure that data architecture is developed in an appropriate manner.

9.1.1 Logical data model stability

Once a system is deployed, the impacts of changing the data model are severe. These changes often impact the budget, schedule, testing, and customer interface.

To see why modifications are difficult, consider the possible types of data model changes:

- Add or remove a class

- Add or remove an attribute from a class

- Change an attribute type

- Move attribute to different class

- Restructure a class hierarchy

With perhaps the exception of adding a new attribute, all of these data changes can create major deployment issues for a system. Almost all will require **upgrading the existing data, the schema, and the software**. This might not be feasible because the new attributes may require some additional information that is not easily obtained. For example, in the banking system there is a need to collect customer information. If email is added as a new attribute, then there is no way to obtain that information easily without contacting all of the customers.

Additional server hardware, networks, and specialized utilities or programs are often required to migrate data from one form to another. This migration requires extensive testing to ensure the resulting data is correct. In addition, the software may be required to support multiple versions of the data to be able to operate during the migration.

In environments that support continuous software operations, both the old and the new versions of the data may need to be available simultaneously. This is because it may not be possible or desirable to upgrade all program components at once, so both forms must be available simultaneously. This makes additions or major modifications to the data much more difficult. Similarly, if a fall-back capability is required during migration, the data in the old form may need to be kept consistent with the data in the upgraded form. Both versions need to be kept synchronized to allow for the situation where the new software fails and the old system needs to be restored.

Attempts to avoid direct dependence on the data model by inserting a procedural layer to encapsulate access to the data do not necessarily help. If this layer is required to support multiple versions of the data interface, now both the application code and the interface layer must change when the data model changes. Changes to the content of the data model will nearly always impact application code. However, a set of infrastructure code to insulate the application developers from the database mechanisms such as session management and transactions can be used to limit dependencies on product-specific database mechanisms.

Finally, there is the issue of retesting. Changes to an underlying data model typically impact systems by forcing full regression testing to ensure the change has not broken existing functionality. This type of testing can be prohibitively expensive to do well. This reason alone may cause data changes to be blocked by project management.

9.1.2   Effects of the stable logical data model

Due to the problems introduced by changes to the data model, it is essential to explore and refine the data model early. The aspects of the data model likely to change need to be identified early in the development process. In this way, the alternatives can be analyzed and potentially prototyped so a decision can be made before the migration issues become a problem.

The stable nature of the data model makes it imperative that the architecture team actively participates in the development of the data architecture. This participation should include frequent technical meetings and reviews to determine the current state of the data architecture as well as approval of the architecture itself. The stability of the data model can also provide several advantages. For example, a stable data model can facilitate the rapid and early development of custom reports. In addition, the data model is one aspect of the design that can become well understood by many team members. This shared understanding provides a basis for communication about the shared portion of the underlying model utilized by the software.

A stable data model also makes a good basis for integration of components, described as data-only integration in Chapter 11. The Repository and Blackboard architecture patterns are examples of utilizing a stable data model for data-only component integration. Another effect of the data-only integration approach is that it often allows for the addition of new disparate functions using new technologies without impact to existing systems. These new functions can be added much more rapidly than might be possible if the existing system had to be modified.

Data models for messaging have somewhat fewer restrictions on their stability than data models for database or file-based data. This is primarily because messages have fewer complex relationships and as a result the impacts of modifications tend to be more isolated. In addition, messaging systems can often be more flexible in handling messages with varying format. This is especially true if the messages use a self-describing format, such as XML or attribute value pairs. However, if the messages are stored in a compact or binary format, the constraints on their stability are much more restricted.

A pitfall to avoid in logical data architecture is taking an incremental deployment approach with a large-scale data model. An incremental approach can be taken during early iterations, but once systems are deployed, all the aforementioned issues with changing the data model become relevant. Incremental deployment can only be achieved if the new elements of a data model are independent of an existing core data model.

9.2   Logical Data Viewpoint

The Logical Data Viewpoint (Table 9.1) provides an overview of all the major data entities in the system. The Logical Data Viewpoint is a UML class diagram focused on modeling attributes and relationships rather than methods and behavior. This view does not need to include all data entities, only those that are shared by multiple components or subsystems. The entities from the Analysis Overall View can serve as the foundation for the Logical Data View. Alternatively, for reengineering tasks an existing database schema, message types, or file contents might serve as the basis for building this view.

Table 9.1   Logical Data Viewpoint

Logical Data Viewpoint	
Purpose	Describe the logical form of data and messaging types for a system.
When Applicable	Design.
Stakeholders	Architecture Team, Developers, Testers, Hardware Architect.
Relation to other Views	Derived from Analysis Overall View.

A typical application of the Logical Data Viewpoint is to create a view of the entities shared among a set of collaborating components. The data entities serve as a point of integration for these components. The data sharing mechanism may use a persistent store such as a database, message passing, or shared memory.

While this viewpoint applies to data views both for messaging and for database or file storage, the views for these two types of data can be quite different in appearance. The views for database or file storage can be quite complex, with a heavy dependence on aggregation and associations. The views for messaging models will be much simpler with little, if any, use of associations and aggregation.

9.2.1 Logical Data View example

Figure 9.1 shows a partial example of a Logical Data View. Derived from the Analysis Overall View, this view has been detailed by defining types for each attribute. This view focuses only on the attributes of the data model and not on the methods elaborated during the analysis. The presumption here is that all the attributes will be available for retrieval and update by clients.

As is customary with views, there is a supporting table that provides descriptions of the entities. Table 9.2 is an example of this.

Part of the analysis of the overall Logical Data View should include dividing the entities in the model and assigning them to different subsystems. The approach generally involves an analysis of the cohesion and coupling of the various data entities. A similar approach is used for the analysis of the Analysis Overall View in the determination of the candidate subsystems, as described in Chapter 12. The process for development of the data view should be considered an extension of the process for the development of the Analysis Overall View. The development of the Logical Data View will often result in modifications to the candidate subsystems.

The logical data design will provide many constraints on the subsystem design. For example, it is important for the subsystem designers to remember that data entities with required bi-directional associations usually need to be created simultaneously. These entities are tightly coupled and should often be assigned to the same subsystem. Attributes of the same entity are automatically coupled.

The assumptions behind attribute coupling need to be examined carefully. For example, in Figure 9.1 if the program is eventually to be expanded to support international locations, the location information will need to change

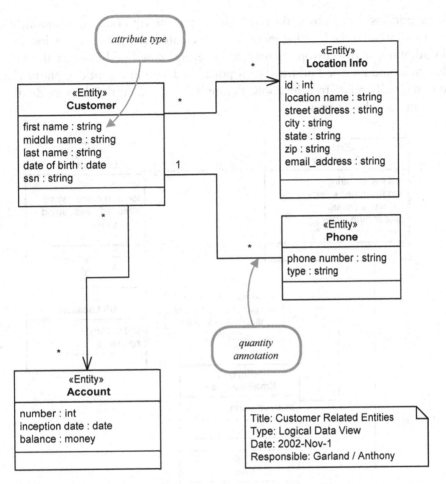

Figure 9.1   Example subset of Logical Data View

Table 9.2   Partial Entity Description Table

Entity	Description
Customer	Provides base information about the customer, including name and social security number.
Account	Entry that serves as anchoring point for all account types. Has a unique id. A customer may have multiple accounts, and an account may be related to multiple people.
...	

since addresses in Europe do not have a state or zip code. In addition, the email address in the existing view must be created along with every location. In addition, many customers may have several email addresses at the same location, and an email address for a portable device like a mobile phone that doesn't really relate to a location. Figure 9.2 is a refactored data model that accounts for these issues.

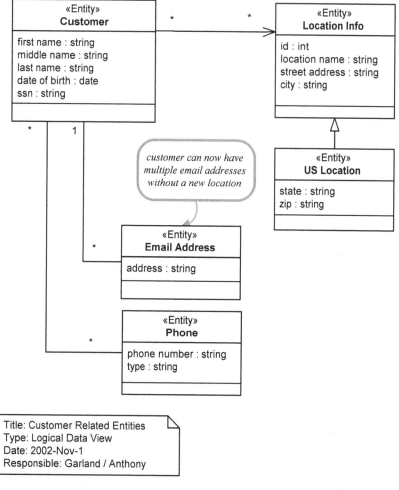

Figure 9.2 Refactored Logical Data View

If the data in the repository or message set is only accessed and used within a single subsystem, then this data becomes part of a subsystem design. This also includes data that is adapted by the subsystem to be communicated on an external interface and not accessed directly by the external subsystem clients. However, some core parts of the domain model may be so critical to the overall system operation that they are treated as system infrastructure and will often be modeled by the architecture team. As an example, the customer or account id will be used as a key field for looking up different types of data associated with a particular customer. Thus, the generation and assignment of the key values is an issue that needs to be addressed by the architecture. Without a consistent approach, integration of components will be difficult.

As another example, in the banking system there are several different identifiers that should be accessible to retrieve the customer information. The home phone number, for example, might be matched by the voice response system to perform an initial lookup of the customer. Similarly, an account number or last name might be used interaction with a customer representative.

9.2.2   Logical Data View for messaging

As described earlier, the Logical Data View can be used to represent messages as well as persistent data. Messages are generally much simpler than persistent classes, in that they have fewer complex associations and aggregations. However, they often have a rich inheritance hierarchy. This allows messages to be sent, received, and routed to message handlers by general-purpose frameworks that deal with the base classes rather than the derived classes.

Figure 9.3 shows an example of a Logical Data View for messages in the banking system. In this model, there is a base message type and several derived types. A group of these message types can be used as the schema for a component data port as described in Chapter 7. The class Message in the diagram forms an abstraction upon which message routing components may be built. The usual description table that accompanies views is omitted for brevity here.

9.3   Data Model Design – Other Considerations

The following sections briefly describe other data model considerations. This includes the interaction with layering, use of reflection for dynamic data models, and mapping objects to relational databases.

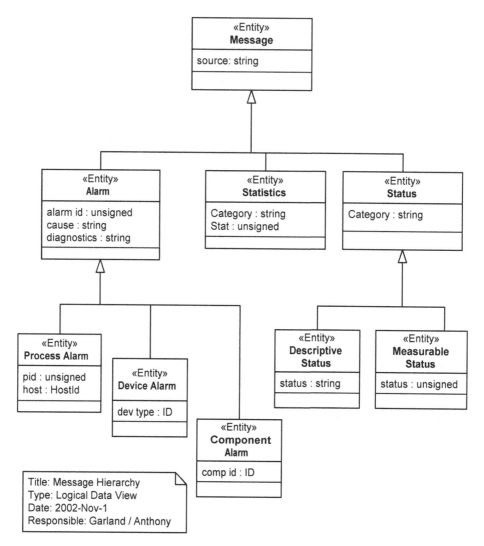

Figure 9.3   Message-based Logical Data View

9.3.1   Data models and layers

Several of the layering strategies for systems interact with the data model. For example, in the *Model–View–Controller* Pattern the data model is usually a large part of the model layer. Many of the entities in this model layer are often either stored in a persistent store or transmitted in messages. This model layer is similar to what we call the 'Domain Layer' in the Layered Subsystem View in Chapter 8.

Figure 9.4 shows an example layering strategy. All of the subsystems associated with the data model form the core of the architecture. Modifications to these subsystems will naturally be the most expensive, potentially requiring changes to the upper layers of the architecture to match with the data changes. In contrast, modifications to the view and control have less impact.

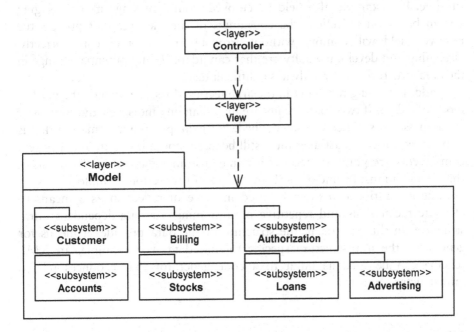

Figure 9.4   Example layering strategy

9.3.2   Data models and reflection

Reflection is a technique that allows systems to provide for flexible data models by providing the software the ability to interrogate the schema at runtime and adapt accordingly. Databases have provided this ability to interrogate the data schema for many years. However, the addition of reflection to languages such as Java makes the implementation of reflection techniques much more feasible. Generally reflection facilitates the implementation of infrastructure software that provides mechanisms for marshaling, parsing, and serialization of data. Without reflection, the creation of the infrastructure software often involves tedious and repetitive programming.

Reflection is an important architectural design strategy that can used to improve the adaptability of systems. However, it is important to realize that reflection by itself doesn't solve the data evolution problem. In particular, all the issues of evolving existing data content still exist.

There are other costs as well. Using reflection often hides software dependencies between components from the build system. Errors that might be found by compilation errors in a system based on reflection must be found at runtime. For example, if a field is removed from a message in a messaging system based on reflection, the consumers of the message that process the removed field will compile without error but may not execute correctly. Designing and developing software that can adapt to any potential change in the data structure is nearly always a difficult task.

In addition, using reflection in the architecture doesn't eliminate the need to model the data. If two components are interchanging messages, the content of those messages still needs to be defined. For example, the information that is to be saved for each customer must still be understood. If two different system components are going to access the same customer data, then the model is shared and it must be understood whether or not reflection is employed.

Code generation can often be used in place of reflection as a means to alleviate the tedious and repetitive programming for data-dependent infrastructure. In this approach, the structure of the data provides a means for generating the infrastructure specific to that data. For example, an XML schema can be used as input to a code generator that produces related infrastructure code.

9.3.3   Mapping objects to relational database

Mapping objects to a relational database is a common architectural issue today because of the extensive use of object-oriented design and relational database systems. As a result, there are many tools and frameworks to support mapping of objects to databases. Unfortunately, the details of this topic are more extensive than can be covered in this book. Here, we will focus on a few major considerations useful for addressing this issue.

One issue when mapping objects to relational databases is that objects are generally referenced based on a unique identifier. Examples of these identifiers include the physical memory address of the object or an identifier generated by an object database. Relational database records are often referenced based on a key, which consists of one or more field values. This basic difference can be problematic when defining a mapping strategy. When mapping objects to relational databases, a scheme for creation of unique identifiers as a field in the record may be utilized. As an alternative, database key values can be stored as object attributes to provide a mapping mechanism.

Unique identifier generation schemes must often be employed in a system to provide unique identifiers for the objects. Object-oriented databases generally provide this capability as part of the facility. Many relational databases also provide a similar capability for providing unique identifiers.

Another basic issue in schema mapping is the relationship between the object model and the tables that implement the model. First, there is the issue of attributes. A primitive attribute is a simple data type such as a number, string, or time that can be directly represented as a single column in a database table. For each primitive attribute in the object model, there must be a corresponding column in a database table.

There are at least three major approaches for mapping tables to classes:

- One table for each class
- One table for each concrete class
- One table for all classes
- Several tables representing a generic data model

When one table per concrete class is employed, any inherited attributes are mapped into the table for the concrete class. If a single table is used many null fields are employed for attributes that do not apply. A generic data model uses reflection (discussed in a later section) to represent all classes in a uniform fashion.

Note that the following diagrams use a specialized icon to represent a table, which is a stereotyped class. In addition, these diagrams are not a view, but simply an illustration.

Figure 9.5 illustrates a simple strategy of mapping the attributes of each class to a table. The derived class gets attribute values from both the Base and Derived tables. To reconstruct a derived class instance requires the joining of the base and derived tables. This diagram provides a simple illustration of the mapping between classes and tables without requiring the detail of showing all the columns or attribute names. If a consistent set of naming conventions is used, the model may not be needed. These naming conventions will allow designers to easily understand the relationship between the data view entities and the database tables.

Unfortunately, designs are not usually this simple. The cost of joining tables

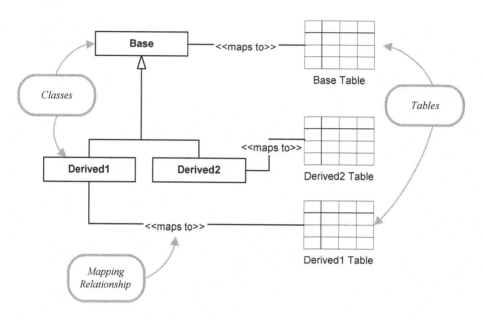

Figure 9.5   Class to table mapping design

or the overhead of extra 'id' attributes may become prohibitive in some cases. Figure 9.6 provides an example of an alternative design. In this case, there is only a single table for all the attributes of all three classes.

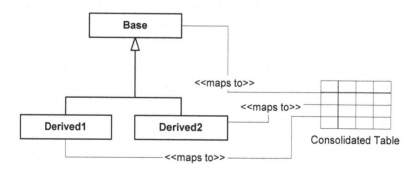

Figure 9.6   Alternative class to table mapping design

Another issue for object to relational database mapping is managing relationships between objects. In Figure 9.7, below, class 1 maps all of its attributes to a single table, class 2 maps all of its attributes to a table, and the association between the classes maps to a third relational table. The associa-

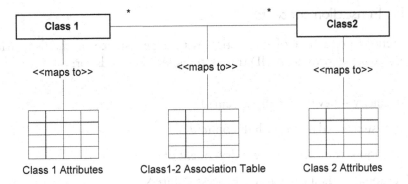

Figure 9.7   Relationship mapping

tion table contains two columns to map the id of a class 1 instance to the id of a class 2 instance.

9.4 Transaction Design

Another critical architectural design issue is the understanding of transactions and component interaction concurrency. Understanding and modeling the transactions of various parts of the system is essential for developing a good architecture. There are several reasons for this fact. First, poorly designed transactions can result in incomplete data in the data store. This incomplete data results in data corruption that can lead to program crashes or at least bad data presented to users. Improper transactions can result in unrecoverable software errors, which is obviously undesirable for software that needs to be robust or highly available. Second, transactions typically span across subsystem, layer, component, and even process boundaries. Thus, the management of the transactional state of the data becomes an implied part of the contract for many operations to behave correctly. The spanning of transactions across components and layers nearly always makes transaction design an architectural issue.

Several architectural issues typically need to be considered when dealing with transactions. These include:

- Which component(s) control the transactions?

- How do transactions relate to interfaces?

- Where are the potential concurrency hotspots?

- What are the transaction rates for updates?

9.4.1 Transaction concepts

Transactions are a unit of interaction with a persistence mechanism. Most database systems provide ACID transactions. ACID stands for:

- Atomicity – never partially executed

- Consistency – data never half committed

- Isolation – transactions are independent of each other

- Durability – data can survive process failures

The main advantage of ACID transactions is that they serve as distinct points where the state of components and processes are saved. Note that a database system is not required to have a system with ACID transactions. ACID transactions can be built with plain files. The advantage of the database system is that ACID transactions are typically built in, thus requiring no additional effort.

To implement ACID transactions typically requires some kind of data locking scheme. That is, transactions that manipulate the same data must be serialized to ensure ACID properties. Locking typically has different properties for reading and writing. Usually a piece of data can have an unlimited number of simultaneous readers and up to one writer. However, there are other locking schemes where any read transaction blocks any write transactions.

An important architectural issue is the unit of locking. Frequently the physical unit of locking does not match the logical unit of locking. Physical data modeling is discussed in Chapter 10. For example, if an application needs to update a customer object it might not be possible to lock only the customer of interest due to the locking mechanisms of the database. If table, page, or file locking is used instead of customer object locking, many other customer objects will be locked besides the customer actually being updated.

A frequent design goal when using databases is to keep update transactions as short as possible. This allows for multiple components to write to the database without blocking for significant periods of time. Keep in mind that not all 'transactions' represent a small amount of work in a short period. For example, in the banking system a billing program might take an entire day to process a set of customers. The billing cycle is not completed until all the records are processed. Internally the system may perform many transactions but if a failure occurs, the system might need to roll back all of the processing.

Some types of systems, such as computer-aided design systems, need transactions to version data rather than replace data. In these systems, the idea of a transaction is separate from the idea of a 'checkout' and 'check-in'.

9.4.2 Modeling transaction dynamics

Transactions may be modeled for several reasons. These include the need to understand and document complex transactional semantics, and as input to the development of component interfaces. Given the need to model transactions, the question arises how best to model them. The first step is to begin to understand where transactions fit into the dynamic model of the system. To model the dynamics there are at least two approaches, one for analysis and one for component interactions. The Component Interaction View is the component perspective on the transaction, where the Analysis Interaction View is the user perspective on the transaction.

Figure 9.8 shows a technique for annotating transactions in an Analysis

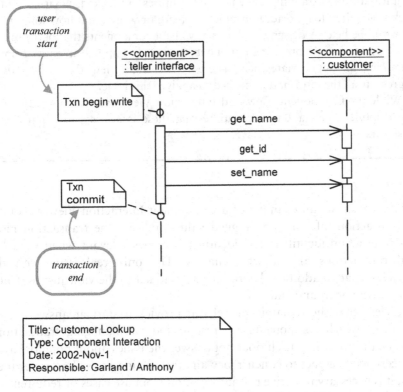

Figure 9.8   Analysis Interaction View of transactions

Interaction View. Here the transaction start and end are simply annotated using comments and attachment lines. This notation is appropriate in Analysis Interaction Views because including transaction servers during analysis creates unwanted implementation entities.

Difficulties in Modeling Transaction Issues

As you can see, we think that the modeling of transactions, whether at the conceptual or at the implementation level, is important to the software design. Unfortunately, figuring out the best way to do this with the UML is difficult. While interaction views can be annotated, as we show in this section, this notation provides only limited help in understanding architectural issues such as concurrent locking and data inconsistencies.

Consider the case of concurrent locking issues. To understand this issue requires an understanding of which data entities are locked, what type of lock is acquired (e.g., read, non-blocking read, or write), and how long the lock will be held. A design that has many client components that perform a blocking read might prevent components that need to update an entity from obtaining an appropriate lock. There is no single view that succinctly represents all the information needed to analyze this issue.

While the Component View and Interaction Views we recommend here are helpful, understanding and addressing these issues is still left to the designers.

Figure 9.9 shows an example of a Component Interaction View annotated with transaction information. Tagged values indicate the transaction mode and a transaction identifier. The identifier becomes relevant when modeling nested transactions and abort scenarios. The only real issue with this approach is that an additional entity must be added to the view just to denote the transaction start and end.

It is clear that the dynamic model can provide a start at answering the question of which components are responsible for managing transactions. However, this model by itself does not answer the issues about potential areas of concern with respect to concurrency and transaction rates. To answer these issues, it is necessary to derive this information from use cases or requirements or by asking stakeholders about the scalability of the system.

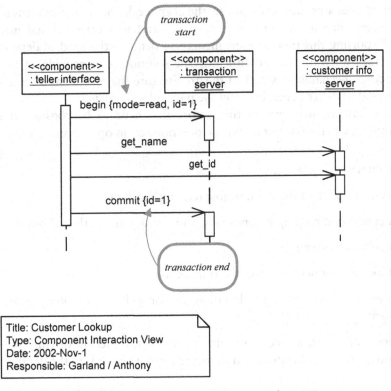

Figure 9.9   Explicit transaction start and commit

9.4.3 Transactions and interface design

A major issue in interface design is whether the transactions are explicit for the client or hidden from the client. For example, if a client is making small individual queries to the database, then each query can have an embedded transaction begin and end. In this way, the client is insulated from knowledge that the transaction exists. However, if the client is about to make several thousand queries, then the performance impact for beginning and ending one transaction for each query may be prohibitive. In this case, the interface should allow the client to control the beginning and end of the transaction. Additionally, the client may need to control transactions for purposes of defining appropriate rollback strategies.

One of the main reasons it is desirable to hide transactions behind an interface is that it is typically difficult to avoid client components from depending on the transaction implementation mechanisms. For example, if the server uses a particular database, the client code that controls transactions will become dependent on that particular database's transactional mechanisms. Exporting this type of implementation detail is the kind of dependence that makes software change difficult. One solution is to provide an abstract transaction mechanism as part of the architecture that clients and servers can use instead of direct dependence on the particular database.

The following are some of the factors that need to be considered when determining whether or not to expose the transaction operations to the client:

- Number of objects retrieved

- Is client updating the data, or just reading the data

- Is concurrent reading by one client and writing by another allowed

- Is performance an issue

- Which component controls the transaction

- How is transaction error handling performed by the interface and the clients

- Does the interface need to utilize an initial transaction to copy the data and a subsequent transaction to merge the data back into the database

9.5 Recommended Reading

Martin Fowler, as part of his Enterprise Application Architecture (formerly known as Information Systems Architecture) Patterns, describes the patterns for concurrency including 'Unit of Work', Optimistic Concurrency, etc. You can find this information on the web. One approach described by Fowler that is especially useful for messaging systems is to use what Fowler refers to as a data transfer object. This is an instance of a class that consists only of attributes and methods to access or modify these data members. These objects are particularly useful for serializing and in sending messages between distributed system components. This type of entity is closely aligned with the data architecture entities we discuss here.

Code generation can often be used as an alternative to reflection. Rettig and Fowler (2001) have a paper with a discussion of reflection versus code generation.

The 'data is just data' quote is the phrase coined by Geoff Buhn in a private conversation.

The use of UML diagrams for documenting database designs can be found in Naiburg and Maksimchuk (2001). In addition, they add the concept of a tablespace as a component. This is not consistent with our definition of a component.

Buschmann (1996) describes Blackboard Pattern. The Repository Pattern is described in Coplien (1995). Buschmann also describes the Reflection Pattern.

Ambler (1999) has written articles describing issues surrounding object to relational mapping issues, including techniques for generation of unique ids. These are available on his web site.

Rational software (2000) has devised a detailed technique for data modeling in UML. A paper describing the details is available on their web site.

10

Process and Deployment Design

This chapter deals with several viewpoints and design topics related to the design and development of large distributed systems. These topics impact several architecture attributes, including reliability, ability to upgrade, fault tolerance, and performance. Enterprise systems, telecommunications systems, and web systems are all examples of the type of systems that require an understanding of the topics in this chapter.

The viewpoints described in this chapter include Physical Data, Process, Process State, and Deployment. Process, Physical Data, and Deployment are variations of the UML deployment diagram. Also included are two examples of solutions to common deployment-related problems, a scalable server and database backup/archive. Views showing process interactions are not shown here, since they are an extension of the Component Interaction Views described in Chapter 7.

Some authors consider many of the viewpoints discussed in this section to be part of the system architecture rather than the software architecture. However, software development teams must often consider the hardware aspects of the design, since they can impact the component design and structure. As an example, there is a direct impact on performance if processing is distributed as opposed to concentrated on a single machine. It is also important to remember that several aspects of the hardware, such as specific hardware configuration information, still remain part of the hardware architecture and will not be included in the viewpoints of interest to the software architect.

10.1 Physical Data Viewpoint

The Physical Data Viewpoint (Table 10.1) illustrates the relationship between servers, components, and data. The physical data organization plays a key role for operational staff understanding and maintaining an enterprise system. For software developers the physical data organization can impact software design and development in several ways. First, it can be critical in determining the performance and availability of an application. In addition, if the data storage is a file or an object database, the application logic may be directly impacted by the need to manage physical data storage locations.

Table 10.1   Physical Data Viewpoint

Physical Data Viewpoint	
Purpose	To describe the layout of the physical database elements. These views are annotated with estimates/measurements of database size, growth rates per factor, and redundancy strategies.
When Applicable	During subsystem and component design and development.
Stakeholders	Architecture Team, Developers, Operations Staff, Hardware Architect, Testers.
Scalability	Can be focused on a chosen subset of the system or can model the overall system.
Relation to Other Views	Nodes and databases may also be shown on the deployment view.

The Logical Data View, described in Chapter 9, shows the relationships among the data entities. These logical views usually stabilize early in the design process and undergo few changes as the system evolves. However, the Physical Data View is something that typically evolves more after system deployment. The physical aspects of how the data is stored and managed tend to be tweaked in order to optimize the storage and performance of data access.

Figure 10.1 shows an example of a Physical Data View. This view shows the set of data stores that are controlled by the main database server node. Each of the data stores is given a stereotype based on the storage mechanism.

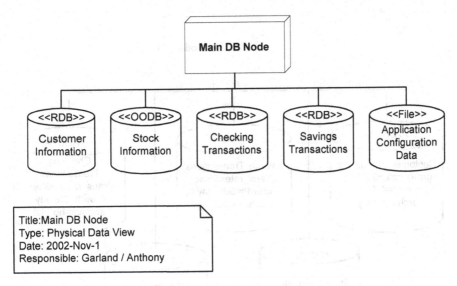

Figure 10.1 Physical Data View

The RDB is for relational databases, OODB for object-oriented databases, and File for regular operating system files. These three stereotypes utilize a 'cylinder' icon to distinguish them clearly from nodes and other components. This particular view is focused on a small set of the data for the entire system. Full-scale versions of this view may be produced for a particular system installation.

10.1.1   Modeling other storage attributes

Besides documenting which databases are managed by a particular server, a frequent need is to understand the basic parameters that will impact the performance of the server. Transaction rates, growth rates, and archive policies have a major impact on the overall performance the server provides. These attributes of the databases can be documented in an auxiliary table or can be provided directly on the view. Figure 10.2 shows a part of the physical database structure annotated with size and growth rates. In addition, several databases are annotated with the archive policy.

The data growth and archive policies provide insight into the storage requirements for the system. The largest and fastest-growing databases and files will require special design attention to ensure that they can be deployed properly. In addition, they may require distribution which requires deciding

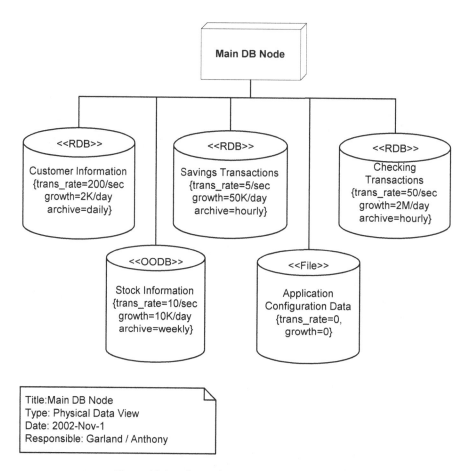

Figure 10.2   Physical Data View with attributes

how to split up large databases into smaller ones and how that impacts on server design. For example, managing a database that grows at a rate of 500 KB per day can be a very different from managing a database that grows at a rate of several terabytes per day.

The transaction rates provide input into the specification of server sizing and scaling. Databases requiring high transaction rates may require specialized server hardware or may need to be distributed across multiple server nodes. Several databases with low transaction rates may be assigned to lower cost hardware or may be combined to use the same database server node.

This same database and attribute information shown in Figure 10.2 is reflected in Table 10.2. If several Physical Data Views must be produced to

Table 10.2 Physical data storage attributes

Database name	Type	Description	Backup strategy	Trans rate	Growth rate	Archive
Customer Information	RDB	Provides basic customer data records.	Replication Server	200/sec	2K/day	Daily
Savings Transactions	RDB	Provides information about savings account transactions.	Journaling log file and periodic backup script	5/sec	50K/day	Hourly
Application Config.	File	Provides application configuration information for various internal applications.	File system backup	N/A	0	Daily
...						

capture a large number of databases, then the table may be preferable to creating these views. In addition, the table can represent additional attributes by adding columns. For example, the table has a backup strategy that is not shown in the view. If all these table attributes were added to the views, they would become too cluttered with detailed database attribute information.

Both the table and the view show the archive strategy for each database. This strategy could involve several levels of archive. The most recent data, a few hours' worth for example, might go to an archive server dedicated for that purpose. From this first level of archive data, another set of data could be archived every few days to a second-level archive server. From there, a final level of archive may involve creation of a tape archive that holds several years of data. In this way, the most recent data would be readily available. Data that is not as recent would require slightly longer to access, and the oldest data may take several minutes or hours to retrieve. A deployment view showing a simple archive strategy, along with a database backup strategy, is shown at the end of this chapter.

10.1.2 Detailed physical storage modeling

Often large systems utilize multiple storage technologies. Some of these technologies, such as files and databases, have physical storage containment hierarchies. These hierarchies may be relevant for several reasons. First, the hierarchy may need to be managed by the applications or database administrators. In addition, in some types of databases this hierarchy may relate to other properties of the database such as locking semantics. For example, in the case of an object database, the database may lock containers when writing. In the case where containment hierarchies are utilized, correct physical organization may directly impact the logical design.

Figure 10.3 shows an example of a Physical Data View of a storage hierarchy for an object database system. In this example, the object database

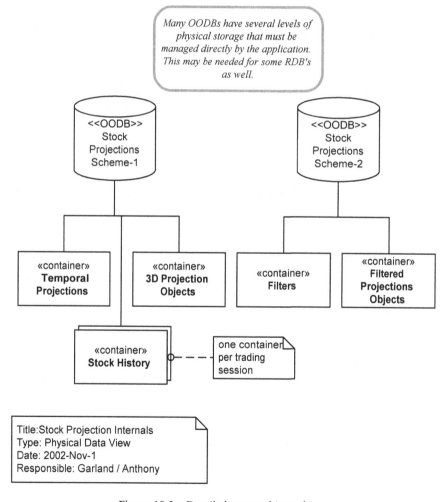

Figure 10.3 Detailed storage hierarchies

physical hierarchy is composed of databases and containers. Containers are important in this environment because they must be allocated by the application to avoid exceeding a fixed number of objects allowed in a container. In the example, a new stock history container is allocated for each trading session.

10.2 Process Viewpoint

Distributed programs are very complex to design. Many difficult process intercommunication issues need to be addressed that do not occur in a system residing in only one operating system process. Examples of these process intercommunication issues include:

- Order of process startup and shutdown

- Process failure and recovery

- Failure and recovery in inter-component communication within the process

- Threading allocation and schemes in a process

Proper design of the process and intercommunication aspects of the software architecture has a direct bearing on the reliability and fault tolerance of the system. This design can also dramatically impact the scalability and performance of the system. To grapple with these issues a view of the process structure and intercommunication between the processes is useful. The Process Viewpoint, summarized in Table 10.3, is useful for analyzing these issues. Process Views are also often useful in reengineering of poorly documented existing systems. Since existing systems are realized as a set of processes, building an initial model of these processes and their interactions provides insight into functionality and its distribution.

Process Views overlap with Component and Deployment Views. If a Deployment View is developed then a Process View is sometimes redundant. However, since Process Views do not contain the detail of physical node mappings, they are often handy if the node mapping does not impact the design task. In systems that have a one-to-one mapping between processes and components, the Component View and the Process View are equivalent.

In the Process Views, we are interested in at least some of the following properties:

Table 10.3 Process Viewpoint

Process Viewpoint	
Purpose	Describe process inter-communication mechanisms independent of physical hardware deployment.
When Applicable	During system design and development. Reengineering of existing systems.
Stakeholders	Architecture Team, Subsystem Developers, Test Team, Software System Engineering Team, Systems Engineering Team, Hardware Architect, Project and Development Managers (to a lesser degree), Operations Staff.
Scalability	Supplement with tables indicating access frequency, response times, data transfer sizes, etc.
Relation to Other Views	This view is an abstraction of a Deployment View that does not include a mapping of processes to nodes. This view is a detailing of the Component View showing the mapping of components to processes.

- Allocation of components to processes and threads
- Performance of process intercommunications
- Quick startup and restart
- Redundancy
- Load balancing
- Minimization of impact on process failure
- Handling of communication failures

In process design, it is important to avoid runtime 'co-dependence'. That is, two processes that require each other to be available for startup often lead to process deadlocks. If the architecture has co-dependent processes they should be combined, or a third process should be created that contains the co-dependent functionality. Cycles on a Process View may signal the potential for this process co-dependence.

Figure 10.4 shows a Process View for the banking system. In this particular system, the Process View is similar to the Component View. The view shows the various system processes and the communication between the processes. The arrow indicates the process from which the communication originates.

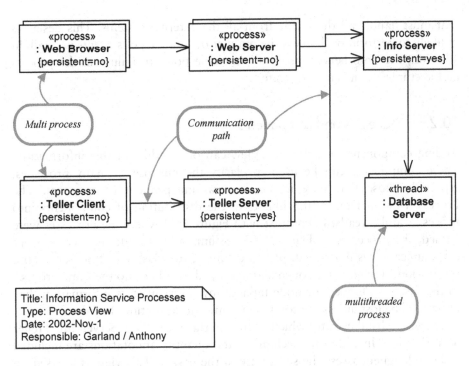

Figure 10.4   Process View

The arrow points toward the receiving process. To be consistent with UML conventions, a line with no arrowheads on either end indicates bi-directional initiation of communication. Alternatively, an arrowhead can be placed on both ends for bi-directional cases.

Each process in Figure 10.4 has a tagged value that indicates if the process is 'transient' or 'persistent'. Server processes tend to be long-running processes that are started and wait for client processes to interact. However, some server processes may be started on demand to serve a client and discarded when the client process interaction is completed. Persistent server processes have the advantage that they can provide faster response since the time to start the process, perform component configuration, and perhaps cache data is completed before the client request. Client processes that are initiated by a user are inherently transient processes. Client processes can also be started by a process management component within the system. These are also generally transient.

In this view, the 'Info Server' and 'Database Server' processes are the most critical processes since all other services ultimately require them to receive customer information. However, the 'Info Server' process is a single process that must handle all the traffic from all the external systems. This design is unlikely to perform well unless the number of simultaneous clients is small. In addition, the 'Info Server' process is a single point of failure in the process architecture since it is not replicated.

10.2.1   Processes and components

Adding components to a Process View can often add valuable information. These components can be used to clarify the purpose of many processes, especially those that may include several independent components. The Process View in Figure 10.5 illustrates the distribution of components into processes and threads. In contrast with Figure 10.4 where the processes were named, the processes in Figure 10.5 are unnamed. In addition, component communication is illustrated. In this example, the Customer Info Server and the Session Manager components are grouped together into the same process. In the case of a process or node failure, any transient state information they utilize will be lost unless the components are checkpointing state data.

The view also illustrates which of the interfaces the 'Web Server' and 'Teller Server' utilize. In addition, mechanism and quantity annotations are included to help designers assess the scalability of the design. This view is focused on the client information use case, but a full system view can also be created using these techniques.

10.2.2   Process and component management

Today, a wide variety of applications are developed using component frameworks. These frameworks often provide standard capabilities for component management. Facilities often include component startup and monitoring, interface discovery, checkpointing, application logging, and load balancing. Since these common facilities are frequently the basis for development, it is important for developers to understand these facilities. A Process View is often helpful in describing the runtime aspects of the common component facilities.

Figure 10.6 shows an example of a simple component management framework. In this framework there are two main elements provided by the framework: the process management component and the component management component. There is one process management component per process and it performs the following functions:

- Configures the process level resources

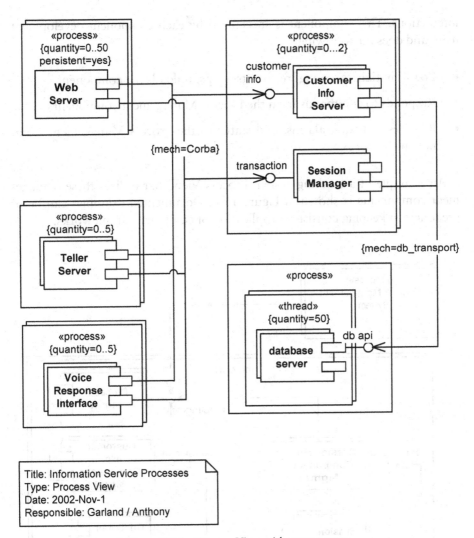

Figure 10.5 Process View with components

- Loads, starts, configures, initializes, reports statistics for each component

- Provides an interface to the management system for status, alarms, performance statistics, configuration changes, and commands (for example, shutdown)

In addition, there is one management component for each application component. This management component handles the component-specific interactions. This component is specialized by each component development team and does the following:

- Loads, initializes, configures, starts, stops, unloads the component

- Responds to commands from the Process Management component

- Provides statistics, alarms, and status to the Process Management Component

An example of a banking system Process View that utilizes these management components is shown in Figure 10.6. Documented examples can be of great help in keeping consistent application of component frameworks.

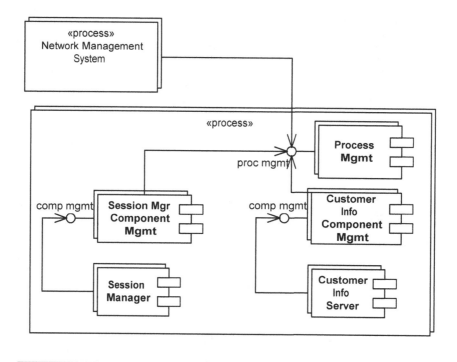

Figure 10.6   Process and component management framework

10.2.3 Process State Viewpoint

While the Process Viewpoint is focused on describing a set of process and component instances, it does not model the dynamics of these processes. Often, to understand the overall interactions of the processes, a view of the process dynamics is required. The Process State View can be used provide this understanding. The viewpoint associated with this view is shown in Table 10.4.

Table 10.4   Process State Viewpoint

Process State Viewpoint	
Purpose	Describe the state transitions and interactions of one or more processes.
When Applicable	During system design and development.
Stakeholders	Architecture Team, Subsystem Developers, Test Team.
Scalability	These views can be provided for a single process or a group of processes.
Relation to other Views	The Process View illustrates the processes of interest for modeling in the Process State View. The Component State View often provides details for a process that executes multiple components.

In many ways, the process state is the sum of the states of the components it executes. Thus in some cases the Component State View is really the view of interest. However, the Process State View may be useful in modeling standard process dynamics that are independent of the loaded components. These dynamics may, for example, be part of a component management infrastructure that loads and controls components in the process.

For process dynamics, it is often useful to think in terms of a standard set of states such as initializing, operating, and shutting down. Figure 10.7 provides an example of just such a canonical state view for a process. In the operating state, the components provided by the process are available for other processes to utilize. When the process is in the other states, the components are not accessible and hence other components attempting to access the process will either block or receive an error. A standard Process State View may become part of the architecture as part of a component management infrastructure or monitoring capability. Note that this view may not apply for processes provided as part of third-party products.

Although all processes may have a canonical set of states, they often

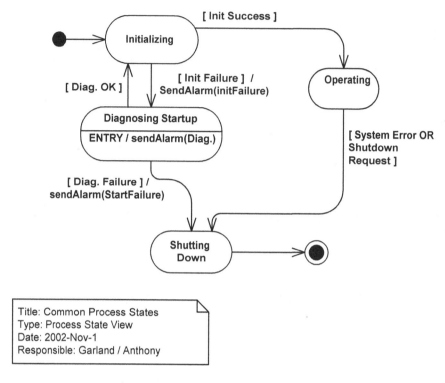

Figure 10.7   Canonical Process State View

perform very different functions while processing in a particular one of these standard states. To understand the specific dynamics of the process, each of the canonical process states needs to be detailed for the different processes in the system. This information is usually captured sufficiently in the Component State View, but the Process View can be used to supplement the component state information. As with Component State Views, these Process Views should only be defined for process states that contain significant state-based behavior.

Figure 10.8 illustrates a state view of the initialization substate for the Customer Information Server process from Figure 10.5. As the view shows, the server will internally start two components after establishing database connections. In addition, the Customer Information Server will fail if the database server process is unavailable. A better behavior might be to send an alarm indicating the failure and to retry until the database becomes available. This would remove the need for restart of this process.

It is important to point out that this type of lower-level state modeling may

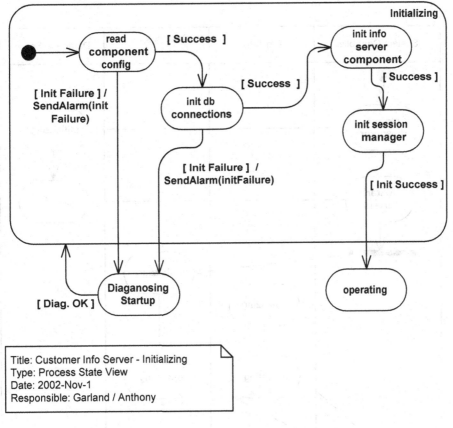

Figure 10.8   State View – process initialization

be better performed by one of the subsystem teams, with close review and participation by the software architecture team. This level of focus by the software architect and the architecture team is a similar issue with component state modeling. The architecture team may want to leave the component state design to be defined by the subsystem team that is implementing that component.

Notice that this substate view is consistent with the state view in Figure 10.7. This means that the events, guards, and actions that enter and exit the initializing substate must be consistent with the ones in the overall state view.

The cross-process and cross-component dynamics illustrated in the Figure 10.8 dependencies are critical to fault tolerance and performance in distributed systems. As the figure shows, a failure to connect to the database results

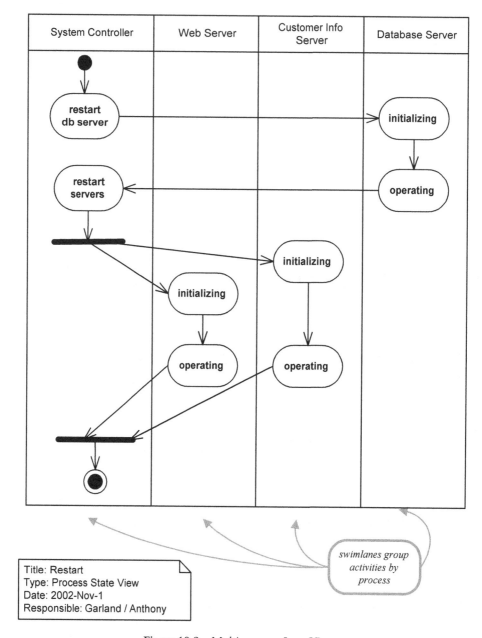

Figure 10.9   Multi-process State View

in a process shutdown and hence a system startup failure. The performance and fault tolerance issues uncovered in dynamic modeling may result in changes to the Process Views and ultimately the Component Views.

While a Process State View focused on a single process is important for understanding the dynamics and potential interactions, it does not show the overall system. For the overall focus, we recommend the utilization of an activity diagram version of the Process State View to show the interactions of several processes.

Figure 10.9 is an example of a multi-process state view for a system restart scenario. Each swimlane in the view corresponds to a process. This view illustrates the actions of various server processes and the parallelism of the restart. The use of this view should be limited to scenarios that explicitly involve process behavior that is independent of the component behavior, such as administrative scenarios for starting or monitoring a process. The Component State View provides a better view of component-specific states.

10.3 Deployment Viewpoint

The Deployment View (described by the viewpoint in Table 10.5) builds on the Process and Component Views by adding a hardware element, called a

Table 10.5   Deployment Viewpoint

Deployment Viewpoint	
Purpose	Describe mapping of processes /components to hardware, may need several of these. May have several views for large systems. Describe runtime component connectivity and communication. Can be applied to performance analysis and later the process interaction design.
When Applicable	After preliminary components are identified, this view can be created as input to making hardware purchase decisions. Updated during construction and transition as components are completed. When reengineering or documenting an existing distributed system.
Stakeholders	Architecture Team, Hardware and Network Architects, Subsystem Developers, Test Team, Software System Engineering Team, Systems Engineering Team, Project and Development Managers (to a lesser degree), Operations Staff.
Scalability	Drawn with scenario or component focus. Also, a node focus can be used for modeling scalable servers.
Relation to Other Views	Builds on process, component, and physical database views by adding in mapping to nodes.

node, which can execute components in processes and threads. In addition, nodes typically have the ability to maintain persistent state via files and databases. This view describes the mapping of processes and components to physical nodes.

Sometimes the Deployment View is not necessary. This occurs when there is an obvious mapping from the Process View to the deployed system. In addition, in some cases a tabular mapping of processes to nodes is sufficient to document the deployment details. If the Deployment View is determined to be necessary, the Process and Component Views should be created first since they provide significant input for the Deployment View.

Figure 10.10 is an example of a Deployment View for the banking system. The view includes node, process, and database information. The focus of this Deployment View is to communicate the mapping of processes to nodes and the utilization of databases with respect to these processes and nodes. The nodes are annotated with the operating system and other special information such as the number of processors and the operating system. As with the Process View, connecting lines between processes show inter-process communication paths.

Figure 10.10 is focused on a specific scenario. However, it is common to have one or more views to capture a specific system configuration. Highly configurable systems may have many different variations that need to be depicted, each requiring a separate view.

Figure 10.11 illustrates a variation of the Deployment View that includes both processes and components. While more complex, this variation of the view provides a clear mapping of components to nodes and processes. In this variation of the Deployment View, we illustrate the component-to-component communication paths. The process-to-process communication paths can then be easily seen, as each component must be mapped to a process.

10.3.1 Scalable node design

One problem that frequently arises when building large-scale systems is the need to create a set of nodes that serve as a point of scalability for the architecture. That is, a particular installation can install as many or as few of these nodes as needed to handle more or less load. In addition, a series of these can be deployed to provide load balancing and fault tolerance. The Deployment View can be used to model the scalable server designs. In this variation of the Deployment View, the internal design of a scalable node is the focus rather than the design of the overall system. This view is important

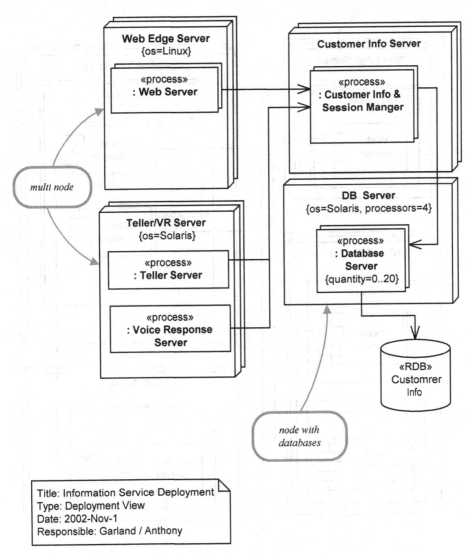

Figure 10.10 Deployment View with annotated nodes

because data and processes must be designed in a way that will allow the system to meet the load and fault requirements.

Figure 10.12 shows an example of a view illustrating a scalable node design. This Deployment View provides additional detail about the monitoring processes and logs files for the scalable node. A shared memory log file system provides a link between a node monitoring process and the customer server. This shared memory is shown as a database that is located on the node

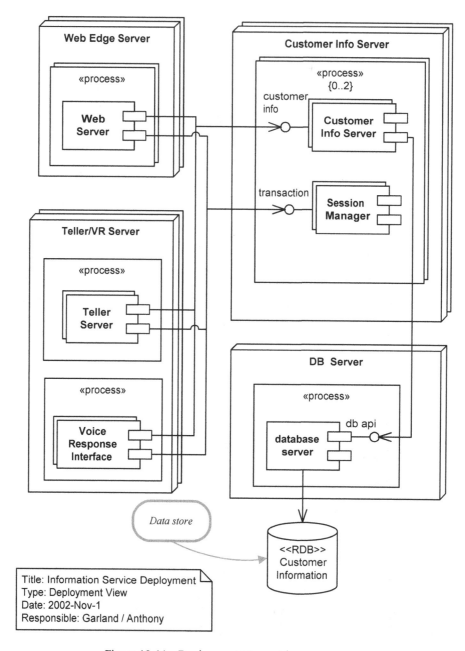

Figure 10.11   Deployment View with components

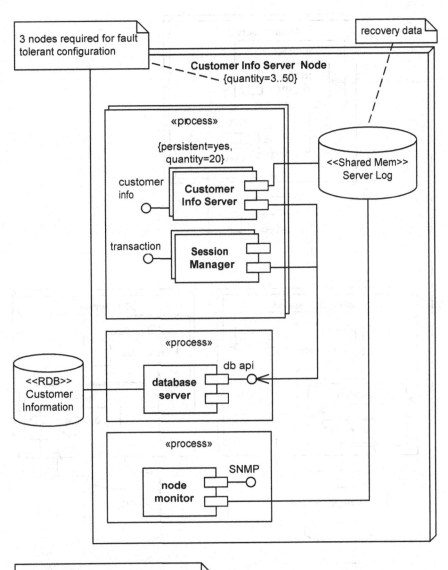

Figure 10.12   Scalable server design

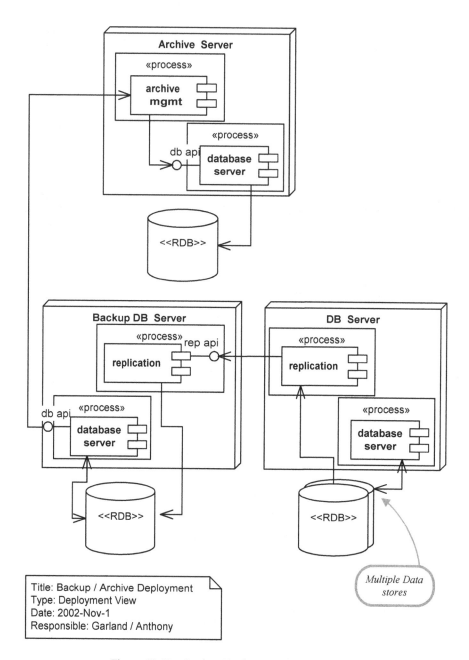

Figure 10.13 Backup/Archive Deployment View

itself. Databases stored on a disk are shown external to the node. Note that the interfaces not attached to internal components are interfaces used by external components not shown in the view.

10.3.2 Backup/archive design

Another deployment view that applies to many large-scale systems is the representation of the backup and archive strategies. In many large-scale systems, these strategies are captured in separate Deployment Views. The backup strategy can be one or more of several approaches. Among these are to make use of vendor capabilities for journaling databases changes to a log file or to make use of a special-purpose replication process. Other approaches include custom scripts to periodically move the data to a backup server. Similarly, vendor utilities can provide archive functionality or the development team may design a custom script or application to perform the archive functionality. As described earlier, several levels of archive nodes and processes may be necessary to store all the necessary archive data.

The Deployment View in Figure 10.13 shows a set of backup and archive nodes and the key processes involved. Notice in this view that the database server processes are shown for each node. Another option is to show each process directly reading from and writing to the database, with the underlying assumption that the vendor's database server process is actually handling the data reads and writes. As with other views shown earlier, this view could be annotated with mechanisms or quantities to better understand the performance characteristics.

10.4 Recommended Reading

On their web site, Bredemeyer discusses how software architecture is not the physical system architecture such as nodes and processors while acknowledging the impact of these on the software architecture. We agree with this, and believe these views need to be included in the software architecture description even though the elements modeled aren't technically part of the software architecture, they are part of the overall environment for the software.

A canonical set of states can also be found in many standards, such as IEEE X.731. This specification specifies operational, usage, administrative, and management states. For example, the administrative states include 'unlocked', 'locked', and 'shutting down'.

Examples of process and deployment diagrams can be found in the UML User Guide (Booch *et al.*, 1999) which uses a cylinder icon for databases. Fowler and Scott (1997) and Hofmeister (1999) also have examples of deployment diagrams.

11

Architecture Techniques

This chapter will provide an overview of a number of techniques that have proven useful for software architects. These techniques include software analysis and design strategies, partitioning strategies, management of dependencies, use of Architectural Patterns, and strategies for system component integration. The proper application of these techniques can reduce the level of complexity of the software architecture, reduce the time spent developing the architecture, and reduce the workload for the software architect and architecture team.

Since this chapter provides information on a wide variety of techniques, the discussions will intentionally provide only a brief overview of each concept. For additional information on these topics, refer to the recommended reading section.

11.1 Architecture Development Techniques

The following sections describe analysis and design techniques that can be helpful in the development of software architectures. The selection of techniques that are best for architecture development will largely depend on the project context. Not all problems are created equal, and as a result, different problems require different techniques. In a large-scale system, several sub-domains with different properties will commonly exist. In these cases, it is desirable to take different approaches to these domains. As a result, these different domains can provide inherent division points in the architecture.

Examples of different domain types include algorithmic domains, data intensive domains, and transactional domains. Thus, the best practice for one project might be nearly useless on another project. Unfortunately, no controlled and quantitative studies of development projects provide guidance on how best to apply these techniques. Our recommendation is to hire an experienced software architect with knowledge of these techniques and experience applying them on several projects.

11.1.1 Commonality and variability analysis

The essence of commonality and variability analysis is to take several things, identify what they have common and what is different, and take advantages of those parts that are common and that vary. This approach was called scope, commonality, and variability (SCV) analysis by Coplien *et al.*

This approach is usually applied to entities within the analysis or design of the system. The primary steps in this approach begin with the identification of the set of entities to be analyzed. For the software architect, this may involve analysis of the functionality in several subsystems, or components. It may also involve analyzing a large number of classes in an Analysis Overall View. This first step establishes the scope. Then the commonalities and variabilities are identified and documented. Following this step, the variabilities are bounded by applying limits to the amount each is expected to change.

The architect then leverages the commonalities in the development of the software architecture. This means that the common aspects of the system will be designed and developed only once. This approach not only prevents duplication of effort, but also provides a standard solution for each common aspect of the system. Finally, the architect identifies ways that the variabilities can be handled by the architecture with minimum impact.

Commonality and variability analysis is useful for many aspects of analysis and design. The commonalities can provide the basis for creating a standard interface, approach, or abstract type. Applying this technique can also assist in the discovery of key abstractions in the architecture. One common use of this technique is to identify reusable aspects of the set of constructs that can be factored out as frameworks or software infrastructure. By analyzing the common aspects of several subsystems, for example, potential frameworks or software infrastructure can be identified for development or purchase.

In addition, the variability analysis part of this technique is useful in understanding the aspects of the system that are likely to change versus those that are not likely to change. The variations should be used to identify possible extension points in the architecture. In addition, potential design modification can be explored to facilitate the extensions and modifications when they occur.

There is no way this book can address this topic in depth. However, in order to develop high quality and modifiable software architectures, the architect should read and learn about this technique.

11.1.2 Design for change

Typically, one of the most critical and difficult aspects of developing a software architecture is understanding what is likely to change and what is not likely to change. The basic idea of change cases is to enumerate the types of changes the architecture will likely need to accommodate. These changes are then used to evaluate whether the current or proposed architecture will easily handle the change. Ask questions like:

- Is the change localized or spread among many disparate subsystems?

- What interfaces or messages will need to be modified to accommodate the change?

- Will the database design need to be updated?

- What is the scope of the change? For example, what is the estimate of how many classes or source code files will need to be modified?

One way to represent change cases is a simple table of one-line descriptions and a relative likelihood. This provides a convenient way to think about the types of changes that will impact the architecture and their relative importance. Table 11.1 gives a simple example of using the technique to elaborate expected variations. Note that this is just a form of commonality and variability analysis applied to requirements. This approach can also be applied

Table 11.1 Simple change case table

Change	Description	Likelihood
Support new printer types	System will need to support new printer types for bill printing as technology evolves.	100%
Web-based interface for customer creation	Support web-based interface for customer creation in addition to the integrated interface.	50%

to use cases by documenting the potential changes that apply to a particular use case.

One of the dangers of change cases is that they require guessing about future events. An expected feature or dimension of change may not be required while adding flexibility to the architecture up front is almost guaranteed to cost time and money. This is a classic engineering risk trade-off. The cost of implementing flexibility up front must be considered against the cost of making the change later by refactoring the design. Items with high probability, high refactoring cost, and low initial cost should be supported up front. Items with low probability and low refactoring costs do not need to be supported by the architecture. Of course, all of the costs and probabilities are imperfect estimates so the decisions are necessarily imperfect.

As with many techniques, there are many levels of possible rigor. The change case process can be completely driven by the experience and knowledge of the architect or can be explicitly documented. The explicit approach takes more time, but has the advantages of typically being more complete and allows the participation of multiple individuals. However, the benefits of experience are critical in making good decisions.

11.1.3 Generative programming techniques

Generative programming techniques can be used to automate the development of software products. There are many different types of generative programming techniques, including advanced application of C++ templates, aspect-oriented programming, custom code generation tools, and domain-specific languages. In addition, code generation from Computer Aided Software Engineering (CASE) tools can also be considered a form of generative programming techniques. This not only applies to the UML, but also can apply to languages like Specification and Design Language (SDL).

Generative techniques provide the ability to customize libraries and components to better meet the needs of the project and to automate the production of some parts of the software. These techniques are particularly relevant if a family of products is to be built from a single architecture.

The architecture team must evaluate whether the use of generative programming techniques will be of value. Most likely, if the project is large enough and important enough to need an architecture team, generative programming techniques will bring value to one or more aspects of the system.

In addition, the architecture team must determine how to represent generative aspects of the system within the architecture. This may be difficult because of the unique nature of generative components. However, stereotypes or other UML extension techniques may be used to facilitate the modeling of generative aspects of the architecture.

The use of some types of components, such as CORBA, promotes the use of generative programming techniques. The tools associated with the CORBA implementations generate elements of the solution that are extended per the normal CORBA practices. For example, the interface is defined using an interface definition language (IDL) specific to CORBA and the IDL compiler generates code in any of a variety of programming languages.

This technique can provide a large boost to developer productivity, but the software architect must make sure the technique is only used in areas where it is applicable. These techniques will rarely apply to an entire large-scale system. In addition, several different generative programming techniques may be applied to different aspects of a large system.

11.1.4 Building a skeleton system

Another proven tactic is to begin the first increment of development by building a skeleton system. This approach builds a single thread of execution across the entire system. This execution thread is the first confirmation of many aspects of the software architecture. Typically, only a few aspects of the architecture need to be in place when the skeleton is developed. Often the skeleton serves as the first iteration of the system to be built. Using this approach has several major advantages:

- Forces integration, which is usually a major development risk, earlier in the process

- Fits well with iterative development approach

- Forces the early development of infrastructure mechanisms

- Can bootstrap end-to-end test automation

Following the completion of the first thread through the system, additional threads can be added and the system functionality can be added incrementally. It is often necessary to use tactical development approaches such as scripts as stand-ins for parts of the system that are needed for the skeleton system, but are not available. This allows the skeleton system to bootstrap prior to having all the components available.

The skeleton system is not intended to be a throwaway prototype, rather it is expected to build some portion of the final system with a focus on breadth. It is important to understand that some aspects of the initial skeleton may need to be refactored as the system evolves. Sufficient time needs to be allocated for this refactoring to ensure that the quality of the design is maintained. Building test automation for the skeleton is an important difference between a skeleton system and prototyping. The initial test automation is a prelude to the development of a continuous integration support that is discussed later in this chapter.

11.1.5   Prototyping

When certain aspects of a large system are unknown, prototyping can often be a powerful technique for developing a concrete understanding of these aspects of the architecture. This approach is discussed as part of the risk reduction strategy and incremental development approach described in Chapter 3.

Several types of prototypes can be built which benefit the understanding of which architectural trade-offs will be the most effective. For example, prototyping of user interfaces is often beneficial to understanding user tasks and building more useable software. In addition, prototypes can be used as part of the analysis and selection of specific COTS or open source products. As a result, this technique is especially powerful if the focus of much of the development is the integration of existing components. The prototyping strategy is also useful to analyze the effectiveness of specific interface mechanisms and designs. Prototypes can be used to identify potential performance bottlenecks in the interfaces themselves and alleviate performance problems early in the development cycle.

One problem with prototyping is the desire to use the prototype as part of, or as the basis for, the final system. While this might seem like a good idea when schedules are compressed, it is nearly always a bad idea. Typically, prototypes have been constructed using many shortcuts that will become liabilities to the architecture later in the development process. Since these liabilities are often the outcome, it is better simply to develop the components in an incremental fashion, recognizing that the first versions may be incomplete in some significant fashion.

11.1.6   Interface development – Design by Contract

One very useful technique for codifying interfaces is called 'Design by Contract'. Bertrand Meyer developed the technique, which is an approach for defining interface specifications for software components. The Eiffel programming language provides first-class support for design by contract. The benefits include:

- A better understanding of object-oriented concepts by the system designers

- A systematic approach to improve quality

- A framework for identifying errors in the software, for testing, and for quality assurance

- An approach for documenting software components, especially the interfaces

- A technique for exception handling

The basic approach is to provide for detailed specification of an interface using preconditions, postconditions, and invariants. These are all types of assertions, or logical conditions associated with a software element. These assertions are generally applied to the classes and methods in the analysis or design views. Interfaces, in this approach, can be defined as specific class methods. A precondition defines an input condition that must be true prior to entry into a method. A postcondition defines an output condition that will be true after the method completes. A class invariant, usually just referred to as an invariant, is a condition that applies to all instances of a class.

Design by contract is based on the use of abstract data types and the concept of business-like contracts. The use of abstract data types makes the interface specification precise and verifiable. The contract concept implies the contract is clear and free of ambiguities. Even if the details of the interface are not all specified using this technique, it is a good way to think about the details of an interface. Message-based protocols can also be developed using design by contract.

One way to extend the design by contract approach is to make use of the fact that the UML contains a specification for the Object Constraint Language (OCL). This language provides a way of specifying the rules of an interface. OCL was added to the UML as a formal language for specifying constraints in a UML model. These constraints include preconditions, postconditions, and guards. One use for the OCL is to allow for constraints between entities in a UML model to be specified. Another use for OCL is to provide a specification for pre- and postconditions of an operation. This is especially useful for definition of the methods in an interface class.

11.1.7 Architectural description languages

One area of interest in the research community is that of architectural description languages (ADL). ADLs are formal languages that can be used to represent and reason about software architectures. These languages also show promise for purposes of analyzing and comparing software architectures. One area of focus is the use of ADLs for specification of component interfaces. While these approaches show promise, they are primarily a research area at this time.

11.1.8 Architecture evaluation

One fundamental task of the software architect and the architecture team is the evaluation of the software architecture. Team members should be constantly analyzing the architecture to see if it meets the goals of the stakeholders. This means assessing if the architecture possesses the desired qualities such as maintainability and testability. Many other attributes of interest for software architects are described in Chapter 1.

Most architecture evaluation is ad hoc, occurring during the normal process of developing a project. For example, reviewing various project work products, including designs and implementations. While reading code, the architect might be surprised to see an unanticipated dependency between subsystems. The architect must evaluate if the dependency violates the principles and structure of the envisioned architecture, reducing the maintainability of the system.

Occasionally, it is useful to have a formal review of the architecture. Usually the review will be targeted at assessing some particular attribute of the architecture. A structured review might include the assessment of a series of use cases if the goal is to assess an operational or performance aspect of the software. However, if the goal is to assess changeability then change cases or other requirements changes may be the focus of the evaluation.

11.2 Software Partitioning Strategies – Separation of Concerns

A fundamental technique for software design can be referred to as 'divide and conquer'. The goal of divide and conquer is to take a large system and break it up into more manageable subsystems or to take a set of subsystems and identify the software components associated with them.

When partitioning a system the elements should be grouped to maximize the cohesive aspects and to minimize the coupling of elements. This is especially critical when partitioning the system into subsystems that will be developed by separate development teams.

The following sections describe various strategies for partitioning a system. These strategies are commonly employed, and might even be considered patterns, but have not been described as such. These are pointed out as approaches that should be considered when evaluating division points for software architecture.

Not all strategies can be used on the same system, but more than one of them will most likely be applicable. Some strategies may also be used as a means to validate aspects of a system decomposition that were identified using another strategy. For example, if an initial partitioning of the system is done by a system engineering organization utilizing functional decomposition, a careful coupling and cohesion analysis can be used to validate the effectiveness of the initial partitioning.

11.2.1 Functional decomposition

Functional decomposition is the process of analyzing the functions performed by a system, using these functions as a means to partition the system, then decomposing each function into lower-level functions. This technique is usually considered the antithesis of object-oriented approaches. However, functional decomposition can still be useful as an initial partitioning of a large system into smaller subsystems.

Some object-oriented practitioners will claim that functional decomposition will lead to an inefficient program structure. However, this is not necessarily the case. Widely disparate functions should be placed in separate system partitions. However, commonality and variability analysis and other techniques may also uncover some shared entities. For example, configuration data might be shared by several different functions. In addition, other techniques may be used to validate the effectiveness of the functional decomposition.

As an example, a system that provides a spell checking capability along with a text editing capability can easily be split initially. The needs of these two functions may share a common model in the document, but are otherwise largely independent functions. This approach is actually more of an intuitive analysis of coupling and cohesion that many experienced system engineers and software architects have been employing for years. There is no reason not to apply this experience and intuition, but care needs to be taken to make sure validation is done on the resulting partitioning.

The biggest danger of functional decomposition is the tendency to use it for several levels of the system decomposition. The thinking is that if the technique is effective for the initial partitioning, it is effective for all levels of partitioning. The reason this approach only works for a potential top-level partitioning is that the coupling of the data and functional behavior is more critical in subsystem-level interfaces. Functional analysis approaches only identify the functions at each level, not the data upon which those functions depend. This encapsulation of data and behavior is one of the cornerstones of the object-oriented design approaches. In addition, interface mechanisms themselves are often best identified in terms of encapsulated objects and behavior. Functional decomposition only has applicability at the highest level because the details of the interfaces are not as critical at this level.

11.2.2   Isolate configuration data

Some of the components may need to share a common set of configuration information. The configuration element serves as a dividing line for the system. The configuration data is a shared set of information that provides a form of integration for the components that depend on the data. For example, a system might have several components that need to understand the structure of nodes in a network. The model of the network structure can be a separate component shared by all the components. This is similar to the Repository Pattern.

Examples of this type of system include a common set of the security symbol information listed on an exchange for various programs that monitor stock trading, or a database of telephone numbers and line features for telephone switching/billing programs.

11.2.3   Isolate hardware-specific components

Isolating hardware-specific parts of a system is a partitioning strategy that has been used by most modern operating systems and many other types of software systems. The idea is to create a software driver or a hardware abstraction that serves as the interface to the hardware. If a system contains a major hardware component, a matching software driver component is a natural partitioning of that part of the system. Similarly, when a software system requires an interface to hardware entities, a separate software component that provides an interface to that hardware insulates the software from the low-level hardware interfaces. This isolation from the hardware interface increases the flexibility of the software to adapt to different hardware interfaces. The modifications to the software are isolated to changes in the interface module.

11.2.4   Isolate time-critical components

Time-critical components are those that have tighter performance constraints than the other parts of the system. For example, the parts of a system that process a real-time data stream are more time-critical than the parts of the system that interact with a human end-user. Time-critical components often have a different development lifecycle and engineering concerns than components that are less time-critical. In order to facilitate the application of techniques that the designers of these components may require, these components need to be separated from the rest of the system as much as possible. Of course, this separation will include the specification of clearly defined interfaces. In this way, several different approaches can be utilized. These could include prototyping, dedicated hardware-specific solutions, and enhanced data storage mechanisms.

11.2.5   Separate domain implementation model from human interface

This is a component design principle targeted at keeping the details of the 'human interaction' separated from the domain implementation model. Part of the reason for this partitioning strategy is that the human interaction might take on multiple forms, such as a web browser interface and a conventional graphical interface. Without this separation, the domain component gets written repeatedly, reducing reuse and increasing cost. This technique is the basis of the Model–View–Controller Pattern.

11.2.6   Separate domain implementation model from implementation technology

The basic concept here is that it is desired to keep the domain model separated from lower-level implementation technology. This strategy is similar to separation of the domain model from the human interface, except that this applies to interfaces to lower-level implementation constructs. Again, this is easier said than done. If a database is used as the primary storage of the domain model, for example, it is usually difficult to keep the database technology separated from the domain model interfaces. Implementation details of the database product may end up exposed to application developers interacting with the domain model. One approach is to represent the domain interfaces with a set of 'handles' to hide the implementation details from the clients.

This may not be possible if the clients need to control implementation semantics related to the domain model. In the database example, this may include transaction management or opening and closing databases.

11.2.7   Separate main function from monitoring

In many large systems, components may require some introspection or monitoring capabilities. The idea of this technique is that the main function of a component should be separated from the component that allows for monitoring of that function. That is, the component should generate data that provides another component with the ability to provide the monitoring function. For example, a web server provides logging information that can be utilized for many purposes. The log analyzer is a completely different function performed by a software component unrelated to the web server itself. The web server provides the log in a specified data format, and the log analysis software provides the desired information about usage.

11.2.8   Separate fault recovery processing

Fault tolerant software systems may include complex logic for handling faults. This logic may include things like monitoring and restarting of processes that are operating correctly. Often this might involve multiple recovery levels, some of which ultimately involve decisions by the human operator.

The fault recovery logic should be separated from the core component logic wherever possible. This keeps the complex recovery strategies from littering the component functional code. However, basic identification and logging of faults and perhaps a first level of fault recovery will necessarily need to be done by individual components. In addition, the component may need to write its state data to a location where it can be used for recovery or restart.

The next level of fault recovery would be for a component management entity to determine a component has failed and initiate shutdown and restart of that component. Additional levels include process and node-level fault recovery. The localization of fault recovery into separate layers as described here is often referred to as making use of fault zones. These zones form an ever-widening set of constructs for detecting and handling faults in the system, thus controlling the propagation of faults.

11.2.9   Adaptation of external interfaces

When a software system has external interfaces that are likely to change, one effective technique is to provide a set of components that adapt the external interface to a common internal representation. For example, an interface based on an evolving telecommunications standard could benefit from this approach so that the internal software components are insulated from changes in the standard. In addition, processing of the interface can be handled by the adaptation components and the key information directed to the appropriate internal components.

This approach can also be used to reduce repeated parsing of the same message. As an example, many telecommunications protocols encode messages in Abstract Syntax Notation (ASN.1) and repeated processing of the complete message by several components in order to extract specific information can be inefficient. A single adaptation component can extract the necessary information from the message and send the appropriate subset of the information to each of the components interested in that subset message data.

Performance and availability considerations, such as load balancing and fail over, can also be allocated to these adaptation components. For example, an adaptation component could be the first contact for an external interface, but would quickly dispatch the handling of the message to a set of components to balance the load and facilitate scalability. If a failure of one of the components occurred, the adaptation component would redirect subsequent messages to another component.

These adaptation components must be highly available and may be paired with another component that can quickly take over. Another approach is to make the adaptation component stateless and quickly restart another if the primary component fails.

11.3   Software Changeability and Dependency Management

Separating software into several smaller elements is a key technique for building large-scale software systems. Ideally, each new element can add a small and clear bit of functionality that fits seamlessly into the larger system.

Usually, no one part of the system creates the functionality directly. Rather, each part contributes an aspect of the functionality and depends on other parts to provide other aspects. However, each new element complicates the system structure, making it harder to document and test. Making this problem harder is the fact that software is rarely static. There is an expectation that the software will evolve over time to support changes in the business rules or other external drivers. Some of these drivers might be technological, including the continuing evolution of computing technology itself. Given that the majority of the lifecycle cost of software is typically after the initial deployment, planning for change is essential.

The previous sections describe a series of different techniques for creating elements based on separating the concerns of software. However, every additional separation will introduce dependencies among the various pieces. There is a constant tension between additional complexity represented by adding a new system element and having a single more complex piece perform the desired function.

Ideally, most change can be localized to a single subsystem. Since subsystems are a unit of delivery, responsibility, and test, localized changes can be done with higher confidence and lower cost. Unfortunately, it is easy to separate the parts in such as way that all elements end up being co-dependent. That is, every part depends on everything else such that every change requires changes to many different parts. It is also easy to replicate functions or policies such that a change to one of these requires changes to many subsystems.

The following sections describe some principles and techniques for managing software dependencies and hence enhancing changeability of the software. This list is not necessarily complete; additional principles and techniques can be found in the references listed in the recommended reading.

11.3.1   The stable dependencies principle (SDP)

Robert Martin describes the stable dependencies principle as 'Depend in the direction of stability'. In essence, the desire is to isolate the software that changes frequently. It is undesirable for otherwise stable software to depend on frequently changing subsystems. The reason is that unchanged subsystems may require to be retested and redeployed if a subsystem upon which they depend has changed. Even with extensive automated internal testing, the retesting and redeployment costs can be high since external customers may be involved.

While we agree with Martin's statement of the principle, we use a different definition of stability. In particular, Martin describes creating stability by creating abstract interfaces. Martin calls this the 'Stable Abstractions Principle'. While this approach solves a certain class of problems, it ignores other subsystem types that provide strictly concrete interface classes and are highly stable.

An example of an infrastructure subsystem for a large project would be a sub-system that provides data-time functionality. The classes in such a subsystem are not abstract. In fact, they are considered 'concrete' classes, yet they are typically extremely stable. The reason for the stability of the date-time subsystem is that for a given project the requirements for date-time do not change frequently. Further, it is desirable that these classes be utilized uniformly throughout the program. Use of this subsystem is desired because application code is simplified. In addition, should the need arise to change the date-time representation, such as during year 2000 rollover, only a single subsystem needs to be modified. While there is still the issue of retesting and deployment it is still far easier to modify a single subsystem and retest than modify many subsystems and retest.

Subsystems that provide shared system data models are also stable. These subsystems cannot always be effectively abstracted and will become difficult to modify, as described in Chapter 9.

11.3.2 Acyclic Dependencies Principle

Another of Martin's principles, the Acyclic Dependencies Principle, states that 'the dependency structure for released components must be a directed acyclic graph'. This means that the components should depend on one another in one direction only, with no loops in the dependency graph. That is, Component A can depend on Component B, which can depend on Component C. However, Component C cannot depend on Component A or Component B, as that would form a loop, or cycle, in the dependency relationships.

This principle can also be applied to subsystems. Since the unit of release is the subsystem, a cyclic dependency in a set of subsystems creates a coupling between all the subsystems in the cycle. The modification of one of the subsystems results in possible impact to all of the subsystems in the cycle.

There are many ways to modify the organization of elements so that this principle is maintained. Among these are moving subsystem entities to another subsystem to break the cycle or moving the entities that are the target of the dependency to a separate subsystem. As a result, following this principle tends to result in smaller subsystems that provide fewer classes and functions. This is primarily because creating smaller subsystems reduces the difficulties of the management of subsystem dependencies.

11.3.3   Interface Separation Principle

The Interface Separation Principle involves the separation of interfaces so that clients of a component do not have functionality in an interface that they don't use. This approach produces a set of minimal interfaces and reduces unnecessary coupling between components. Lack of application of this principle causes unnecessary dependencies at build time. In addition, development teams that are clients of a particular interface are required to review and inspect aspects of the interface definition that they do not use.

11.4   Using Architectural Patterns

Patterns have now become an essential tool in developing large-scale systems. Patterns document a solution to a recurring problem, providing a problem context and solution trade-offs. Patterns have many uses, including inspiration for design, communication of a design, gathering of design ideas, and reviewing of designs. The main benefit of patterns is their ability to extend the experience of the team. Simply reading the trade-offs and solutions as documented by other development teams may lead to the consideration of trade-offs that would otherwise go unnoticed. Eventually patterns may do more, but it is currently time-consuming to research and understand which patterns might apply to a particular problem.

One interesting question is which patterns are most relevant to the practice of software architecture. Buschmann defines an Architectural Pattern as 'expressing a fundamental structural organization schema for software systems. It provide a set of predefined subsystems, specifies their responsibilities, and includes rules and guidelines for organizing the relationships between them'. This section will briefly describe just a few of the Architectural Patterns. However, architects should be fluent in their understanding of patterns well beyond those categorized as architectural.

Other kinds of patterns, such as Process and Organizational Patterns, influence software architecture. Many of the aspects of these patterns were discussed in Chapter 3 and, as a result, they will not be addressed here. Refer to the recommended readings section here and in Chapter 3 for references to these types of patterns.

In smaller systems or at the subsystem level a single Architectural Pattern may be a dominant theme. Shaw and Garlan have called this an architectural style. However, most large-scale systems will incorporate many patterns. Thus, it is usually impossible to describe a large system with a single architectural style. The incorporation of several styles into a single system is likely an Architectural Pattern that has yet to be documented.

Some of the commonly described architectural styles include *Pipes and Filters, Black Board or Repository*, and *Layered Architecture*. As described previously, different viewpoints provide some of the views described by these Architectural Patterns. For example, the Subsystem Layered View provides an overview of the subsystem and layers in the software architecture.

While patterns can be tremendously useful, they can be misused. One pitfall is lengthy arguments over whether a certain pattern fits the design or vice versa. These debates are typically off topic and are not terribly useful to producing the final system. In addition, the software architect must be careful that a pattern is applicable to the problem at hand and wasn't selected because a zealous designer had a desire to apply the pattern. This desire may be fueled by the fact that the pattern looked interesting or because it was used successfully on another system.

The following paragraphs describe only a few of the many software Architectural Patterns that may prove to be useful. Discussion of a complete set of Architectural Patterns would fill several books the size of this one. In fact, Architectural Patterns have been the topic of, or included in, several books already. Several of these can be found in the recommended readings at the end of the chapter.

Model–View–Controller (MVC) is an Architectural Pattern that provides for the separation of the interface from the underlying domain model. This approach divides a system that requires a human–computer interface that manipulates an underlying set of information into three components. The model defines the domain information in the system, independent of how the user interacts with the information. The view defines the way the information is presented to the human and the acceptable set of manipulation capabilities. The controller processes and sequences human input. A mechanism is also provided to ensure consistency by propagating changes from the interface to the model.

One common Architectural Pattern, called *Reflection*, can be used to build powerful systems. This pattern provides a means for the structure and behavior of the system to be changed dynamically. This capability is facilitated by the ability of objects within a system to be self-described and to allow this description to be dynamically modified. This is done by storing meta-information about the objects in the system. This meta-data can then provide information about attributes, methods, and other information. As a result, software can be written that is not dependent on the structure of the system. This provides for a more generic and less fragile approach to architecture definition. Reflection is most useful in systems where the structure of the data is not known in advance and a generic system needs to access and analyze the data. Examples include data schema browsers and general-purpose displays of device attribute information.

Several patterns describe the trade-offs involved in creating a layered architecture. The *Layers* Pattern described by Buschmann involves structuring the system by organizing the elements into groups at different levels of abstraction. The goal is to structure the system into an appropriate number of layers, with the highest level of abstraction at the top layer and the lowest level of abstraction at the bottom layer. This approach is similar to the one used in the Layered Subsystem Viewpoint. While the *Layers* Pattern is sometimes considered as one option for architecture definition, we view the Layered Subsystem Viewpoint as one of the viewpoints that can be applied to nearly all large-scale software systems.

Pipes and Filters pattern is useful for the design of flexible processing of data streams. In this pattern, the system is divided into a sequence of processing tasks called filters. The data travels through pipes that connect the filters to one another. The output of one task is input to another. The input to the system is some type of data source, for example a set of sensors in a process control system. The output usually flows to a set of displays, possibly in conjunction with a database system. *Pipes and Filters* can be used in large-scale systems that handle large amounts of data, for example a live data feed for a financial management system.

11.5 Integration Strategies

The potential ways by which the various parts of the system will communicate are often referred to as integration strategies. There are frequently different options available for component integration. For example, both COTS and legacy systems serve as constraints on the software architecture by defining approaches for integration with other parts the system. Integration strategies that utilize minimal build-time coupling are often most effective for integration with COTS and legacy systems.

In some systems, the selection of an integration strategy may have only a minor impact on the overall architecture of the system. However, in many systems the integration approaches are critical to consider early in project development as they may substantially change the determination of development to be done versus purchasing or reusing existing system elements. In addition, a major aspect of many projects that is essential to the effectiveness of the software architecture is the selection and development of the system integration facilities.

Many of these integration approaches are difficult to apply, especially when the system functionality requires predictable response times or fault tolerance. This is because many integration strategies that utilize a clear separation of elements do not provide predictable bounded response times, nor do they enable fault tolerance. However, even systems that require these features can often use these integration strategies in parts of the system where predictable response times or fault tolerance is not required. The following sections describe two of the most common component integration strategies that require minimal build-time coupling.

11.5.1 Data-only integration

A data-only integration strategy provides for loose coupling of software components. A data-only integration scheme means that the system will provide data and a form suitable for import into another program. There is no direct invocation of one component by another. As a result, this strategy has the following properties:

- Works with unchanged COTS and legacy code
- No build-time coupling
- Components need not share a common platform
- A database or shared memory may be used to store the data to be exchanged

As an example, a system might provide the ability to export data to a comma-separated value list. This type of file can be imported into custom analysis tools or popular spreadsheet products where the data can be analyzed. Similarly, export of a report into HTML provides the ability for any web browser to display the data. Alternatively, a new system component might import a data file produced from a spreadsheet program to alleviate the need for the creation of a user interface. The advent of XML has increased the ease of implementation of this approach by providing developers access to a common set of tools for handling complex data.

The downside of the data-only integration approach is that the user is often directly involved in the management of files and in controlling the execution of the COTS or legacy program after generating a data file. For tasks that occur infrequently, this approach works well but may be cumbersome if the task occurs frequently, for example if users are required to frequently exchange data between components.

Adding a central database as a repository of data exchange will often make the use of existing products more difficult. On the other hand, some of the direct management of data storage and exchange is removed. In addition, the database often provides security and query features more directly than a file-based approach.

For this sort of integration, there is often little impact to the software architecture task unless a data exchange format and the associated database schema needs to be defined, or the data exchange between components is bi-directional. Approaches for this task are described in Chapter 9. In addition, if the approach uses a database, then a database system needs to be acquired and integrated into the system design.

One issue to consider is to try to select relatively stable data exchange formats. If a new version of a COTS product does not recognize the old data import or export format then the system components will need to be changed to match or to support multiple formats as the new version of COTS becomes available.

11.5.2 Executable integration

In executable integration, a stand-alone executable component is used to perform a specific function in the system. The executable component is partially controlled by either another component or a scripting infrastructure within the larger system. The controlling component will need to depend on an execution infrastructure that allows the controlling component to start the executable component and to exchange data with that component. The execution infrastructure may be anything from operating system process execution facilities to a web protocol. This integration approach has the following properties:

- No build-time component coupling

- Dependency on component invocation platform

- Usually builds on a data integration foundation

- Is not required to share a common platform, but often this is the case

As an example, a system might generate a data file and then use a COTS spreadsheet product to provide data graphing capabilities. The creation of graphs may be driven by a script that provides the spreadsheet product with the necessary data from the system to draw the desired user graphs.

A big advantage of this approach is that the direct role of the user can often be eliminated. Thus, even if a data file is the primary basis of integration between two components, the ability of one component to execute another can automate an end-to-end task for a user.

With this sort of integration, the architecture concern is in the interactions between components as well as the design of the supporting component execution infrastructure. The execution infrastructure is often part of the selected platform or is provided by a cross-platform execution facility.

11.6 Establishing Architecture to Support Development

The architecture of a software system inevitably impacts and is impacted by many critical development support functions. The following sections will describe some of development support functions impacted and enabled by the software architecture. Establishing the relationship between support functions and the architecture is often critical to keeping a large project agile enough to succeed.

11.6.1 Configuration and change management

Establishing configuration and change management practices is essential to the success of large-scale systems. Configuration management systems provide for the versioning and management of changes to source code and other software artifacts. A mapping of the subsystems to a build-tree provides a good basis of source code configuration management.

Change management systems record defect and feature requests that drive the development process. Inevitably, the setup of these development support systems is impacted by the software architecture. In particular, as defects are reported, they will often be isolated to a certain subsystem or subsystems. The assignment of a development group to investigate and make the necessary changes usually involves determining the subsystems involved and assigning the work accordingly.

Inevitably, some changes will involve coordination across multiple subsystems that are the responsibility of different parts of the organization. These types of changes are fundamentally more expensive since communication and coordination are required. Again, there is inevitably some mapping between the software architecture and the organizational responsibility.

11.6.2   Build management

Establishing consistent and automated build practices is essential to the success of large-scale systems. By build, we mean the process of compiling source code, creating libraries and executables, and transforming these products into an installable software package. The subsystem structure usually provides the basis for automated build systems.

The agility of the build process is significantly impacted by the software architecture. Reduction of build times is an important way that the architecture facilitates development. For example, in a good architecture that leverages layers, the lowest layers will change the least. These lower layers can be pre-built and made available for developers to utilize. This relieves individual developers from the time needed to constantly build these stable elements of the software. In a good architecture, the majority of changes will only require modification of a single subsystem. When this is the case, the build and test cycles are minimized. This means that more work can be accomplished by the same number of developers. Add the effect of these efficiencies over many developers and extended periods, and the benefits of a good architecture become clear.

As new builds of the software are created, the architecture description must be updated to match. This usually involves an automated update of the detailed design information, as well as validation that the subsystem and higher-level architecture are still consistent with the code that was delivered. As an example, the subsystems map to the build-tree within which the libraries and executables for the system are generated. If new subsystems are created, or additional dependencies between the subsystems are added, automated tools can flag this change and notify the architecture and development teams.

11.6.3   Continuous integration

In large systems with many developers, software changes can happen at a rapid rate. Continuous integration is a process for managing changes and detecting incompatibilities between changes rapidly. As developers integrate changes into the system, a series of regression tests is performed to ensure that the changes have not broken some existing capability. These tests go beyond the subsystem-level tests typically performed as changes are being made.

A typical realization of this process is a daily build and test process. In reality, most large projects will perform multiple builds in a given day since management of multiple different versions is needed to manage complex delivery constraints. For example, a single change may be propagated to several release versions that support external customers as well as internal development versions of the software. The build and test process may need to be run across all of these versions. In addition, some complex changes may require days or weeks to complete. In this case, a daily build and test may be required on a feature development branch as well.

The most important aspect of continuous integration is that failures in the automated tests detect system integration issues almost immediately following the change is made. This early detection ensures that the change is still fresh in the mind of the developer and avoids expensive rework cycles typically involved with integrating large numbers of unchecked changes.

The architecture of the software heavily impacts the continuous integration process. Ideally, the daily build and test process will run smoothly. Changes will be made, and no errors will be found by the automated tests. If the daily build and tests are constantly unstable, this is an indication that developers are unable to isolate work appropriately. It is often the sign of a poor architecture.

Development of a skeleton system, as described earlier, can provide the start for the development of a continuous integration process. Likewise, the skeleton system is a technique for incrementally building up the software architecture.

11.6.4   Anticipate multi-language development

In today's software development environments, there are many different languages available for development. These include C++, Perl, Python, Java, SQL, Visual Basic, and others. Different languages and environments have different strengths and weaknesses. The widespread use of databases and web-based infrastructure almost guarantees that a large system will have multiple development languages. It is an important architectural concern to determine where and how language boundaries impact the software design.

Choosing the correct language and environment for addressing various problems can provide cost-effective solutions. For example, SQL might be used to create data in a database that is retrieved by a C++ application. Since

C++ never needs to update the data, time and energy are saved since the C++ application only needs to implement database-reading capabilities.

One common approach to the multi-language environment is to describe the cross-language interfaces using middleware such as the Common Object Request Broker Architecture (CORBA). The tools provided with CORBA implementations generate much of the cross-language binding and marshaling. However, there are many other cross-language mechanisms, including other libraries that provide the ability to execute a program written in one language from another language. For example, a Perl script can be executed from within a C++ program by loading a Perl interpreter within the C++ executable. The Perl program might then call functions written as part of the C++ program. This type of approach might be used to enable custom reports written in Perl to retrieve data from the C++ API.

One of the big downsides to multi-language development is increased complexity in both the operational and development environments. In addition, a badly partitioned system will end up with intertwined application logic written in multiple languages. Therefore, one goal of the architecture is to isolate specialty languages to solving the problems for which they are appropriate. This might involve restricting the language to a particular layer of the system such as the application user interface. For example, the application logic should generally not be written as stored procedures in a database system.

11.6.5 Anticipate tactical development (scripting)

A topic that is related to multi-language development is the enabling of tactical development features. Tactical development is the rapid development of a short-lived capability which is very specific to a certain customer or context. The scripting approach provides many benefits, including the ability to develop one-of-a-kind or one-use programs.

Scripting may be used to mine data, fix a database corruption, recover from a software failure, or perform other complex jobs that would otherwise be difficult to accomplish manually. For example, the ability to create a report from a database to gather data for resolving a software bug is an example of a potential one-time feature. The software problem may be unique, and hence the report is only valuable one time. However, having the ability to quickly develop scripts for data mining and other purposes may allow for quick resolution of the problem.

Often the features developed using tactical development techniques will not require the same level of formal review as software that forms the core of the system. As a result, it might be important for the architecture to support and limit the risk of this type of software. For example, a Perl binding to a database for report generation might be limited to reading of the database. This would prevent the destruction of data created by a flawed script.

Software architectures that facilitate scripting can be created using several approaches. For example, a software architecture might provide scripting interfaces to data stores that allow for various monitoring and reporting capabilities. In many large-scale developments, providing for scripting is an essential component of success. Modern scripting languages provide the ability to develop new features in real time that could not be anticipated up front.

11.7 Recommended Reading

The applicability of Scope, Commonality, and Variability (SCV) Analysis as well as domain analysis for product families is described in Weiss and Lai (1999). As a general-purpose approach for software engineering, SCV is described in both the paper by Coplien, Hoffman, and Weiss (1998) and the book by Coplien (1998). The use of Commonality and Variability Analysis for identification of frameworks is described in Mili *et al.* (2002).

Feature modeling, as described by Czarnecki and Eisenecker in their generative programming book (2000), is a formal version of commonality and variability analysis. Feature modeling provides a formal basis for the development of frameworks and product families.

Bertrand Meyer (1997) has the definitive discussion on design by contract. There are also several good discussions on the Interactive Software Engineering web page and in the paper by Meyer (1992).

Bass *et al.* (1998) describes building a skeletal system as the first step.

Many papers on Architecture Description Languages can be found at the CMU SEI web site. Shaw and Garlan (1996) have done a lot of work in this area. Garlan and Allen (1994), as well as several other authors on the topic of ADLs, have been focusing on describing interfaces using ADLs.

The paper by Niklaus Wirth (1971) on stepwise refinement provides a good overview of early thinking on the divide and conquer approach.

Hofmeister (2000) includes several effective strategies. Among them are Encapsulate Domain-Specific Hardware, Isolate Time-Critical Components, and Separate Domain Model from Human Interface.

In a series of articles, Robert Martin discussed several key principles, including the Dependency Inversion Principle, the Interface Segregation Principle, and the Open Closed Principle. The articles describing these principles are also available at his web site. The book by Lakos (1996) also discusses package levelization, a similar to dependency inversion.

Buschmann (1996) has a very good description of many Architectural Patterns. These include *Pipes and Filters, Blackboard, Model–View–Controller*, and *Reflection*. While Buschmann introduced the idea of an Architectural Pattern, Shaw and Garlan (1996) had an earlier discussion of what came to be called patterns and architectural style. Monroe *et al.* (1997) also had a paper that discussed architectural styles and design patterns.

Douglass (1999) discusses the use of Architectural Patterns for real-time software.

The Specification and Description Language (SDL) is in the ITU Z.100 Specification (1999).

The Repository Pattern is described in Coplien (1995).

The SEI has done a significant amount of work on architecture analysis and evaluation. This work includes the Architecture Tradeoff Analysis Method (ATAM) and the Software Architecture Analysis Method (SAAM). Information is available from the SEI web site.

Garland, Anthony, and Lawrence (1999) provide a more detailed description of the factors that impact the quest for the creation of stable software in an OOPSLA position paper.

Martin Fowler has a good description of continuous integration at his web site. There is also a description of continuous integration at the C2 Wiki site.

12

Applying the Viewpoints

The following sections sketch how to use the previously described viewpoints to facilitate architecture development. In addition, we provide some concluding thoughts about becoming a software architect, the current state of the practice, and some thoughts about the future.

It should be noted that the amount of time required to perform a full iteration through these processes might range from hours to months. The length of time required will depend on the size of the system and the focus of the participants. An expert designer focused on a small part of the system might progress through a series of views and directly to implementation all in a single session. These views might be simply sketched on a whiteboard to support development of either a prototype or skeletal system. An architecture team in the first phase of a very large and complex system development might spend a month. Every project and situation is a bit different.

12.1 Bottom-Up Architecture Development

One of the more structured approaches for architecture development starts with domain analysis as described in Chapter 6. This overall process is illustrated in Figure 12.1. Note that the figure only illustrates the structural views. The dynamic views are used in conjunction with these structural views as described in the earlier chapters.

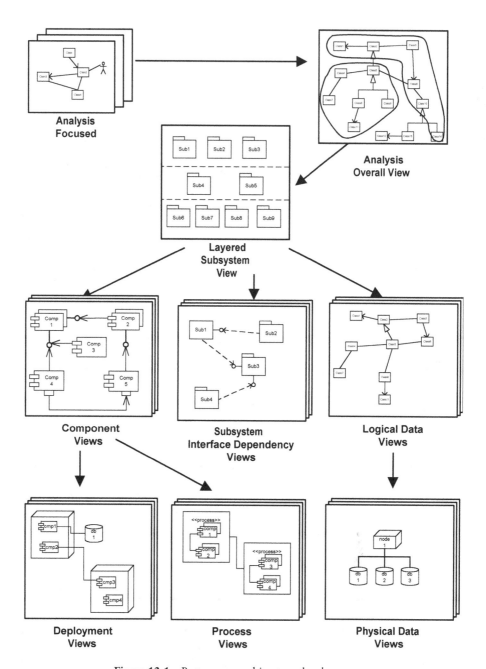

Figure 12.1   Bottom-up architecture development

A list of use cases is the driver for development of analysis and subsequent design views. The domain analysis process produces the Analysis Overall View. The next step is to partition the analysis view into domains. This partitioning is accomplished by rearranging the Analysis Overall View and grouping the classes based on coupling and cohesion, as described in Chapter 11. The classes that are closely coupled should be grouped together into a cohesive set. The goal is to minimize the number of associations and aggregations between the groups of classes. Each group forms the basis for a candidate subsystem.

One approach for identifying the set of subsystems is to add implementation details to the Analysis Overall View until the key implementation classes are added. This is similar to the process of evolving an object-oriented analysis into a design. From this more detailed Analysis Overall View, the subsystems are then identified by following a similar grouping process. Another, more rigorous approach, is to go back to the use-case elaboration step and add implementation constructs to all the Analysis Focus Views and eventually to a view that is more implementation focused. Once again, this view is used for identification of the subsystems based on grouping of the classes in the Analysis Focused View.

Regardless of which approach is used, the result will be the set of subsystems. The subsystems can be represented in the Layered Subsystem View. As subsystem interfaces are identified, the Subsystem Interface Dependency View is developed. At this point off-the-shelf infrastructure subsystems and other technical mechanisms are added. The Component View is often developed following the definition of the Subsystem Interface Dependency View in order to understand the preliminary runtime structure for the candidate subsystems. For systems using a shared data design, the Logical Data View should be developed starting from the Analysis Overall View.

Mapping to processes and hardware can be derived by starting with Component Views and creating Process Views and Deployment Views. Remember from Chapter 10 that both types of views may not be needed since Deployment Views can also capture processes.

12.2 Top-Down Architecture Development

A completely different approach from the bottom-up approach is to identify a preliminary set of system components, develop the interfaces, and then begin to analyze the details of the subsystems and entities required to support each component. This 'top-down' approach has many benefits. First, it reduces the

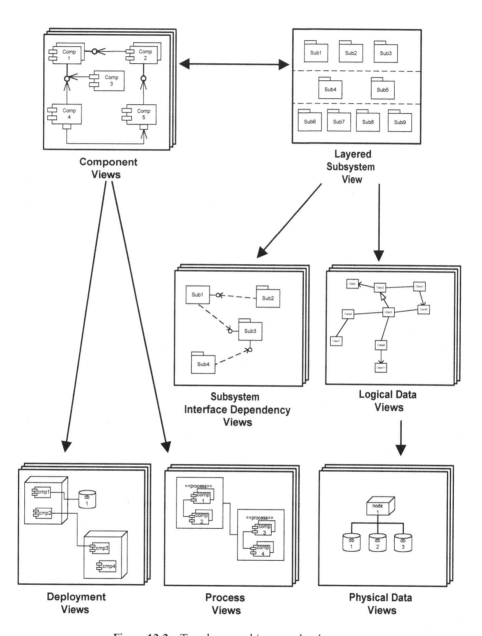

Figure 12.2   Top-down architecture development

time required for analysis and design because it ignores many details required by the bottom-up analysis approach. Second, software architecture development is often not undertaken for a completely new system but for an existing system. Existing systems consist of well-defined components that can be rapidly modeled. In addition, the requirements for a new system might specify the use of some existing components, thus fixing the solution space. Finally, a system based on standards will often predefine specific components and interfaces, again limiting the solution space.

Figure 12.2 provides an overview of this approach. As with the bottom-up approach, use cases can be used to elaborate Component Views. The focus in the top-down approach is on splitting the system functions into components and detailing a set of message-based or interface-based interactions. The interface design process is discussed in more detail in the next section.

After defining Component Views for the key use cases, one option is for all the components in the use case focused views to be brought together into a single Component View representing all the components and component interactions. This Component View can then be used to identify candidate subsystems that will build the components. The layers and interfaces associated with these subsystems can then be identified and the Layered Subsystem View and Subsystem Interface Dependency Views can be generated. The Logical Data Views can then be generated from the Component Views along with the Layered Subsystem View. The Deployment and Process Views can be defined, based on the component definition. In addition, the Physical Data View can be defined based on the Logical Data Views.

12.3   Message Protocol and Interface Development

Interface and message protocol development is a critical part of architecture definition. The process of defining an interface or a messaging protocol involves detailing the sequence of events between two or more components. Chapter 11 describes a number of useful techniques, including Design by Contract and prototyping, that can be useful for refining the details of an interface or messaging protocol.

Figure 12.3 shows a structured technique for developing interfaces and message protocols. In this method, the use cases drive the development of a set of Component Interaction Views. Component Views may be developed as well, but it is the interactions that are fundamental to the understanding of the interfaces and message protocols.

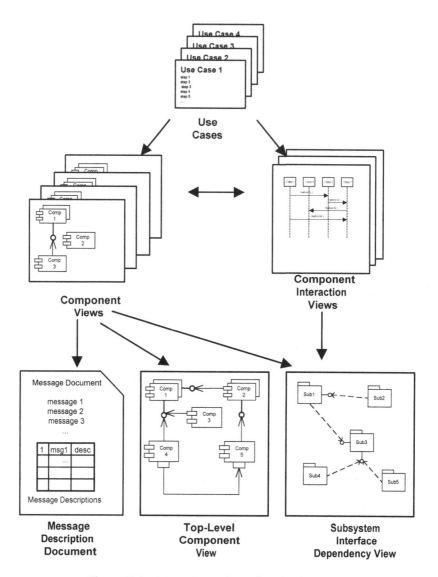

Figure 12.3   Messaging and interface development

From these Component Views, the component interface detail can be captured at a high level in the Subsystem Interface Dependency Views, and in the overall Component View. In addition, information concerning the messages and ports can be captured at a lower level of detail in a Message Description or Interface Document. The detailed description of interfaces that accompanies the Component Views, along with the message detail contained in the Message Description Document, is then used to drive the design and development of the software.

Interface development is typically supported either by prototyping or done within the context of skeleton system development. All of the aforementioned views provide a useful start to both of these efforts.

12.4 Reengineering Existing Systems

A frequent problem faced by development teams is the need to understand existing systems for reengineering, evolution, or integration with new systems. In this case, the Process, Deployment, and Component Views are useful in getting an understanding of the as-is system. The Process and Deployment Views provide an understanding of the physical layout of the system and the Component Views provide a logical layout. Other views, such as the Logical Data View, may also be created to understand and document database schemas for existing systems.

Once the as-is system is documented, the next step is to describe the as-desired system. This usually involves discussing the implementation constraints of the current system that are preventing it from fulfilling the desired requirements. For example, an existing system may not be capable of supporting desired scalability and deployment scenarios because of a monolithic component design. In this case, some components may need to be split into multiple components that can be replicated at runtime. Developing Component and Deployment Views of the as-desired system supports this type of redevelopment.

In the end, the best selection of views depends on the particular problem. And as usual, the development of views is typically only an intermediate step prior to code refactoring or a rewrite. To be effective, designers need to constantly evaluate what information will be learned by creating another view.

12.5 Documenting the Architecture

In order to document the software architecture, a top-level software design document (TLSDD), sometimes referred to as the software architecture document, should be produced and maintained by the software architecture team. This document will communicate the software architecture to the stakeholders. If the project is utilizing a CASE tool, as much of this document as possible should be generated from that tool. However, certain text sections may need to be edited by hand and included in the generated document.

The following views and information should be included in the document. Along with nearly all views, a textual description and/or a set of tables that are similar to the ones we describe along with the viewpoints should also be included. The TLSDD should include all of the relevant architectural views and related information. However, it should not be stuffed with so much detail that it cannot be used as a reference by the stakeholders, nor should it contain views for which there are no stakeholders. The following information is typical of what should be included in the TLSDD:

- Overall description of the software system under design

- Identification of the major design constraints as they relate to the key top-level requirements

- Overall design principles, key abstractions, and overarching considerations

- References to other key documents defined by the architecture or process teams

- Context view

- Top-Level Subsystem Interface Dependency View – This will define the organizational boundaries and dependencies. If a single view will not fit in the document, then produce a smaller set of views to capture the relevant information or use the Layered Subsystem View.

- Other focused Subsystem Interface Dependency Views, potentially one for each development subsystem with that subsystem as the focus

- One or more views of the composite components – These may be focused on key use cases or other critical interactions. If possible, one overall Component View should be produced.

- Other Component Views, again focused on use cases or other interactions

- Logical Data Views

- Deployment Views, focusing on sets of nodes or processes that are involved in specific interactions or that need to be grouped for other reasons

- Key design decisions that drove this version of the software architecture

- Outstanding issues or concerns with the overall architecture

A typical TLSDD should be fifty to one hundred pages. This is small enough to be quickly read, but deep enough to cover the system. If the document becomes too large, think about ways to move details to other documents.

12.6 Conclusions

12.6.1 Becoming an architect

Becoming a good software architect is a difficult job requiring a large breadth of knowledge and many years of experience. It requires becoming an expert in software development. It also means learning many social skills. It requires becoming an expert in the domain of the project.

The following are some characteristics of great software architects:

- Well versed in software analysis and design techniques, as well as architectural and design patterns

- Fluent in several programming languages

- Excellent verbal communication and writing skills

- Excellent at critical thinking and knowledge acquisition

- Ten or more years of experience in software development

With the exception of experience, the skills required to become an architect can be taught. People can learn new languages, read about design, and take classes to improve communication skills. The following paragraphs expand on these topics.

Ten years ago, very little literature existed about applied software design. Thanks to the pattern movement and many other authors, a large body of literature has been developed about software design. There is certainly no lack of advice. New software architects should read widely and try out ideas that look promising. Patterns are especially valuable for several reasons. First, they typically provide an end-to-end capsule of thought about a particular design aspect. Both the abstractions and the implementation are available for study in a concise and specific write-up. Second, patterns describe trade-offs and alternatives. Finally, they are based on repeated experience and hence represent practical designs.

The architect should be fluent in several programming languages. The first reason for this is that the software architect of a large project will be faced with implementations using many languages. Architects will often be involved in helping to sort out which languages are applied to which problems. In addition, architects will need to read and review interface implementations and other source code. Consider the need to evaluate if an existing C library can serve as the foundation for a Java interface. Being fluent in several different languages makes the job of learning unfamiliar programming languages much easier.

Excellent writing and presentation skills are critical for software architects. Software architects need to interact with many types of people. Extracting the important essence of the information from a discussion or other communication is an important skill. Be prepared to make regular presentations as a software architect. Sometimes highly technical topics need to be communicated to non-technical audiences. At other times the architect much interface directly with technical experts. Sometimes these presentations may be to a hostile audience, making the interactions stressful. All of these skills can be nurtured by taking classes or participating in organizations focused on the development of communications skills.

Software architects need to be good critical thinkers. The various roles of an architect require evaluation of the merits of everything from requirements to code structure. Being able to distinguish between good arguments and spurious rationale helps in making good technical choices. While being critical, it is important to keep an open mind. Few designs are categorically good or bad. Most designs have various strengths and weaknesses. The critical question is whether the strengths and weaknesses are in alignment with the needs of the project and the stakeholders. Architects that work on a broad range of systems often need to rapidly get an understanding of the domain of a new system. This means digging in and understanding new terminologies and processes. It means also means not being afraid to ask questions and admit a lack of knowledge.

Finally, there is no substitute for experience. It is important for aspiring architects to dig in, get their hands dirty by doing design and development. For example, the architect should try to implement a reusable library in his or her spare time from the ground up. The architect should also write and review Design Patterns in order to become accustomed to looking at the different perspectives. The architect should also be a frequent product tester. These experiences will help the aspiring architect to:

- Balance trade-offs in a design

- Learn to move on before perfection is achieved

- Learn how to estimate well in the face of great uncertainty

- Learn how to see the customer perspective

Throughout this book we have pointed to many sources of information about software architecture and related topics. This list of sources is only a small fraction of what we have actually read and learned from over the years. Reading widely is another required behavior for a software architect.

12.6.2   State of the practice

Over the past ten years there have been dramatic changes in the practice of software development. Some of the changes include:

- Less software developed from scratch

- Emergence of object-oriented, scripting, and special-purpose languages

- Rise of the Internet and networked applications

- Consensus that software design matters

More often than not, projects are either rewriting existing capabilities or adding web interfaces onto existing systems. In addition, the libraries and frameworks available for developers have expanded dramatically. The availability of good libraries has reduced the amount of time devoted to the development of basic data structures and other low-level details. This allows more attention to be paid to the development of the application. On the other hand, the expectations of users have dramatically increased due to more sophisticated user interfaces and to advanced functionality becoming an expectation rather than an exception. As a result, the job of software development is becoming more about putting together in new ways software that already exists in various pieces.

Internet and network applications have become much more prevalent as the Internet has grown. This has resulted in an increase in complexity compared with non-networked applications.

Object-oriented languages such as Java and C++ are the predominant development languages. These languages have features that allow for more sophisticated architectures than the functional languages that preceded them. Less recognized has been the expansion of widely available special-purpose programming languages and general-purpose scripting languages such as Perl and Python. These languages can provide highly effective development environments for integration, testing, and development of tactical functionality. Frameworks that apply generative programming techniques have become rather commonplace.

In the area of the modeling and representation of software architecture, a significant advancement was the emergence of the UML as a standard. Prior to the standardization of the UML, the object-oriented design community was attempting to promote widely disparate approaches and modeling notations.

One other interesting change is that companies developing software have decided that having a design is important. Most companies now expect that software projects will include design as well as code products. There is recognition that a bad architecture can result in significant downsides for a project, including cost overruns and even project abandonment. This is all meaningful for the software architect, as it means many organizations will now provide for and support the software design effort.

All of these factors have changed the issues for software architects. Today, it is more important than ever to understand the advantages and limitations of off-the-shelf components. Integration and augmentation of existing components is a common problem.

The good news is that projects that have an early and consistent focus on software architecture and that provide the necessary resources for the definition of an effective architecture will realize the benefits throughout the project lifecycle. For this reason, more projects are making use of architecture-centric processes and are achieving these benefits. While the architecture-centric approach is being used more often, providing tremendous improvements in the state of the art of software development, many projects are still attempting significant development efforts without the definition of a software architecture. In fact, many projects are still being attempted without any documented software architecture at all.

12.6.3   Looking forward

While the information in this book and others like it will assist the software architect in doing his or her job, there is still much to be done to improve software architecture definition. Some areas where advancement might be reasonably expected include:

- Improved design and development tool support

- Improved documentation and usability of architecture patterns

- Improved architecture definition language support

Software engineering tools have never been better, and they are continually improving. For example, several programming environments now integrate coding and design tools. However, there are still plenty of issues with tools. As an example, most tools provide extremely limited support for automated layout of diagrams. This requires designers to spend time 'tweaking' the diagrams to look good. It should be reasonable to expect that a sophisticated program can relieve designers of the tedium of diagram layout. It should also be reasonable to expect design tools to automatically generate and maintain a view based on model information and some sort of template specification. Like many of today's applications, we can expect design tools to become truly networked enabled providing first-class support for geographically distributed development teams. Finally, direct support for design-level refactoring within a tool that directly modifies code will magnify the impact of expert designers.

As mentioned previously, **Software Patterns** are still in an early stage of development. Many patterns have been written, but much less work has been done to unify patterns into a coherent system. Figuring out how best to apply patterns today requires an immense effort. The development of **Pattern Languages** should provide deeper insight into how various patterns relate and how to use them together effectively.

Some of the original Design Patterns are increasingly becoming the building blocks for the next generation of reusable components. Patterns such as Abstract Factory and Singleton have been married with design tools and generative programming techniques to provide powerful configurable libraries. This moves the practice of design to a new level by automating the implementation based on a set of configuration options. This allows architects and designers to have more control over the quality and consistency of the final implementation. In the past this was not possible because libraries made design decisions incompatible with a new architecture. All too frequently this meant rewriting the library. By leveraging documented patterns these libraries build on previously successful designs. With these new techniques, reuse seems like a much more achievable goal. As more repetitive and infrastructure code can be configured for specific needs and reused directly, more time and focus can be applied to improved application architecture and development.

The adoption of IEEE 1471 and the upcoming release of the UML 2.0

should help improve the future practice of software architecture. Having a common vocabulary for discussion is typically the first step to common understanding. We hope that this book will provide some insights for discussing other improvements. Some of the proposals for Architectural Description Languages may also make a major impact on the practice of software architecture.

This book has attempted to provide a set of practical techniques and approaches for defining a software architecture that achieves the product and organizational goals. In addition, we stress the importance of producing only architectural views for which there are stakeholders in order to prevent the architecture definition process from becoming too heavyweight. We have been successful in building architectures using these techniques. In many cases, the full benefit was not initially achieved as we were still learning how to apply the notations and techniques effectively. The message this book is intended to convey is that successful large-scale projects can be developed and have a software architecture that reflects the needs of the users.

12.6.4   Final thoughts

Developing software is one of the most complex tasks in which humans can be engaged. To develop this software without a blueprint or set of overriding principles makes the task nearly impossible. The goal of the software architect is to develop and communicate this blueprint based on a vision of how the system should evolve into the final product.

With a well-defined architecture and the guidance of a knowledgeable software architect, large-scale software can be a much more satisfying experience for all who are involved.

In this book, we provided both the experienced and the aspiring software architect with techniques and a set of viewpoints, which have proven to be valuable in several large-scale and smaller projects. Our hope is that you have found this book useful. We hope that armed with the knowledge gained by reading this book and the recommended readings you will:

- Extract the pieces that apply to the particular project and organization

- Supplement this information with your own experience and study

- Mentor other aspiring software architects

- Promote best practices in software architecture and design

- Add to the growing body of Architectural Patterns

- Document and publish your knowledge and experiences as a software architect

- Find other ways to further advance the state of software architecture

12.7 Recommended Reading

The process described here for the creation and partitioning of the Analysis Overall View was referenced in the Unified Process, but little detail was provided.

Andrei Alexandrescu (2001) has implemented several of the original Design Patterns using policy-based design in C++.

Appendix: Summary of Architectural Viewpoints

This appendix includes a summary viewpoint table, based on the tables found in Chapter 1, along with the Viewpoint tables from each chapter. The summary is found in Table A.1.

Table A.1 Software Architecture Viewpoint Summary

Viewpoint	UML diagram type	Description	Chapter
Analysis Focused	Class	Describe system entities in response to a scenario. Often referred to as a view of participating classes or VOPC.	6
Analysis Interaction	Interaction	Interaction diagram between objects for analysis.	6
Analysis Overall	Class	Combination of all classes from all focused analysis viewpoints.	6
Component	Component	Illustrate component communications.	7
Component Interaction	Interaction	Interactions among components.	7

(continued overleaf)

Table A.1 *(continued)*

Viewpoint	UML diagram type	Description	Chapter
Component State	State/Activity	State transition/activity diagram for a component or for a set of components	7
Context	Use Case	Show the external system actors and the system under design.	6
Deployment	Deployment	Mapping of software to hardware for distributed systems.	10
Layered Subsystem	Package	Illustrate layering and subsystems design.	8
Logical Data	Class	Show critical data views used for integration.	9
Physical Data	Deployment	Physical view of a particular database.	10
Process	Deployment	Show the processes of a particular system instance.	10
Process State	State	Show the dynamic states of a process.	10
Subsystem Interface Dependency	Class	Illustrate subsystem dependencies and interfaces.	8

The descriptions for each of the viewpoints shown in the summary are shown in Tables A.2 to A.15.

Table A.2 Analysis Focused Viewpoint

Analysis Focused Viewpoint	
Purpose	Illustrate a set of actors, classes, attributes, methods, and associations for a specific use case, set of use cases, or subset of an Analysis Overall View.
When Applicable	Primarily prepared during analysis, along with use case development. Generally not maintained, unless a product family is being developed.
Stakeholders	Software Architecture Team, Software Systems Engineering Team, Subsystem Design Leads, Developers, Testers.
Scalability	The focused views will be used to produce an overall view that can be used to drive the software architecture definition.
Relation to Other Views	Should be consistent with the initial overall views, but will most likely not be maintained as the overall views evolve.

Table A.3 Analysis Interaction Viewpoint

Analysis Interaction Viewpoint	
Purpose	Illustrate a set of classes, attributes, methods, and associations for a specific path through a use case.
When Applicable	Prepared during analysis, along with use case development. Generally not maintained.
Stakeholders	Software Architecture Team, Software Systems Engineering Team, Subsystem Design Leads, Developers, Testers.
Scalability	The interaction views will be used to produce a focused view for that use case.
Relation to Other Views	Should be consistent with the initial focused views, but will most likely not be maintained as the focused views evolve.

Table A.4 Analysis Overall Viewpoint

Analysis Overall Viewpoint	
Purpose	Illustrate the set of key actors, classes, attributes, methods, and associations for a system. This viewpoint should not contain implementation details.
When Applicable	Primarily prepared during analysis, along with use case development. Generally not maintained, unless a product family is being developed.
Stakeholders	Software Architecture Team, Software Systems Engineering Team, Subsystem Design Leads, Developers, Testers.
Scalability	The overall view is seldom small enough to fit onto a single sheet of paper. Subsets of the classes, actors, and associated information can be extracted to produce focused views that convey a key concept or set of concepts.
Relation to Other Views	Should be consistent with the initial analysis focused and interaction views, but generally evolves to contain additional information.

Table A.5 Component Viewpoint

Component Viewpoint	
Purpose	Describe runtime component connectivity and communication. Can be applied to performance analysis and later the process interaction design.
When Applicable	During system design and development, as analysis views and subsystems are identified.

(continued overleaf)

Table A.5   (*continued*)

Component Viewpoint	
Stakeholders	Architecture Team, Subsystem Developers, Test Team, Software System Engineering Team, Systems Engineering Team, Project and Development Managers (to a lesser degree)
Scalability	Drawn with scenario or component focus. Can make use of composite components.
Relation to Other Views	The Component Views should be consistent with components shown in the Process and Deployment Views.

Table A.6   Component Interaction Viewpoint

Component Interaction Viewpoint	
Purpose	Validate structural design via exploration of the software dynamics.
When Applicable	Throughout project lifecycle. Primarily prepared during design and analysis, but can also be used and expanded during development.
Stakeholders	Software Architecture Team, Software Systems Engineering Team, Subsystem Design Leads, Developers.
Scalability	Based on scenarios, can be scaled to higher levels by using composite components.
Relation to Other Views	Should be consistent with Component, Process, and Deployment Views.

Table A.7   Component State Viewpoint

Component State Viewpoint	
Purpose	Model the state of a component or group of components.
When Applicable	Throughout project lifecycle. Primarily prepared during design and analysis, but can also be used and expanded during development.
Stakeholders	Software Architecture Team, Software Systems Engineering Team, Subsystem Design Leads, Developers, Testers.
Scalability	State-based views, based on individual components, can be scaled up to composite components. Activity-based views can be applied to single component or several components.
Relation to Other Views	Should be consistent with other dynamic views as well as interface and message definition.

Table A.8   Context Viewpoint

Context Viewpoint	
Purpose	Model the set of actors with which the system interacts and the interfaces between the system and these entities.
When Applicable	Throughout project lifecycle. Primarily prepared during the first stages of design and analysis, but is updated as information about external interfaces changes.
Stakeholders	Software Architecture Team, Software Systems Engineering Team, Subsystem Design Leads, Developers, Testers, Systems Engineers, Marketing, or others who are interested in or negotiate external interfaces.
Scalability	The system should always be located in the middle of the view. The external actors should be surrounding the system. If the number of actors becomes too large, they may need to be grouped into higher-level actors. Multiple Context Views should only be used as a last resort.
Relation to Other Views	Should be consistent with other static views that show external interfaces. For example, the subsystem interface, component, process, or deployment views.

Table A.9   Deployment Viewpoint

Deployment Viewpoint	
Purpose	Describe mapping of processes/components to hardware, may need several of these. May have several views for large systems. Describe runtime component connectivity and communication. Can be applied to performance analysis and later the process interaction design.
When Applicable	After preliminary components are identified, this view can be created as input to making hardware purchase decisions. Updated during construction and transition as components are completed. When reengineering or documenting an existing distributed system.
Stakeholders	Architecture Team, Hardware and Network Architects, Subsystem Developers, Test Team, Software System Engineering Team, Systems Engineering Team, Project and Development Managers (to a lesser degree), Operations Staff.
Scalability	Drawn with scenario or component focus. Also, a node focus can be used for modeling scalable servers.
Relation to Other Views	Builds on process, component, and physical database views by adding in mapping to nodes.

Table A.10 Layered Subsystem Viewpoint

Layered Subsystem Viewpoint Synopsis	
Purpose	Provide top-level view of the subsystem and layer build-time architecture
When Applicable	Throughout project lifecycle
Stakeholders	Program and Project Managers, Software Architecture Team, Development Team, Test Team, Customers
Scalability	Omits detailed dependency information
Relation to other Views	Abstraction of the Subsystem Interface Dependency View.

Table A.11 Logical Data Viewpoint

Logical Data Viewpoint	
Purpose	Describe the logical form of data and messaging types for a system.
When Applicable	Design
Stakeholders	Architecture Team, Developers, Testers, Hardware Architect.
Relation to other Views	Derived from Analysis Overall View.

Table A.12 Physical Data Viewpoint

Physical Data Viewpoint	
Purpose	To describe the layout of the physical database elements. These views are annotated with estimates/measurement of database size, growth rates per factor and redundancy strategies.
When Applicable	During subsystem and component design and development.
Stakeholders	Architecture Team, Developers, Operations Staff, Hardware Architect, Testers
Scalability	Can be focused on a chosen subset of the system or can model the overall system.
Relation to Other Views	Nodes and databases may also be shown on the deployment view.

Table A.13   Process Viewpoint

Process Viewpoint	
Purpose	Describe process inter-communication mechanisms independent of physical hardware deployment.
When Applicable	During system design and development. Reengineering of existing systems.
Stakeholders	Architecture Team, Subsystem Developers, Test Team, Software System Engineering Team, Systems Engineering Team, Hardware Architect, Project and Development Managers (to a lesser degree), Operations Staff.
Scalability	Supplement with tables indicating access frequency, response times, data transfer sizes, etc.
Relation to Other Views	This view is an abstraction of a Deployment View that does not include a mapping of processes to nodes. This view is a detailing of the Component View showing the mapping of components to processes.

Table A.14   Process State Viewpoint

Process State Viewpoint	
Purpose	Describe the state transitions and interactions of one or more processes.
When Applicable	During system design and development.
Stakeholders	Architecture Team, Subsystem Developers, Test Team.
Scalability	These views can be provided for a single process or a group of processes.
Relation to other View	The Process View illustrates the processes of interest for modeling in the process state view. The Component State View often provides details for a process that executes multiple components.

Table A.15   Subsystem Interface Dependency Viewpoint

Subsystem Interface Dependency Viewpoint	
Purpose	Describe subsystem dependencies and interfaces. Will most likely be one of these for overall system, potentially one for each top-level subsystem complex enough to require a view of its own.
When Applicable	During system design and development, as subsystems are identified.
Stakeholders	Project and Development Managers (primary stakeholders for top-level subsystem views), Architecture Team, Development leads, Test Team.
Scalability	Can be focused on individual subsystems or scenarios. Layers also provide for hiding of detail.
Relation to Other Views	These views should be consistent with the Layered Subsystem View.

Bibliography

The following books and papers provide a good source of information on software architecture. URLs mentioned in the recommended reading may be found on the web site.

Alexandrescu, Andrei. *Modern C++ Design: Generic Programming and Design Patterns Applied.* Addison-Wesley, 2001.

Ambler, Scott, 'Distributed Object Design', *Software Development*, June 1999.

Anthony, Richard, Jeff Garland, and Bill Lawrence, 'An Analysis of the Advantages of Application and Enterprise Frameworks'. Position Paper for the Workshop on Achieving Bottom-Line Improvements with Application and Enterprise Frameworks at OOPSLA 1999.

Bass, Len, Paul Clements, and Rick Kazman. *Software Architecture in Practice.* Addison-Wesley, 1998.

Beck, Kent, and Ward Cunningham, 'A Laboratory For Teaching Object-Oriented Thinking'. From the *OOPSLA'89 Conference Proceedings*, October 1–6, 1989, and the special issue of *SIGPLAN Notices*, **24**, No. 10, October 1989.

Bellin, David, and Susan Suchman Simone. *The CRC Card Book.* Addison-Wesley, 1997.

Booch, Grady, Ivar Jacobson, and James Rumbaugh. *The Unified Modeling Language User Guide.* Addison-Wesley, 1999.

Bosch, Jan. *Design and Use of Software Architectures.* Addison-Wesley, 2000.

Brown, William J., Hays W. McCormick, and Scott W. Thomas. *Anti-Patterns in Project Management.* John Wiley, 2000.

Brown, William J. (Editor), Raphael C. Malveau, and Hays W. McCormick, III. *Anti-Patterns: Refactoring Software, Architectures, and Projects in Crisis.* John Wiley, 1998.

Buschmann (Editor), Frank, Regine Meunier, Hans Rohnert, Peter Sommerlad and Michael Stal. *Pattern-Oriented Software Architecture: A System of Patterns.* John Wiley, 1996.

Cockburn, Alistair. *Writing Effective Use Cases.* Addison-Wesley, 2000.

Coplien, James O. *Multi-Paradigm Design for C++*. Addison-Wesley, 1998.

Coplien, James, Daniel Hoffman, and David Weiss, 'Commonality and Variability in Software Engineering', *IEEE Software*, November/December 1998, **15**, No. 6.

Coplien, James O., and Douglas C. Schmidt (Editors). *Pattern Languages of Program Design*. Addison-Wesley, 1995.

Czarnecki, Krzysztof, and Ulrich W. Eisenecker. *Generative Programming – Methods, Tools, and Applications*. Addison-Wesley, 2000.

Department of the Army, 'Joint Technical Architecture – Army', Version 6.0, 8 May 2000.

Dikel, David M., David Kane, and James R. Wilson. *Software Architecture: Organizational Principles and Patterns*. Prentice-Hall, 2000.

Douglass, Bruce Powel. *Doing Hard Time: Developing Real-Time Systems with UML, Objects, Frameworks and Patterns*. Addison-Wesley, 1999.

Egyed, Alexander, and Nenad Medvidovic. "Extending Architectural Representation in UML with View Integration". In *Proceedings of the Second IEEE International Conference on the Unified Modeling Language (UML99)*. IEEE Computer Society Press.

Ericsson, Maria, 'Developing Large-scale Systems with the Rational Unified Process', Rational Software, Rational White Paper, 2000.

Fagan, M.E., 'Design and Code Insptections to Reduce Errors in Program Development', *IBM Systems Journal*, **38**, Nos 2–3, 1999.

Foote, Brian, Neil Harrison, and Hans Rohnert. *Pattern Languages of Program Design 4*. Addison-Wesley, December 1999.

Foote, Brian, and Yoder, Joseph, 'Big Ball of Mud'. In *Pattern Languages of Program Design 4*. Addison-Wesley, 2000.

Fowler, Martin, 'Reducing Coupling,' *IEEE Software*, July/August 2001.

Fowler, Martin, and Jim Highsmith, 'The Agile Manifesto', *Software Development Magazine*, August 2001.

Fowler, Martin, and Kendall Scott. *UML Distilled, Applying the Standard Object Modeling Language*. Addison-Wesley, 1997.

Garlan, David, and Robert Allen, 'Formalizing Architectural Connection', 71–80. In *Proceedings of the 16th International Conference on Software Engineering*, Sorrento, Italy, May 16–21, 1994. IEEE Computer Society Press.

Garland, Jeff, 'Representing Software Architectures for Large-Scale Systems'. Position Paper for the OOPSLA 2001 Workshop on Representing Architectures.

Garland, Jeff, Richard Anthony, and Bill Lawrence, 'Accomplishing Software Stability'. Position Paper for the OOPSLA 99 Workshop on Accomplishing Software Stability.

Highsmith III, James A. *Adaptive Software Development*. Dorset House, 2000.

Hofmeister, Christine, Robert Nord, and Dilip Soni. *Applied Software Architecture*. Addison-Wesley, 1999.

IEEE Std. 1471-2000, 'IEEE Recommended Practice for Architectural Description of Software-Intensive Systems', 2000.

ISO/IEC, 'The Reference Model for Open Distributed Processing', ISO/IEC DIS 10746-1:1995.

ITU-T Recommendation X.731 | ISO/IEC 10164-2, 'State Management Function'.

ITU-T, 'Z.100, Specification and Description Language (SDL) Specification', November 1999.

ITU-T, 'Z.120, Message Sequence Chart (MSC) Specification', November 1999.

Jackson, Daniel, and John Chapin, 'Redesigning Air Traffic Control: An Exercise in Software Design', *IEEE Software*, May/June 2000, pp. 63–70.

Jacobson, Ivar. *Object-Oriented Software Engineering: A Use Case Driven Approach*. Addison-Wesley, 1992.

Jacobson, Ivar, 'Use Cases in Large-Scale Systems', *ROAD*, **1**, No. 6, 1995.

Jacobson, Ivar, Grady Booch, James Rumbaugh. *The Unified Software Development Process*. Addison-Wesley, 1999.

Jacobson, Ivar, K. Palmkvist, and S. Dyrhage, 'Systems of Interconnected Systems', *ROAD*, **2**, No. 1, 1995.

Kandé, Mohamed Mancona, and Alfred Strohmeier, 'Towards a UML Profile for Software Architecture Descriptions'. In *Proceedings of UML '2000 – The Unified Modeling Language: Advancing the Standard, Third International Conference*, York, UK, October 2–6, 2000. Springer Verlag.

Kerner, Judy, 'Joint Technical Architecture: Impact on Department of Defense Programs', CrossTalk, *The Journal of Defense Software Engineering*, October 2001.

Kruchten, Philippe, 'The 4+1 view model of architecture', *IEEE Software*, **12**, No. 5, 1995.

Kruchten, Philippe, 'Modeling Component Systems with the Unified Modeling Language'. A Position Paper presented at the 1998 International Workshop on Component-Based Software Engineering.

Kruchten, Philippe. *The Rational Unified Process*. Addison-Wesley, 1999.

Lago, P., and P. Falcarin, 'UML Requirements for Distributed Software Architectures'. In *Proceedings of the 1st International Workshop on Describing Software Architecture with UML* (co-located with ICSE'2001), Toronto, Canada, May 2001.

Lakos, John. *Large-Scale C++ Software Design*. Addison-Wesley, 1996.

Lawrence, Bill, Dick Anthony, and Jeff Garland, 'A Process for Developing Reusable Software'. Position Paper submitted to the OOPSLA '99 Workshop on Patterns in Software Architecture: The Development Process.

Maier, Mark W., and Eberhardt Rechtin. *The Art of Systems Architecting*. CRC Press, 1996.

Maier, M.W., D. Emery, and R. Hilliard, 'Software Architecture: Introducing IEEE Standard 1471', *Computer*, **34**, No. 4, April 2001, pp. 107–109.

Martin, Robert C. *Designing Object Oriented C++ Applications Using The Booch Method*. Prentice-Hall, 1995.

McCarthy, Jim. *Dynamics of Software Development*. Microsoft Press, 1995.

Medividovic, Nenad, and David S. Rosenblum, 'Assessing the Suitability of a Standard Design Method for Modeling Software Architectures'. In *Proceedings of the First Working IFIP Conference on Software architectures (WICSA1)*, San Antonio, TX, February 22–24, 1999.

Medvidovic, Nenad, David S. Rosenblum, Jason E. Robbins, and David F. Redmiles, 'Modeling Software Architectures in the Unified Modeling Language', *IEEE Computer Magazine*, January 1999.

Medividovic, Nenad, and Richard N. Taylor, 'Separating Fact from Fiction in Software Architecture'. In *Proceedings of the Third International Software Architecture Workshop (ISAW-3)*, pp. 105–108, Orlando, FL, November 1–2, 1998.

Meyer, Bertrand, 'Applying Design by Contract', *IEEE Computer*, **25**, No. 10, October 1992, pages 40–51.

Meyer, Bertrand. *Object-Oriented Software Construction*. Prentice-Hall, 1997.

Meyers, B. Craig, and Patricia Oberndorf. *Managing Software Acquisition: Open Systems and COTS Products*. Addison-Wesley, 2001.

Mili, Hafedh, Mohammed Fayad, Davide Brugali, David Hamu, and Dov Dori, 'Enterprise Frameworks: Issues and Research Directions', *International Software Practice & Experience (SP&E) Journal*, March 2002.

Monroe, Robert T., Andrew Kompanek, Ralph Melton, and David Garlan, 'Architectural Styles, Design Patterns, and Objects', *IEEE Software*, January, 1997, pp. 43–52.

Naiburg, Eric J., and Robert A. Maksimchuk. *UML for Database Design*. Addison-Wesley, 2001.

Ousterhout, John K., 'Scripting: Higher Level Programming for the 21st Century', *IEEE Computer*, March 1998.

Parnas, D.L., 'On the Criteria To Be Used in Decomposing Systems into Modules', *Communications of the ACM*, **15**, No. 12, December 1972, pp. 1053–1058.

Paulish, Daniel J. *Architecture-Centric Software Project Management: A Practical Guide*. Addison-Wesley, 2001.

Pryce, Nathamid G., 'Component Interaction in Distributed Systems'. PhD Thesis, Imperial College of Science, Technology and Medicine, January 2000.

Putman, Janis, R. *Architecting With RM-ODP*. Prentice Hall, 2000.

Rettig, Michael J., and Martin Fowler, 'Reflection vs. Code Generation', *Java World*, November 2001.

Riel, Arthur J. *Object-Oriented Design Heuristics*. Addison-Wesley, 1996.

Rising, Linda, and Norman S. Janoff, 'The Scrum Software Development Process for Small Teams', *IEEE Software*, July/August 2000.

Rosenberg, Doug, and Kendall Scott. *Use Case-Driven Object Modeling with UML*. Addison-Wesley, 1999.

Rumbaugh, James, Ivar Jacobson, and Grady Booch. *The Unified Modeling Language Reference Manual*. Addison-Wesley, 1999.

Schmidt, Douglas, Michael Stal, Hans Rohnert, and Frank Buschmann. *Pattern-Oriented Software Architecture, Volume 2, Patterns for Concurrent and Networked Objects*. John Wiley, 2000.

Sewell, Marc, and Laura Sewell. *The Software Architect's Profession: An Introduction to the 21st Century*. Prentice-Hall, 2001.

Shaw, M., and P. Clements, 'A Field Guide to Boxology: Preliminary Classification of Architectural Styles for Software Systems'. In *Proceedings of Computer Software and Applications Conference 1997 (COMPSAC '97)*, 1997, pp. 6–13.

Shaw, Mary, and David Garlan. *Software Architecture: Perspectives on an Emerging Discipline*. Prentice-Hall, 1996.

Smith, Douglas, 'Realizing Architecture Through Realizing Use Cases'. In *Proceedings of UML World 2000*, June 12, 2000, New York. Published by CMP Media, pp. 1131–1168.

Soni, Dilip, R.L. Nord, and Liang Hsu, 'An Empirical Approach to Software Architectures'. In *Proceedings of the Seventh International Workshop on Software Specification and Design*, 1993, pp. 47–51.

Taylor, P., 'Adhocism in Software Architecture – Perspectives from Design Theory'. In *Proceedings of the International Conference on Software Methods and Tools 2000 (SMT 2000)*, pp. 41–50.

Vaughan, Jack, 'UML Hits the Streets', *Application Development Trends*, 8, No. 9, September 2001, pp 18–23.

Weinberg, Gerald M. *The Psychology of Computer Programming, Silver Anniversary Edition. Dorset House Publishing.* February 2000.

Weiss, David M., Chi Tau Robert, and Lai, *Software Product-Line Engineering: A Family-Based Software Development Approach.* Addison-Wesley, 1999.

Wirth, Niklaus, 'Program Development by Stepwise Refinement', *Communications of the ACM*, **14**, No. 4, April 1971, pp. 221–227.

Yourdon, E. *Modern Structured Analysis.* Prentice-Hall, 1991.

Index